THE YOUNG ELIZABETH

THE
YOUNG
ELIZABETH

ALISON PLOWDEN

STEIN AND DAY / *Publishers* / New York

First published in 1971
Copyright 1971 © by Alison Plowden
Library of Congress Catalog Card No. 70-151289
All rights reserved
Printed in the United States of America
Stein and Day/*Publishers*/7 East 48 Street, New York, N.Y. 10017
ISBN 0-8128-1367-7

To Joe Burroughs
In Happy and Grateful Memory

Contents

Contents

List of Illustrations

between pages 112 & 113

ACKNOWLEDGEMENTS

The author and publishers are grateful to the following for permission to reproduce the illustrations: by gracious permission of H.M. the Queen: 5, 7, 11; Marquess of Bath, 10; the Bodley Librarian, 14; Lord Brooke, 1; Dean and Chapter of Westminster, 3; Lord Hastings, 12; Mansell, 8, 13; National Monuments Record, 6; National Portrait Gallery, 2; Prado, Madrid, 9; Marquess of Salisbury, 15; Walker Art Gallery, Liverpool, and the Earl of Bradford, 4.

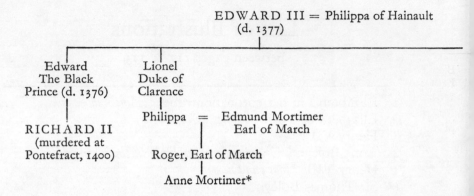

EDWARD III = Philippa of Hainault
(d. 1377)

Edward
The Black
Prince (d. 1376)

RICHARD II
(murdered at
Pontefract, 1400)

Lionel
Duke of
Clarence

Philippa = Edmund Mortimer
Earl of March

Roger, Earl of March

Anne Mortimer*

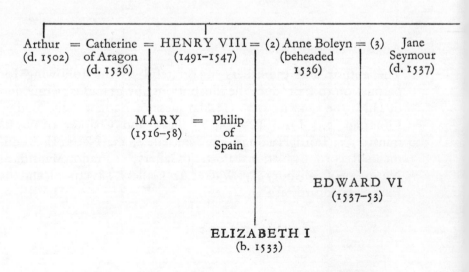

Arthur = Catherine = HENRY VIII = (2) Anne Boleyn = (3) Jane
(d. 1502) of Aragon   (1491–1547)   (beheaded   Seymour
           (d. 1536)   1536)   (d. 1537)

MARY = Philip
(1516–58) of
           Spain

EDWARD VI
(1537–53)

ELIZABETH I
(b. 1533)

Simplified Genealogical Table Showing
the Descent of the House of Tudor

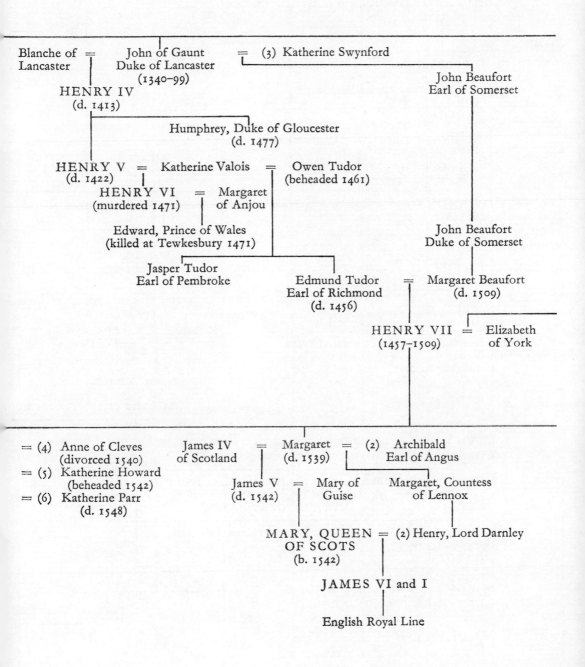

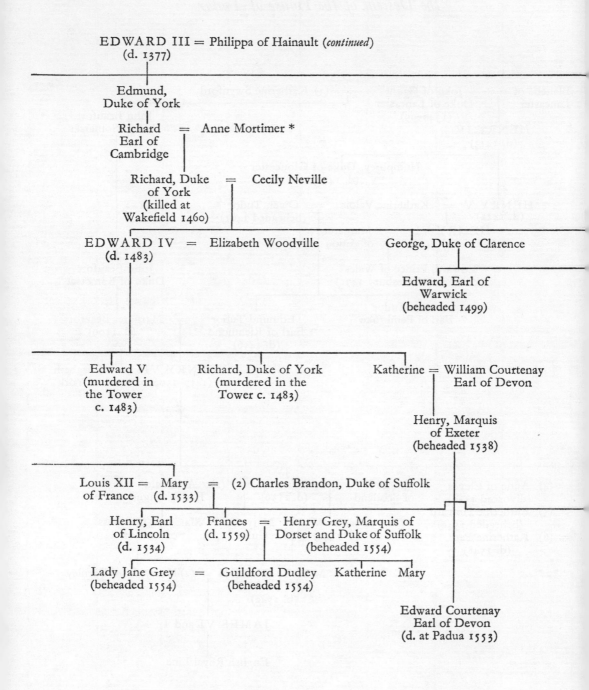

EDWARD III = Philippa of Hainault (*continued*)
(d. 1377)

Edmund,
Duke of York

Richard = Anne Mortimer *
Earl of
Cambridge

Richard, Duke = Cecily Neville
of York
(killed at
Wakefield 1460)

EDWARD IV = Elizabeth Woodville   George, Duke of Clarence
(d. 1483)

Edward, Earl of
Warwick
(beheaded 1499)

Edward V   Richard, Duke of York   Katherine = William Courtenay
(murdered in   (murdered in the   Earl of Devon
the Tower   Tower c. 1483)
c. 1483)

Henry, Marquis
of Exeter
(beheaded 1538)

Louis XII = Mary   =   (2) Charles Brandon, Duke of Suffolk
of France   (d. 1533)

Henry, Earl   Frances = Henry Grey, Marquis of
of Lincoln   (d. 1559) Dorset and Duke of Suffolk
(d. 1534)   (beheaded 1554)

Lady Jane Grey = Guildford Dudley   Katherine Mary
(beheaded 1554)   (beheaded 1554)

Edward Courtenay
Earl of Devon
(d. at Padua 1553)

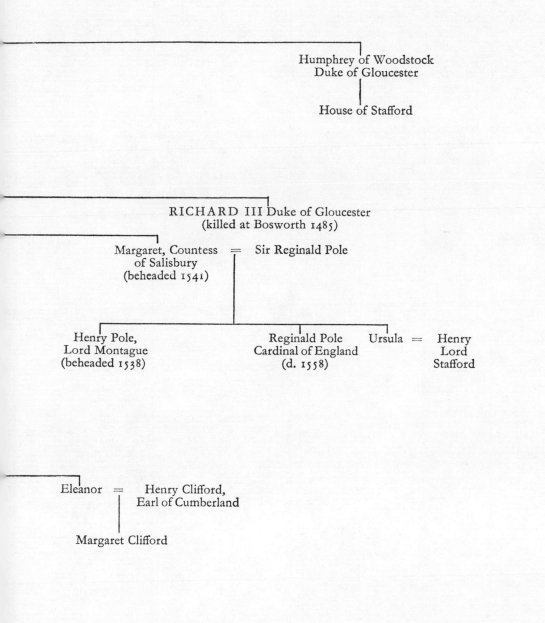

Humphrey of Woodstock
Duke of Gloucester

House of Stafford

RICHARD III Duke of Gloucester
(killed at Bosworth 1485)

Margaret, Countess = Sir Reginald Pole
of Salisbury
(beheaded 1541)

Henry Pole,   Reginald Pole   Ursula = Henry
Lord Montague   Cardinal of England   Lord
(beheaded 1538)   (d. 1558)   Stafford

Eleanor = Henry Clifford,
Earl of Cumberland

Margaret Clifford

Prologue

At three o'clock in the afternoon of Thursday, 29 May 1533, Queen Anne Boleyn, Marquess of Pembroke, 'most dear and well-beloved' wife of Henry VIII, embarked at Greenwich for the journey up-river to the Tower at the beginning of her coronation celebrations. She was escorted by an impressive contingent of the nobility and by the Lord Mayor and Aldermen, with all the crafts of the City of London in barges sumptuously decorated with banners and streamers and cloth of gold, and plentifully supplied with bands of musicians 'making great melody'.[1] According to one awed foreign spectator, there were so many boats and barges, and so many ladies and gentlemen that it was a thing to wonder at. He added that, although it was four English miles from Greenwich to London and the river was quite wide, nothing else could be seen all the way but boats and barges draped with awnings and carpeted. On arrival at the Tower, the Queen was greeted by a salvo of more than a thousand guns so that it seemed to the same foreigner 'verily as if the world was coming to an end'.[2] In fact, such was the gunners' enthusiasm, that not a single pane of glass survived either in the Tower or neighbouring St Katherine's.

On Saturday, the thirty-first, came the recognition procession through the City to Westminster, and no expense had been spared to make it a memorable occasion. The great cavalcade, shimmering with gold and crimson, silver and purple and scarlet, wound its way through freshly gravelled and gaily decorated streets. The Queen herself, dressed in white cloth of tissue and 'sitting in her hair' as one observer put it, rode in a litter of white cloth of gold drawn by two palfreys caparisoned to the ground in white damask. At every point of vantage along the route pageants and tableaux were presented, children spoke carefully rehearsed pieces in welcome and praise, and all afternoon the conduits and fountains ran with wine.

The climax of splendour was reached on the following day, Whitsunday, with the coronation ceremony itself when

> Queen Anne was brought from Westminster Hall to the Abbey of St Peter's with procession, all the monks of Westminster going in rich copes of gold with thirteen abbots mitred; and after them all the King's Chapel in rich copes with four bishops and two archbishops mitred, and all the Lords going in their Parliament robes, and the crown borne afore her by the Duke of Suffolk, and her two sceptres by two Earls, and she herself going under a rich canopy of cloth of gold, apparelled in a kirtle of crimson velvet powdered with ermines and a robe of purple velvet furred with powdered ermines over that, and a rich coronet with a caul of pearls and stones on her head, and the old Duchess of Norfolk bearing up her train, and the Queen's Chamberlain staying the train in the midst.[3]

In the Abbey itself, set in her 'seat royal' before the high altar, Anne Boleyn was anointed and crowned Queen of England by the Archbishops of Canterbury and York, 'and so sat crowned in her seat royal all the Mass and offered also at the said Mass'. Afterwards, at the banquet in Westminster Hall, she occupied the place of honour at the high table under the Cloth of Estate, served by the nobility of England, while the minstrels made 'goodly sweet harmony' in the background and the King looked on from a place which he had had made from which he could see without being seen.

This was Anne's moment of triumph – a moment which for six years she had worked and schemed to bring about, conducting a dangerous and difficult campaign with cold-blooded courage, tenacity and skill. It only needed now for the child she was so visibly carrying to be a healthy boy and her tremendous gamble – a gamble which had brought the former maid-of-honour to the second highest place in the land – would finally have paid off beyond all possibility of doubt.

CHAPTER I

A Gentleman of Wales

THE story of Elizabeth Tudor began just over a hundred years before she was born. It began with a love story – with the romance of a young widowed queen and 'a gentleman of Wales'.

Katherine of Valois, called 'the Fair', daughter of the King of France, had been married to that notable warrior, King Henry V of England, hero of Agincourt, in June 1420 – a marriage designed to seal the Treaty of Troyes which was to inaugurate 'perpetual peace' between the two countries. Two years later, on the last day of August 1422, Henry died of dysentery at the Castle of Vincennes just outside Paris. Katherine became a widow shortly before her twenty-first birthday, and her son, 'Harry born at Windsor' who was destined to lose all the glory his father had gained, became King Henry VI at the age of nine months.

The youthful Queen Dowager, stranded in a foreign country and probably both bored and lonely, presently found diversion with one of the gentlemen of her household, Owen Tudor, her Welsh Clerk of the Wardrobe. 'Following more her appetite than friendly counsel and regarding more her private affections than her open honour', as the chronicler Edward Hall put it. Understandably perhaps, for Owen is described by Polydore Vergil as being 'adorned with wonderful gifts of body and mind', and by Hall as 'a goodly gentleman and a beautiful person garnished with many godly gifts both of nature and of graces'. Another (earlier) chronicle was less complimentary, referring to him tersely as a man of neither birth nor livelihood.

Years later, Owen's grandson, the first Tudor king, was to be somewhat embarrassed by certain 'reproachful and slanderous assertions' about the deficiencies of his pedigree, and felt it necessary to appoint a commission consisting of the Abbot of Valle Crucis, Doctor Owen Poole, canon of Hereford, and John King, herald, to enquire into the matter. After visiting Wales and consulting the bards and other authorities, these seekers after knowledge drew up their master's 'perfect genelogie' from the ancient Kings of Britain and Princes of Wales. The Tudors, they said, could prove lineal descent by issue male, saving one woman (an artistic touch), from Brute the Trojan – mythical first King of the Britons, who was supposed to have given his name to the land.

In actual fact, however, the founder of the family fortunes appears to have been Ednyfed Fychan, who served the rulers of Gwynedd – the principality of North Wales – as seneschal or steward, from approximately 1215 to his death in 1246. Ednyfed was evidently highly thought of by his employers, for they rewarded him with extensive grants of land in Anglesey and Caernarvon. He also acquired estates in West Wales, and he and his relatives were allowed the unusual privilege of holding their lands free from restriction, excepting homage and military service in time of war.

The conquest and subjugation of Wales by England in 1282 does not seem to have adversely affected Ednyfed's descendants. On the contrary, by the middle of the next century, the seneschal's great-great-grandson, Tudur ap Goronwy, had emerged as a considerable landowner. Like a number of other Welsh magnates, he probably supported the English crown and Goronwy, eldest of his five sons, served with the army in France. It was the unsuccessful revolt of Owen Glendower in the early 1400s which brought about the family's downfall. Through their mother, Tudur's sons were first cousins to Glendower. Old loyalties reasserted themselves and the remaining four brothers (Goronwy had died in 1382) threw in their lot with the rebel chieftain. The consequences were disastrous. Rhys, the middle brother, was executed in 1412 and all the family estates were confiscated; though the property at Penmyndd in Anglesey was later returned to Goronwy's heirs.[1]

Owen Tudor was the son of Maredudd, youngest of the brothers, who held some office under the Bishop of Bangor and was escheator of Anglesey. Owen was born about 1400, and despite the ill-judged activities of his relations became a page and subsequently a squire in the household of Henry V. It was probably then that he found it convenient to adopt an English-style patronymic, but for some reason chose to take his grandfather's instead of his father's name. There is a tradition that young Owen was present at Agincourt, but this seems rather unlikely, because in 1415, when the battle was fought, revolt against English rule was still simmering in the Welsh hinterland. Two years later, however, Glendower's only surviving son was pardoned and shortly afterwards appointed Squire of the Body to the King. It may have been through his influence that Owen Tudor was taken into the royal service.[2]

The circumstances surrounding Owen's courtship of the Queen Dowager are unfortunately obscure. As Clerk of the Wardrobe, his duties would have included guarding Katherine's jewels and buying and paying for the materials for her dresses – duties which no doubt provided plenty of opportunity for them to get acquainted. It is said that on one occasion he was called upon to dance before the Queen and her ladies. He overbalanced and fell into Katherine's lap, and her reaction to this familiarity led the onlookers to suspect there was something between them.

No record survives of when or where they were married; but, as Katherine bore her second husband three sons and one, possibly two, daughters before her death in 1437 and their legitimacy seems never to have been questioned, the ceremony cannot have taken place much later than 1429, the date generally assigned to it.

It would be fascinating to know more about the private life of this oddly assorted couple. Katherine's own early childhood had been unsettled, with a background of disruption and war. Her father, Charles VI of France, was subject to long and recurring fits of insanity, during which he was liable to tear his clothes, smash the furniture and imagine himself to be made of glass, so that he dared not move for fear of breaking. Her mother, Isabeau of Bavaria, acquired a considerable reputation for loose living and general bad character. She is said to have neglected her younger children to such an extent that for a time they went ragged and hungry. Katherine's short-lived marriage to Henry V was a matter of high politics and one hopes she found happiness with her Welshman.

Their wedding took place without the knowledge or consent of the Duke of Gloucester – Protector of the realm during the King's minority – and several accounts declare that it was not discovered until after Katherine's death. It is straining credulity

somewhat to believe that the Queen Dowager could have successfully concealed at least four pregnancies, even if she was living
away from the court. A more probable explanation seems that her
unsuitable marriage was tolerated by tacit consent during her
lifetime, rather than precipitate a scandal involving the King's
mother. Owen may also have had influential friends, for in 1432
he was granted letters of denizenship which relieved him of some
at any rate of the penal legislation then in force against the Welsh
people. Towards the end of 1436, however, the family broke up.
Katherine retired, voluntarily or otherwise, into the Abbey of
Bermondsey, where she died the following January at the age of
thirty-five – possibly giving birth to a daughter who did not survive. The Abbess of Barking took charge of the other Tudor
children – Edmund and Jasper, then about six and five years old,
Owen, who later became a monk, and a girl of whom nothing is
known except that she, too, entered the religious life.

Their father's subsequent career contains all the ingredients of
an old-fashioned adventure-story. Deprived of his wife's protection, he evidently thought it wiser to remove himself from the
vicinity of the Duke of Gloucester. He was at Daventry when, not
long after Katherine's death, a summons was issued by the
Council requiring 'one Owen Tudor the which dwelled with the
said Queen Katherine' to come into the King's presence. Suspecting a trap, Owen refused to obey unless he was given an assurance
in the King's name that he might 'freely come and freely go'.
According to a minute of the Privy Council's proceedings dated
15 July 1437, a promise to this effect was conveyed to him by a
certain Myles Sculle, but Owen was not entirely satisfied. He
came to London 'in full secret wise' and took sanctuary at Westminster, where 'he held him many days'. This despite the fact that
'divers persons stirred him of friendship and fellowship to have
comen out thereof, and some in especial to have disported him
in [the] tavern at Westminster gate.' Owen, no doubt wisely,
resisted these persuasions. However, some time later, hearing that
the King was 'heavily informed of him', he suddenly appeared in
the royal presence and

> declared his innocence and his truth, affirming that he had nothing
> done that should give the King occasion or matter of offence or
> displeasure against him, offering himself in large wise to answer as

the King's true liege man should to all things that any man could or would submit upon him. And so submitted himself by his said offer to abide all lawful answer.[3]

He was allowed to depart 'without any impeachment' but shortly afterwards was arrested and committed to Newgate. The Council felt it necessary to justify their action in a somewhat specious memorandum, saying that Owen's 'malicious purpose and imagination' were not known to the King or the Duke of Gloucester when the safe conduct was issued. They added piously that it was 'thought marvellous' that one of the King's liegemen should desire any such surety before coming to his presence, and anyway Owen *had* been allowed to go free – for a time. There was no statute engrossed on the Parliamentary Rolls forbidding the marriage of a subject to a queen dowager, and no indication in the Privy Council minute as to what Owen was accused of. Polydore Vergil says that he was committed to ward by the Duke of Gloucester, 'because he had been so presumptuous as by marriage with the Queen to intermix his blood with the noble race of kings'. Possibly Gloucester was just paying off old scores, but his victim proved a slippery customer.

An entry in the Chronicle of London for the sixteenth year of the King's reign records that Owen 'brake out of Newgate against night at searching time, through help of his priest, and went his way, hurting foul his keeper; but at the last, blessed be God, he was taken again'.[4] This was probably in February. He was recaptured by Lord Beaumont and temporarily consigned to the dungeons of Wallingford Castle in Berkshire, but later returned to Newgate with his servant and the priest. On 4 March 1438, Lord Beaumont received twenty marks to cover his expenses, and the sum of eighty-nine pounds which was found on the priest was handed over to the Exchequer.[5] It would be interesting to know if this enterprising cleric was the same priest who had married Owen and Katherine.

Newgate was evidently not strong enough to hold the Welshman. He escaped again, and on 29 July 1438 the sheriffs of London were pardoned for not having prevented it. It is not clear which escape this refers to, but all contemporary accounts agree that Owen broke out of prison twice. The second time he got clear away and probably took refuge in Wales.

When Henry VI reached his majority the fortunes of the Tudor family improved. The gentle, devout, ineffectual King seems to have been fond of his Welsh relations. He provided for the education of his two elder half-brothers; and, as soon as they outgrew the Abbess of Barking, Edmund and Jasper were brought up 'chastely and virtuously' by discreet persons. Their father received a pension of forty pounds a year which the King, moved by 'certain causes', paid out of the privy purse 'by especial grace'. On Christmas Day 1449 the Tudor brothers were knighted. Four years later they were created Earls of Richmond and Pembroke respectively. The King was also apparently instrumental in providing a wife for the Earl of Richmond. In 1455 Edmund Tudor married fourteen-year-old Margaret Beaufort – a union which was to have far-reaching consequences.

The Beaufort family was the result of a long-ago liaison between John of Gaunt, Duke of Lancaster, third son of Edward III, and Katherine Swynford, a lady of Flemish extraction who had been governess to the Duke's daughters. Their four children were indisputably born on the wrong side of the blanket, but after the death of his second wife John of Gaunt proceeded to make an honest woman of Katherine. His Beaufort progeny (so called after the castle in France where they were born) were legitimated by the Pope, by Letters Patent granted by Gaunt's nephew Richard II, and for good measure by Act of Parliament. The Beauforts grew rich and powerful – Cardinal Beaufort, the last survivor of Katherine Swynford's brood, had governed England with the Duke of Gloucester during Henry VI's long minority – and after the King and his heirs they represented the royal and ruling family of Lancaster. Margaret, heiress of her father, John, Duke of Somerset, great-granddaughter of John of Gaunt and later to develop into a remarkable personality in her own right, was a matrimonial prize by any standards – especially for the son of an obscure Welsh squire.

Their marriage coincided with the outbreak of that long-drawn-out dynastic struggle among the all too numerous descendants of Edward III, which is known to history as the Wars of the Roses. The quarrel had its roots in the *coup d'état* of 1399, when Henry Bolingbroke, John of Gaunt's eldest son, wrested the crown from his cousin Richard II; and it became progressively more bitter and more complicated – as family quarrels usually do. It was fought out on one side by the pathetic Henry VI's tigerish Queen, Margaret of Anjou; and on the other, first by the Duke of York and later his son, Edward, Earl of March, representing a senior branch of the royal house, but whose descent had twice passed through the female line.

Edmund Tudor did not live to see the outcome. Neither did he live to see his son. He died at Carmarthen early in November 1456, at the age of twenty-six, leaving his young wife six months pregnant. Jasper at once took his brother's widow under his protection, and Margaret Beaufort's child was born at Pembroke Castle on 28 January 1457. He was given, prophetically as it turned out, the royal English name of Henry but at the time the birth attracted little attention. Henry Tudor was said to be a delicate baby. His future looked uncertain.

Meanwhile the deadly power-game of York and Lancaster continued unabated. The Duke of York was killed at Wakefield in December 1460, but his son remained to carry on the struggle. Jasper Tudor, Earl of Pembroke, brave, energetic and loyal, was a leading supporter of the Lancastrian cause; so, too, his father, quite an old man by this time. Nevertheless, Owen Tudor was present, fighting under Jasper's banner, at the battle of Mortimer's Cross near Wigmore on 2 February 1461. The Lancastrians were defeated by the young Earl of March, and Owen, not quite so spry as he had once been, was among those captured. He was brought to Hereford and executed there in the market-place. It seems he could not believe his luck had turned at last for, one old chronicle says, he trusted

> all away that he should not be headed till he saw the axe and the block, and when that he was in his doublet he trusted on pardon and grace till the collar of his red velvet doublet was ripped off. Then he said 'that head shall lie on the stock that was wont to lie on Queen Katherine's lap' and put his heart and mind wholly unto God and full meekly took his death.

Afterwards his head was displayed on the highest step of the market-cross and 'a mad woman combed his hair and washed away the blood of his face and she got candles and set about him burning more than a hundred.'[6] It was a sad but perhaps suitably bizarre end for the adventurous gentleman of Wales who had sired a dynasty of kings, whose great-granddaughter's descendants occupy the English throne to this day, and whose great-great-granddaughter was to be the most complex and fascinating personality ever to occupy it and give her name to a whole glittering epoch of English life.

1461 was a black year for the House of Lancaster. On 4 March the nineteen-year-old Earl of March was acclaimed as King Edward IV in Westminster Hall, and his victory over Queen Margaret at Towton at the end of the month confirmed his position. Margaret fled to Scotland, taking Henry VI and their young son with her. For a while she succeeded in keeping the fight alive, but four years later King Henry, reduced by this time to a wandering fugitive in the North Country, was betrayed to his enemies and deposited in the Tower. The Queen and the Prince of Wales sought refuge abroad. The Yorkists appeared triumphant.

Jasper Tudor, who had inherited all his father's slipperiness, escaped after Mortimer's Cross and was reported 'flown and taken to the mountains'. For the next few years he led the life of an underground resistance-leader, moving from one safe house to another in Wales, then turning up in Ireland, then Scotland, over in France, back in Wales again. 'Not always at his heart's ease, nor in security of life or surety of living' he remained unswerving in his devotion to the cause of Lancaster, and lost no opportunity, however slight, of stirring up trouble for the new régime.

The task of subduing Wales had been entrusted to William Herbert, himself a Welshman, who was rising in the councils of Edward IV. Pembroke Castle surrendered on 30 September 1461, and in February of the following year Herbert was granted the wardship and marriage of Henry Tudor then five years old. Whether or not the child actually came into the hands of his new guardian at this time is uncertain. Harlech Castle was still holding out for the Lancastrians and provided a convenient shelter for refugees – little Henry may well have been among them. But in 1468 Harlech was besieged, and despite an attempt by Jasper to come to its rescue the Castle finally surrendered on 14 August. Jasper got away again but William Herbert was rewarded with his earldom of Pembroke.

In the following year there was another reversal of fortune. Edward IV fell out with his powerful ally, Richard Neville, Earl of Warwick, 'the Kingmaker'. Warwick defected to the other side and in the summer of 1470 came to an arrangement with Queen Margaret, still chafing in exile. Edward, caught unawares, fled abroad in his turn, escaping capture by a hair's breadth. Once more the Lancastrians were in the saddle. The wretched, apathetic Henry VI was brought out of the Tower, dusted off and once more installed in the royal apartments at Westminster.

Another captive was set at liberty by the new turn of events. Jasper Tudor lost no time in recovering his young nephew. According to Polydore Vergil, he found him 'kept as a prisoner, but honourably brought up with the wife of William Herbert'. Jasper, again according to Vergil,

> took the boy Henry from the wife of the Lord Herbert, and brought him with himself a little after when he came to London unto King Henry. When the King saw the child, beholding within himself without speech a pretty space the haultie disposition thereof, he is reported to have said to the noblemen there present, 'This truly, this is he unto whom both we and our adversaries must yield and give over the dominion.'

'Thus', added Vergil, 'the holy man showed it would come to pass that Henry should in time enjoy the kingdom.'

There was a long road to travel before this pious (and most probably apocryphal) prophecy was fulfilled. Without the help of a crystal-ball, not even the most optimistic well-wisher of Henry Tudor would have foretold in 1470 any other future for him than that of an honoured and profitable career in the service of Henry VI and his heirs. In fact, the Lancastrian revival was short-lived. Barely six months after his flight, Edward was back in England, re-proclaiming himself King. On Easter Day 1471, he defeated Warwick at the battle of Barnet which, appropriately enough, was fought in thick fog. The Kingmaker was killed and Henry VI, 'a man amazed and utterly dulled with troubles and adversity', was taken back to the Tower.

On the day that Barnet was being lost and won, Queen Margaret and her son landed at Weymouth, too late to save the situation. Together with the Lancastrian lords who had rallied to them, they marched up the Severn valley, hoping to join forces with Jasper Tudor and his Welshmen coming down from North

Wales. But Edward, with his usual speed and tactical skill, intercepted them at Tewkesbury, an encounter which ended in disaster
for the House of Lancaster. The last surviving male members of
the Beaufort family lost their lives and the Prince of Wales, for
whose sake his mother had struggled so long and so valiantly, was
killed trying to escape. On 21 May, Edward IV re-entered London
in triumph with the Queen, her spirit broken at last, a prisoner in
his train. That same night 'between eleven and twelve of the
clock' Henry VI was released from his earthly troubles with the
help of a Yorkist sword.

When Jasper heard that Queen Margaret 'was vanquished in a
foughten field at Tewkesbury and that matters were past all hope
of recovery', he retired to Chepstow (where he had yet another
narrow escape from capture and death). He had been unable to
help the cause in battle but there was still one important service
he could perform. In the person of his fourteen-year-old nephew
was now represented the last surviving male of the Lancastrian
line – the last slender hope for the future. At all costs Henry
Tudor must be kept from falling into Yorkist hands. Margaret
Beaufort had confided her son to Jasper's care – a trust which he
faithfully performed – and now that there was no possibility of
'any comfort or relief to be had for the part of poor King Henry'
she asked her brother-in-law to take the boy out of the country
to safety.

Jasper made for Pembroke and was immediately besieged. But
once again his luck held, and after eight days he was able to make
his way through 'ditch and trench' with the help of one David
Morgan. He then

> departed forthwith to a town by the sea side called Tenby, where
> having a bark prepared out of hand he sailed into France with his
> brother's son Henry Earl of Richmond, and certain other his friends
> and servants, whose chance being to arrive in Brittany he presented
> himself humbly to Francis, duke there, and, reporting the cause of
> his coming, submitted himself and his nephew to his protection. The
> Duke received them willingly, and with such honour, courtesy and
> favour entertained them as though they had been his brothers,
> promising them upon his honour that within his dominion they
> should be from thenceforth far from injury, and pass at their
> pleasure to and fro without danger.[7]

Nevertheless, the young Earl of Richmond was to have at least two very nasty moments during his exile. Edward IV made several attempts to persuade the Duke of Brittany to part with his guest – 'the only imp now left of King Henry VI's blood' – and on one occasion very nearly succeeded, sending ambassadors 'laden with great substance of gold' and with instructions to tell the Duke that he intended to arrange a marriage for young Henry which would unite the rival factions 'by affinity'. Duke Francis was convinced, either by the sight of the gold or the smooth-talking ambassadors, and delivered the Earl of Richmond into their hands, 'not supposing that he had committed the sheep to the wolf, but the son to the father'. Edward's ambassadors set off with their prize towards the coast, but Henry 'knowing that he was carried to his death, through agony of mind fell by the way into a fever'. (Or was he desperately playing for time, in much the same way as his granddaughter was to do in later years?) Fortunately the Duke was warned in time that 'the Earl of Richmond was not so earnestly sought for to be coupled in marriage with King Edward's daughter, as to have his head parted from his body with an axe.'[8] Henry was snatched back at St Malo and thereafter more closely guarded by his host – partly for his own safety and partly to appease the English government, who continued to pay the Bretons handsomely to keep him prisoner.

It cannot have been a very cheerful existence for the young man, helpless to defend himself, knowing that his life depended on the goodwill of a protector who might at any time be subjected to heavy financial and political pressures from outside (though, in fact, Duke Francis was to prove a good friend) and with little apparent prospect of ever being able to lead a normal life and enjoy even the fruits of his own earldom.

Then, suddenly, in April 1483, Edward IV was dead. His two young sons fell into the hands of his brother, Richard Duke of Gloucester, who proceeded to declare the King's marriage to have been defective and his children bastards. The Princes were lodged in the Tower and shortly afterwards disappeared permanently and mysteriously from sight. In June, Richard of Gloucester was King of England. He was not popular. In an age not noted for squeamishness many of his subjects were repelled by persistent rumours that he had had his nephews murdered, and the future of the exile in Brittany looked unexpectedly brighter. Margaret

Beaufort, now married for the third time to Lord Stanley, a powerful magnate generally regarded as a Yorkist supporter, set to work to build up a following for her son – no doubt beginning with her husband. She also quietly approached Edward IV's widow, Elizabeth Woodville, who had been stripped of her royal dignity by Richard, suggesting that a marriage between Henry Tudor and the widow's eldest daughter, Elizabeth, would solve a great many problems, by uniting the rival factions once and for all and ousting the usurper. The Queen and her daughter were agreeable. Other people, too, alarmed by the ferocity of the new King's behaviour, had begun to think in terms of Henry Tudor as a possible replacement. The Duke of Buckingham declared in his favour and messengers were sent to Brittany inviting the Earl of Richmond to come and claim his bride and his kingdom.

With the help of Duke Francis, Henry gathered a force of fifteen ships and 5000 mercenaries and embarked for England in October. But the rising was still-born. Richard fell on the conspirators with his usual violence. Buckingham was executed and even Margaret Beaufort had a narrow escape. Fortunately for her son, the winds had scattered his small fleet, driving it back on the coast of France. He himself got as far as Plymouth, but 'viewing afar of all the shore beset with soldiers' and realising that it would be suicidal to land, 'hoisted up sail' and returned to Brittany. But despite this setback, the tide was running in his favour. Fugitives from Richard's rule began to gather round him, and on Christmas Day 1483 Henry Tudor swore a solemn oath in the cathedral at Rennes 'that so soon as he should be King he would marry Elizabeth, King Edward's daughter'.

All the same, his troubles were not yet over. The following September he was to have a very narrow escape indeed. King Richard, like King Edward before him, had already done his best to ensure that Henry should at least be kept a permanent prisoner in his Breton sanctuary. But after the Buckingham episode the King, 'more doubting than trusting in his own cause, was vexed and tormented in mind with fear almost perpetually of the Earl Henry and his confederates' return; wherefore he had a miserable life'.[9] Determined 'to rid himself of this inward grief', Richard despatched another embassy to Brittany. Unfortunately, Duke Francis had 'become feeble by reason of sore and daily sickness' and the ambassadors were received by his treasurer, Peter

Landois. They offered the yearly revenues of the earldom of Richmond, together with those of the other English nobles who had fled since the rising, in return for Henry's surrender. Peter Landois, a man 'of sharp wit and great authority', was ruling 'all matters as he list' in the incapacity of his master, and as a result had aroused considerable hostility among his own countrymen. According to Polydore Vergil, he felt that the King of England would be a powerful ally against his enemies at home, and for that reason and not any personal spite he agreed to betray Henry Tudor.

Once again the luck held. Henry heard about Landois's plans and, 'thinking it meet to provide for his affairs with all diligence', applied for and got a safe conduct from the King of France. He sent word to the faithful Jasper to get himself and the other English refugees across the frontier into Anjou without delay, and set about arranging his own escape. He gave out that he was going to visit a friend who lived near by;

but when he had journeyed almost five miles, he withdrew hastily out of the highway into the next wood and donning a serving man's apparel he as a servant followed one of his own servants (who was his guide in that journey) as though he had been his master, and rode on with so great celerity that he made no stay anywhere, except it were to bait his horses, before he had gotten himself to his company within the bounds of Anjou.[10]

Not a moment too soon, for when Peter Landois, 'who wanted no subtlety', heard that Henry had gone

he sent out horsemen incontinent every way to pursue, and if they could overtake him, to apprehend and bring the earl to him. The horsemen made such haste as that there was never thing more nigh the achieving than the overtaking of the earl; he was scarce an hour entered the bounds of France when they came thither.[11]

It is pleasant to know that Duke Francis recovered, and when he heard that 'Henry was so uncourteously entertained as that he was forced to fly out of his dominion' was very angry with Peter Landois, at least so Polydore Vergil says. It is also salutory to remember that the whole future of the dynasty and the very

existence of Elizabeth Tudor may well have depended on that
quick change in a Breton wood, and a dash to safety with barely
an hour to spare.

The fugitives were welcomed in France and the exile began 'to
have good hope of happy success'. By the following summer the
time seemed ripe for another attempt on England. At best it was
likely to be a desperate venture, and delay might indeed be fatal.
There was no knowing how much longer Elizabeth of York
would be allowed to remain unmarried, the loyalty of the English
refugees – many of them discontented Yorkists – could not be
relied on for ever and France might yet prove inhospitable. Henry
borrowed money, 'a slender supply' from the French King, and
more where he could get it, and left Paris to start collecting a
fleet. On 1 August 1485 – 'thinking it needful to make haste, that
his friends should not be any longer kept in perplexity between
hope and dread, uncertain what to do' – he sailed from the mouth
of the Seine with 2000 armed men and a few ships, and 'with a
soft southern wind' behind him. A week later he landed at Milford
Haven and began his march up through Wales towards the
Midlands, gathering support as he went. The local gentry came in
to join him, less because he was the last Lancastrian than because
he was Owen Tudor's grandson and Jasper's nephew. 'He was
of no great stature', this unknown Welshman, the adventurer
come to conquer if he could, 'his countenance was cheerful and
courageous, his hair yellow like burnished gold, his eyes gray,
shining and quick.'[12]

Henry had sent messages to his mother but he still did not
know how the powerful Stanley family was going to react, and
as he approached the English heartland he heard that King
Richard 'with an host innumerable was at hand'. The final confrontation, the great gamble on which everything depended, took
place on 22 August at the village of Market Bosworth, 'a little
beyond Leicester'. After two hours' fierce fighting it was all over.
The naked corpse of the last Plantagenet king had been carried
ignominiously away, slung across the back of a horse, to be buried
in the Franciscan Abbey at Leicester. The crown had been found
in a hawthorn bush and placed on Henry Tudor's head by Lord
Stanley.

The new King was twenty-eight. He had had no practical experience of government or of warfare. As he himself is supposed

to have said, he had been either a prisoner or a fugitive since he was five years old. Apart from one brief visit in his boyhood, he had never set foot in England before. His hereditary title was not impressive and devolved entirely from his mother. If descent from Edward III through the female line was admitted, then there were Yorkist claimants alive with unquestionably better titles in law, not least Henry's intended bride, Elizabeth, eldest surviving child of Edward IV. But the majority of his subjects were less concerned with the legality of Henry VII's claim to the crown than with his ability to hold on to it. The dynastic struggles of the past thirty years had not unduly affected the life of the country as a whole. It had not been a civil war fought over some fundamental principle of the kind that tears a nation apart. Ordinary people had been able to conduct their affairs more or less undisturbed, while the great pursued a more than usually stimulating form of bloodsport. But, in an age when the government was the King, continued uncertainty as to who was likely to be occupying the throne next was unsettling. It was bad for business, bad for the orderly administration of justice, and bred dangerous habits of disrespect for the rule of law. The crown was weakened and impoverished, the nobility were becoming disagreeably powerful and England had lost prestige abroad. If the new dynasty could establish a strong central authority, it would be assured of support from the solid middle block of the population with a stake in stability and prosperity.

In January 1486, Henry redeemed the pledge given at Rennes two years before and married Elizabeth, King Edward's daughter. In the veins of the second and third generations of Tudor monarchs would flow the blood of Plantagenet, both York and Lancaster, of Valois and Mortimer, Neville and Woodville, of the lady from Flanders and the seneschal to the princes of Gwynedd.

Like her bridegroom, Elizabeth was very much a child of the warring factions. She had been twice hurried into sanctuary with her mother; had suffered the grief of the unexplained disappearance and sinister end of her two brothers, and all the other alarms and anxieties of Richard's reign. She was a pretty, fair-haired girl in her early twenties at the time of her marriage, sweet-tempered, docile and affectionate; generous to her less fortunate younger sisters and kind to her mother, who was by all accounts a rather tiresome woman with an unlucky talent for making enemies.

Henry allowed his wife no share in the executive power, but there is no indication that she ever expected it or resented the fact that he wore a crown which should rightfully have been hers. Elizabeth of York seems to have been perfectly content with the role of Queen Consort, and certainly nobly fulfilled her prime function, giving birth to eight children before her death in 1503. Only one son and two daughters survived into adult life, not a very good omen even in an age of high infant-mortality, but it was enough to secure the succession.

Henry VII has been likened to a man who, starting from virtually nothing, built up a flourishing family business. His spirit, says Polydore Vergil, was distinguished, wise and prudent, his mind brave and resolute. John Stow thought him 'a prince of marvellous wisdom, policy, justice, temperance and gravity'. In private life he was a devoted son, an affectionate husband and a conscientious father. He was fond of music, a keen sportsman and generous to those in trouble. In spite of his early disadvantages, he was a cultured man, a patron of literature and the arts with a taste and talent for royal magnificence. His public abilities as king and statesman are beyond dispute, but he remains essentially a lonely figure – cold, secret and remote. His precarious youth had taught him to trust no one completely, to keep his own counsel and, above all, the importance of holding on to what he had won. He was admired, feared and respected by his contemporaries, but not loved. The first Henry Tudor lacked the precious gift of personal magnetism possessed in such abundance by his granddaughter Elizabeth, who in many other ways so closely resembled him, but he laid the foundation without which her achievement would have been impossible.

When he died the country was at peace. The crown was solvent. Despite some determined challenges, his dynasty was established and accepted. Reputable foreign monarchs were prepared to marry their children into it. There was a healthy male heir of full age ready to take over. Few men could have done more.

CHAPTER II

The King's Great Matter

O N one point everybody was agreed: the youthful Henry VIII was a most magnificent specimen of manhood, who seemed to embody all the gifts and graces of the ideal Christian monarch. When he succeeded to his father's throne in the spring of 1509 his contemporaries went wild with delight over this 'new and auspicious star', this 'lover of justice and goodness', their dazzling eighteen-year-old King. 'If you could see how all the world here is rejoicing in the possession of so great a prince,' wrote William Mountjoy to Desiderius Erasmus,

> how his life is all their desire, you could not contain your tears for joy. The heavens laugh, the earth exults, all things are full of milk, of honey and of nectar! Avarice is expelled the country. Liberality scatters wealth with bounteous hand. Our king does not desire gold or gems or precious metals, but virtue, glory, immortality.[1]

The country was ready for a change. In his last years Henry VII had become 'a dark prince, infinitely suspicious' and his subjects, forgetting the many solid benefits he had brought them, complained loud and bitterly about the shocking extortions of his tax collectors. In 1509 it really seemed as if a new era – 'called then the golden world' – had dawned, and few English kings have ever embarked on their reigns in such a general atmosphere of goodwill and buoyant optimism than the future father of Elizabeth Tudor – 'our natural, young, lusty and courageous prince and sovereign lord, King Harry the Eighth'.

As a physical type, the new King resembled his maternal grandfather, Edward IV, who was 'very tall of personage, exceeding the stature almost of all others' and 'of visage lovely, of body mighty, strong and clean-made. Howbeit in his latter days, with over-liberal diet, somewhat corpulent and burly. . . .' Descriptions which could equally well have been applied to his grandson.

The descriptions of Henry's own appearance as a young man were
lyrical. Piero Pasqualigo, the Venetian Ambassador Extraordinary, writing in 1515, declared that 'His Majesty is the handsomest potentate I ever set eyes on; above the usual height, with
an extremely fine calf to his leg, his complexion very fair and
bright, with auburn hair combed straight and short in the French
fashion, and a round face so very beautiful that it would become
a pretty woman.'[2] Four years later, Sebastian Giustinian, another
Venetian, was just as complimentary. Nature could not have
done more for the King, he said. He was much handsomer than
any other sovereign in Christendom, very fair and his whole frame
admirably proportioned.

Henry took after his grandfather Edward in other ways. The
Yorkist king had been noted for his popularity and, as Polydore
Vergil rather disapprovingly remarked, 'would use himself more
familiarly among private persons than the honour of his majesty
required'. Edward had fully realised the truth of the somewhat
cynical observation that 'the common people oftentimes more
esteem and take for greater kindness a little courtesy, than a great
benefit'. Henry knew this too, whether consciously or not. He
mingled freely with the common people, and when he chose to
exert his charm he could be irresistible. Thomas More put his
finger on it when he wrote to John Fisher: 'the king has a way
of making every man feel that he is enjoying his special favour,
just as the London wives pray before the image of Our Lady by
the Tower till each of them believes it is smiling upon *her*'.[3]

Henry had also inherited the prodigious energy of his Plantagenet forbears, and to his admiring subjects there seemed no end
to the skills and accomplishments of their glorious prince.
According to the Venetians, he could draw the bow with greater
strength than any man in England and jousted marvellously. He
was a capital horseman, inordinately fond of hunting, and capable
of tiring out eight or ten horses in one day. He was an enthusiastic
tennis-player, 'at which game', wrote Sebastian Giustinian, 'it is
the prettiest thing in the world to see him play, his fair skin
glowing through a shirt of the finest texture'.[4] The King was, in
fact, a first-rate all-round sportsman – wrestling, tilting, shooting,
hawking, dancing, running at the ring, casting of the bar – whatever form of physical exercise he engaged in, he excelled at.

Nor was his prowess only athletic. Henry had plenty of native

shrewdness and a good brain, when he stood still long enough
to use it. He had been well educated. He was an enthusiastic
amateur theologian. He spoke fluent French and Latin, some
Spanish and a little Italian. He enjoyed the company of scholars
and liked to display his own learning. A music-lover like his
father, he was himself a talented musician. He played the lute,
organ, virginals and harpsichord, could sing 'from book at
sight' and composed two five-part masses, a motet and many
instrumental pieces, rounds and part songs.

> Pastance with good company
> I love and shall until I die

he sang to his own accompaniment and, thanks to old Henry's
careful counting of the pennies, 'such grace of plenty reigned'
that young Henry was able 'to follow his desire and appetite'
to his heart's content. With the unselfconscious absorption of a
child, he threw himself into the delightful business of cutting a
dash in the world. He received the Venetian ambassadors under
a canopy of cloth of gold, wearing a doublet of white and crimson
satin and a purple velvet mantle lined with white satin. Round
his neck was a gold collar from which hung a diamond the size of
a walnut, while his fingers 'were one mass of jewelled rings'.
Mounted on a warhorse caparisoned in cloth of gold with a raised
pile, he looked like St George in person. On board his new
warship, named in honour of his sister Mary, he acted as pilot,
wearing 'a sailor's coat and trousers made of cloth of gold, and
a gold chain with the inscription "Dieu *est* mon Droit", to which
was suspended a whistle, which he blew nearly as loud as a
trumpet'.[5] He had a passion for dressing up – as Robin Hood;
'in Turkey fashion'; 'in white satin and green, embroidered and
set with letters and castles of fine gold in bullion'; in an abbreviated suit of 'blue velvet and crimson with long sleeves, all cut
and lined with cloth of gold'.[6] 'Youth will needs have dalliance,'
sang the King; and tournaments, pageants, banquets, revels and
'disguisings' followed one another in an unending, untiring
stream, so that life was spent 'in continual festival'.

From across the centuries one's mind balks at the splendours,
the superlatives, the super-human energy, the sheer prodigality
and over-exuberance of it all. He was more than life-size, this

amazing young man: a great, sumptuous, heraldic beast, rampant
on a field of scarlet and gold, 'disposed all to mirth and pleasure',
innocently exulting in his own magnificence. There were not many
signs as yet of that other beast, the cold-hearted egotist, tricky,
violent and cruel, which lurked behind the smooth pink and white
countenance with its intermittent aureole of fluffy red beard. Some
people caught a glimpse of it. George Cavendish, Thomas
Wolsey's gentleman usher, watching his master's rise to power,
noticed indulgently enough that the King 'loved nothing worse
than to be constrained to do anything contrary to his royal will
and pleasure'. Thomas More saw deeper. Even in the unclouded
days when Henry used to send for him to discuss 'astronomy,
geometry, divinity, and such other faculties'; and when 'for the
pleasure he took in his company' would visit More at his house
at Chelsea and walk in the garden with him, an arm flung round
his shoulders, Sir Thomas had no illusions. He told his son-in-
law, William Roper, that if his head could win the King a castle
in France 'it should not fail to go'.[7]

One of Henry's first actions had been to get himself a wife.
Barely six weeks after he came to the throne he married his
brother's widow, the Spanish princess Catherine of Aragon,*
daughter of those redoubtable monarchs Isabella of Castile and
Ferdinand of Aragon – *los Reyes Catolicos* – the Catholic Kings
of Spain. Catherine had come to England in 1501, when she was
fifteen, to be married to Arthur, Henry's elder brother, then
Prince of Wales. Not quite five months after the wedding young
Arthur was dead and, in order to preserve the Anglo-Spanish
alliance, Catherine had been betrothed to Henry, then rising
eleven years old, their marriage to take place when he was fifteen.
Then Isabella of Castile died. The political situation in Spain
looked less stable. Henry VII, always cautious, had hesitated,
wondering if after all he might do better for his one remaining
son. The marriage was postponed and Catherine remained a
widow, a pawn in the game of dynastic politics and the victim of
a not very edifying dispute over the payment of the second instal-
ment of her dowry. For seven years she waited; stoically enduring
the humiliating position of a guest who had outstayed her wel-

---

* I have spelt Catherine of Aragon's name with a 'C', coming, as it does, from
the Spanish 'Catalina'. For the other, numerous, Katherines who appear in this
story, I have followed the English spelling at the time.

come. Cold-shouldered and neglected, dependent on the reluctant provision of her father-in-law, Catherine had no money to pay her servants, hardly enough money for food and clothes, but she refused to despair. She had come to England to be married, to serve Spain with her own body, and in England she would stay. Even in her teens, Catherine of Aragon had a will of iron. In 1509 she got her reward. In the best tradition of all fairy tales, Prince Charming came into his own, rescued the forlorn princess and carried her off in triumph. It certainly looked like a happy ending.

Catherine was not startlingly beautiful but she was a good-looking girl, small and slender, with clear grey eyes and a mass of russet-coloured hair. She was also intelligent and thoughtful, and in the early days Henry relied on her a good deal, respecting her opinion and listening to her advice. Many of his most extravagant entertainments were planned, so he said, for her pleasure and Catherine never failed to be suitably appreciative. He wore her favour in the lists; heard vespers and compline every day in her chamber; read the latest books with her and hurried to bring her any titbits of news he thought would interest her.[8]

The King found his diversions, of course; that was to be expected. There was Elizabeth Blount who bore his bastard son in 1519. Later there was Mary Boleyn. There may well have been others. All the same, despite his highly coloured reputation, Henry was no Don Juan. By the standards of royal behaviour at the time, he was a faithful husband, at any rate in those early years, and Catherine repaid him with steadfast loyalty and devotion. Well bred, virtuous and dutiful, she had every quality of an ideal Queen Consort except the all-important one: she could not produce a healthy son.

The tragedy of the Queen's child-bearing began in 1510 with a still-born daughter. A son arrived on New Year's Day 1511, but lived only a few weeks. Time went by and more pregnancies ended in miscarriages, in babies born dead, babies who lived only a few days. Then, in February 1516, a child was born at Greenwich, alive and healthy. It was a girl, christened Mary. The King was philosophical, at least in public. 'We are both young', he said to a congratulatory ambassador; 'if it was a daughter this time, by the grace of God the sons will follow.' In the autumn of 1517 Catherine miscarried again. In November 1518 she was delivered of a still-born child. It was her last pregnancy.

By the early 1520s Henry was seriously worried about the
succession. In June 1525 he created his bastard Henry Fitzroy,
then six years old, Duke of Richmond – a semi-royal title. There
was even talk of a marriage between Richmond and the legitimate
heiress, Princess Mary. Henry's love affair with his wife had long
since grown cold. Catherine was nearly forty now, her prettiness
faded, her slender figure thickened and spread – although ambassadors still remarked on her beautiful complexion. Henry no
longer needed her as audience and confidante. Her very nationality
had become a liability, as English foreign policy, under the
guidance of Thomas Wolsey, leaned more and more towards a
French alliance. And there were no sons.

In the early spring of 1527, something or someone led the King
to open his Bible and turn to the Book of Leviticus. There, in the
twentieth chapter, he read: '. . . if a man shall take his brother's
wife, it is an unclean thing . . . they shall be childless'. According
to Henry's own account, once his attention had been drawn to
these alarming words, he began to have qualms (that famous
scruple which 'pricked' his conscience) soon to grow into an
unalterable conviction that his marriage was against God's law;
that for eighteen years he had been living in incestuous adultery
with his brother's wife. And the fact that they were childless, or
as good as childless, was surely, he reasoned, a sign of God's
displeasure. After all, Henry asked himself, why else should God
who had favoured him in all things, and whom he regarded very
much in the light of a senior partner, deny him living sons? Obviously something must be done, and the King turned to Cardinal
Wolsey, always so reliable, so devoted to his master's interests and
anxious only to satisfy his royal will and pleasure. Wolsey, confronted with what was in effect a command to arrange the
removal of the Queen with a minimum of scandal and incon-
venience, did his usual efficient best to oblige and in May 1527
instituted the divorce proceedings, or, to be more exact, the
nullity suit which was to have such incalculably far-reaching
effects on the whole course of English life.

The first tentative steps in 'the King's great matter', as it was
carefully referred to by those in the know, were taken in an
atmosphere of elaborate secrecy; but it was not long before news
of it leaked out. By midsummer the whole affair, as the Spanish
ambassador scornfully remarked, was 'as notorious as if it had

been proclaimed by the public crier'. By the end of the summer it was being freely rumoured that the pricking of the King's conscience was not the only spur prompting him to question the validity of his marriage to Catherine of Aragon. No one knows exactly when Henry first became enamoured of Anne Boleyn, but certainly by September what George Cavendish described as 'the long hid and secret love' between the King and Mistress Anne was a secret no longer.

The rise of the Boleyn family, who came originally and obscurely from Sall in Norfolk, had followed the classic pattern. Early in the fifteenth century, Geoffrey Boleyn, second son of a tenant farmer working some thirty acres of land, came up to London to seek his fortune. In 1428 he was admitted to the freedom of the City in the art of hatter, but subsequently changed his trade to become a mercer. In 1446 he was Sheriff of London and also of Middlesex. He married the daughter of Lord Hoo and Hastings; held the office of Lord Mayor in 1457 and before his death in 1463 had firmly established the family fortunes – acquiring the property of Blickling Hall in Norfolk from Sir John Fastolf and the manor and castle of Hever from the Cobhams of Kent. His son William had no need to concern himself with commerce. He was created Knight of the Bath at Richard III's coronation and was able to lead the pleasant life of a wealthy country squire. The Boleyns were now well on the way up the social ladder and William married into the noble Anglo-Irish family of Butler. His wife Margaret was the daughter and co-heir of Thomas Butler, last Earl of Ormonde. William Boleyn's son, Thomas, came to court to make his way in the royal service – one of the new men of the new dynasty. Thomas Boleyn had all the qualifications of a capable underling and by 1512 he was being entrusted with diplomatic missions abroad. He also made a useful marriage – to Lady Elizabeth Howard, one of the daughters of the second Duke of Norfolk. There were three surviving children of this marriage, George, Mary and Anne, who was born in 1507. Thomas was a careful father. In 1514 he managed to obtain for his elder daughter a much sought-after place as maid-of-honour in the suite of the King's sister Mary, when she crossed the Channel to marry old King Louis of France. Anne, then a child of seven, may have gone too, her mother being dead by this time. She certainly went to France at some stage in her childhood (most

probably she travelled over with her father in 1519, when he was
appointed ambassador) and entered the household of Queen
Claude, wife of Francis I, much as a girl of a socially ambitious
family nowadays is sent abroad to be 'finished' at a fashionable
boarding school.

Anne was back in England by early 1522. There was a plan,
arranged ironically by the King and Wolsey, to marry her to Sir
James Butler, an Irish chieftain and claimant to the earldom of
Ormonde, on which the Boleyns were also casting a covetous eye.
But Butler's price was too high and the negotiations fell through.
Anne's father then 'made such means that she was admitted to be
one of Queen Catherine's maids; among whom, for her excellent
gesture and behaviour, [she] did excel all other, in so much', said
George Cavendish, 'as the King began to kindle the brand of
amours, which was not known to any person, ne scantly to her
own person'. Certainly Anne was not thinking about the King at
this time. A well-grown girl of fifteen or so, she was looking
round for a husband and her choice fell on young Henry Percy,
son and heir of the Earl of Northumberland. This rather thick-
witted youth was attached to Wolsey's entourage and 'when it
chanced the Lord Cardinal at any time to repair to the court, the
Lord Percy would then resort for his pastime unto the Queen's
chamber, and there would fall in dalliance among the Queen's
maidens, being at the last more conversant with Mistress Anne
Boleyn than with any other'.[9] The young people soon reached
an understanding, but this promising romance was ruthlessly
blighted by Wolsey who, in a public scolding, reduced the
unfortunate Percy to tears for his 'peevish folly' in so far forgetting himself as to become entangled with 'a foolish girl yonder
in the court'. The Cardinal may or may not have been acting on
instructions from the King (the Butler marriage was still being
negotiated), but Anne never forgave the insult. She showed her
annoyance so openly that she was sent away from court for a while
in disgrace.

It is a little hard to understand just what Henry saw in her. She
was certainly not an especially beautiful girl. Her complexion is
variously described as sallow or 'rather dark'. She had a slight
deformity – a rudimentary sixth finger – on one hand and a mole,
or strawberry mark, on her neck. The Venetian ambassador, a
reasonably detached observer, wrote in 1532: 'Madam Anne is

not one of the handsomest women in the world; she is of middling
stature, swarthy complexion, long neck, wide mouth, bosom not
much raised, and in fact has nothing but the English King's great
appetite, and her eyes, which are black and beautiful.'[10] Her eyes
seem to have been her best feature; another ambassador remarked
enigmatically that they 'invited to conversation'. She also had
quantities of thick, glossy black hair. She sang well, played the lute
and was a graceful dancer, but apart from her French education
appears to have had no special advantages or accomplishments to
distinguish her from many other young women of her time and
class. She is said to have had a ready wit, but no record of it has
survived. Nevertheless, attractive she undoubtedly was. Thomas
Wyatt, the able and sophisticated courtier and poet, unquestionably found her so. Probably her fascination lay in that special
quality of sexual magnetism which eludes description, defies por-
traiture and has very little to do with physical beauty. She also
had a venomous temper, rapacious ambition and a definite
tendency to hysteria. It proved a highly explosive mixture and
Elizabeth Tudor's mother was to leave a trail of wrecked lives
behind her.

Henry must presumably have started in serious pursuit of Anne
Boleyn some time towards the end of 1526 and became 'so
amorously affectionate that will bare place and high discretion
was banished for the time'. But the King soon made the surprising
discovery that Anne had no intention of becoming his mistress.
Her sister Mary had already filled that position and gained little
as a result. Thomas Boleyn's younger daughter, from her vantage-
point as maid-of-honour, had been able to watch the Queen's
influence weakening and had begun to realise that if she kept her
head and played her cards skilfully she might conceivably win for
herself an unimaginably greater prize. Whatever her faults, Anne
had courage, vision and tremendous strength of will. Henry, now
in his mid-thirties, was still an extremely attractive man – foreign
ambassadors were still writing eulogies about his angelic appearance. He also had the almost magical aura of his kingship, quite
apart from the famous charm. It would have taken very considerable resolution on the part of an insignificant girl of nineteen to
refuse to give him what he wanted; not to mention the tact and
finesse needed to make him accept her rebuff without resentment. This is remarkable enough. Even more astonishing is the

undoubted fact that she contrived to go on resisting (and enthralling) him for six years – sometimes repulsing, sometimes encouraging, meek, imperious, seductive, pettish by turns. In another age, Anne Boleyn might have found an outlet for her energy and talent on the stage. Her daughter Elizabeth certainly inherited her very considerable histrionic talent.

Henry was not used to being refused, and what he could not have he wanted with furious concentration. Having satisfied himself that Anne was only interested in marriage, he made up his mind with majestic simplicity to give her marriage. Here, he decided, was a woman worthy to be the mother of his sons. He did not, however, tell Wolsey about his matrimonial intentions when he first broached the subject of divorce in the spring of 1527. That September, when the Cardinal (who had been hoping to replace Queen Catherine with a French princess) saw what was in the wind, he was 'extremely annoyed at a circumstance which boded no good to him'. But Wolsey concealed his feelings. Anne Boleyn was not the only person in England who disliked him, and his position depended almost entirely on the King's goodwill. The King must therefore be given what he wanted.

In normal conditions this should not have presented insuperable problems. The ending of a marriage – especially a royal marriage – by a decree of nullity was by no means without precedent, and provided a reasonably viable case could be made out the Pope would be unlikely to disoblige so dutiful a son of the Church as the King of England. Unfortunately for Henry, conditions were not normal. In Italy, one of the interminable wars between France and the Habsburg empire was in progress, and in the early summer of 1527 Rome suffered occupation and sack by a Habsburg army. The Pope was virtually a prisoner of the Habsburg Charles V, the most powerful monarch in Christendom, Holy Roman Emperor, ruler of Spain, the Spanish Netherlands and a whole patchwork of German states. And Charles, who had a strong sense of family loyalty, was Queen Catherine's nephew. As soon as Catherine heard about her husband's intentions – and she heard about them sooner than he meant her to – she appealed energetically to her nephew for help, begging him to prevent any hearing of the case in England and especially any hearing of it by Wolsey. Henry was by now sending a procession of envoys to Rome, all badgering the Pope for a commission giving Wolsey full powers to hear the case and pronounce judgement on it without fear of reversal. The Holy Father shed tears and tore his beard. He temporised. He hesitated. Eventually, however, as the French advanced and the Emperor's army of occupation retreated in disorder, he agreed to send Cardinal Lorenzo Campeggio to England with a decretal commission authorising him and Wolsey jointly to enquire into the validity of the King's marriage and declare it null and void if the facts seemed to warrant it – a document so worded that it virtually directed the verdict in Henry's favour. But Campeggio was also given instructions not to let the commission out of his possession. He was to take no irrevocable action without reference to Rome. He was to delay matters as much as possible and, if possible, persuade the King to abandon the whole idea.

Campeggio arrived in London on 9 October 1528. He found Henry restive and impatient for action. He was not amenable to persuasion and appeared so completely satisfied with the justice of his cause that, after a long interview with him, Campeggio reported that he believed an angel descending from heaven would be unable to persuade him otherwise. Henry based his argument on the text in Leviticus and on the contention that the Pope who had originally issued dispensations for his marriage to Catherine (or any other Pope for that matter) had no authority to dispense the law of God. Catherine's main line of defence was simple. Her marriage to Prince Arthur had never been consummated, she told Campeggio. She had come to Henry *virgo intacta*. Therefore, the question of the Levitical prohibition and the Pope's powers to dispense it did not arise; although, as she pointed out, this had all been carefully gone into at the time of her second betrothal. She refused all bribes, all attempts to induce her to retire gracefully into a convent. She was unmoved by threats. She believed herself to be Henry's lawful wife. If she blasphemed against the sacrament of marriage, she would be damning her immortal soul and consenting to the damnation of her husband's. She would be admitting that she had lived in sin for nearly twenty years and that her daughter was a bastard. She would also leave the way open for Anne Boleyn. All her instincts as a woman, wife, mother and Queen were outraged.

By the following summer Campeggio had run out of delaying tactics. In June 1529 the legatine court, which was to consider the

King of England's marriage, opened at Blackfriars and cited
Henry and Catherine to appear. It was an extraordinary occasion,
and one unprecedented in England. The King did not appear to
notice that he was admitting the right of a foreign power to set
up a court in his own realm and to summon him before it as a
private individual. Nothing mattered, it seemed, if he could only
get his divorce. Honest George Cavendish, watching the progress
of events from his place in Wolsey's shadow, was deeply shocked.
In his Life of his master, he lamented the wilfulness of princes
against whose appetites no reasonable persuasions would suffice.
'And above all things', he went on, 'there is no one thing that
causeth them to be more wilful than carnal desire and voluptuous
affection of foolish love.'

On 18 June the Queen lodged a formal protest against the
jurisdiction of the legatine court, and appealed to the Pope to
advoke the case to Rome. Three days later she made her famous
appeal to Henry himself. In the great hall at Blackfriars, before
both cardinals and the whole bench of bishops, she knelt at her
husband's feet and begged him, for all the love that had been
between them, to do her justice and right and to take some pity
on her. 'And when ye had me at the first', she said, 'I take God
to my judge that I was a very maid without touch of man; and
whether it be true or no, I put it to your conscience.' There was
silence. Henry looked straight ahead, stony-faced. Catherine
finished her speech. She rose from her knees, curtsied and turned
to go, ignoring the repeated summons from the court crier. 'And
thus she departed out of that court without any further answer at
that time or at any other, nor would never appear in any court
after.'[11]

After Catherine had gone, Henry repeated the same speech he
had already made several times to various audiences. How he
valued all the Queen's noble qualities and what an excellent,
virtuous and obedient wife she had always been; but how greatly
his conscience troubled him and how he feared himself in danger
of God's indignation. How it behoved him to consider the state
of the realm and the danger it would stand in for lack of a prince
to succeed him. It was hardly necessary to remind his hearers
again of the 'mischief and manslaughter' which had prevailed
between the Houses of York and Lancaster in the time of their
fathers and grandfathers. He had therefore thought it proper to

'attempt the law therein' to see if he might take another wife by whom God would send him male issue. He was not moved, he said, by any carnal concupiscence nor by any misliking of the Queen's person. It was an effective speech, moving and dignified. It was also sincere. Henry had long since convinced himself that he was acting in purest good faith. Not everybody, though, was similarly convinced. 'The common people being ignorant of the truth and in especial women and others that favoured the Queen, talked largely and said that the King would for his own pleasure have another wife.'[12] Catherine had always been popular with the common people, just as they always cordially hated Anne Boleyn.

At Blackfriars the Queen was declared contumacious and the proceedings continued in her absence. Catherine had been quite right when she said that she would never get a fair hearing before any court in England. Only one person – John Fisher, Bishop of Rochester – had the courage to speak cogently in her defence, and much of the court's time was taken up by a somewhat prurient attempt to prove that her first marriage had been fully consummated. It was all to no purpose, however, for the European scene was changing. On 21 June the French had been decisively defeated in battle. A week later the Pope came to terms with the victorious Emperor. In July he agreed to revoke the authority of the legatine court. The King of England's divorce case would now, after all, be decided at Rome.

It was the end of Wolsey. Predictably, he became the scapegoat for Henry's rage and disappointment. Scenting blood, his enemies gathered for the kill, and that autumn, Eustace Chapuys, the Emperor's new ambassador in London, reported that the downfall of the Cardinal was complete.

The King's domestic arrangements at this time were unusual. Anne now accompanied him wherever he went, and as George Cavendish remarked kept an estate more like a Queen than a simple maid. She had her own apartments at Greenwich and was receiving all the attentions due to a royal bride-to-be; while in another part of the palace Queen Catherine, outwardly unperturbed, continued to preside over the household, mending her husband's shirts and quietly attending to his comforts.

In December 1529, Thomas Boleyn, already Viscount Rochford, was further rewarded with the earldoms of Wiltshire and Ormonde. His daughter became Lady Anne Rochford. At a splendid banquet held to mark the occasion, Lady Anne took precedence even over the Duchesses of Suffolk and Norfolk and, according to the indignant Chapuys, 'was made to sit by the King's side, occupying the very place allotted to a crowned Queen, which is a thing never done before in this country. After dinner there was dancing and carousing, so that it seemed as if nothing were wanting but the priest to give away the nuptial ring and pronounce the blessing'.[13]

But the struggle for the divorce went on, and the ultimate prize seemed as far away as ever. Time was passing, as the Lady Anne did not scruple to remind her frustrated lover, while for his sake she sacrificed her youth and her chances of making an honourable marriage elsewhere. The case was still pending at Rome, and despite the pressure exerted by the Emperor's agents, despite repeated pleas from Catherine herself, the Pope remained inactive. Henry had already threatened schism if judgement were to go against him. If he carried out that threat, it would mean a loss to the Papacy in revenue and prestige which it could ill afford – especially at a time when heresy was spreading alarmingly in Europe. As long as the matter was left undecided, the King might hesitate to do anything rash. One of the disputants might die. Henry might tire of Anne. Few people had yet realised the exact nature of her hold on him. Her will was law, reported one ambassador. There were occasions when the King even seemed rather frightened of her. Her sharp tongue and arrogant behaviour had made her a lot of enemies, but Henry was still fascinated – almost, it sometimes appeared, against his will.

It was during the year 1530 that the King first began to evolve the plan which would solve both his marital problems and the financial difficulties now besetting him. If the Pope would not give him his divorce – and it was becoming pretty clear that he would not – then he must manage without the Pope, although remaining, at least in his own estimation, a good Catholic. If he were to take on himself the supreme religious power in his own realm, the clergy would come to realise that they could no longer look to Rome for protection and would be dependent only on the King. They would then be eager to do the King's bidding. The appearances of law could be maintained and the wealth of the English Church would be at the disposal of the crown.

Henry had found a new councillor by this time – Thomas

Cromwell, once a rather shady underling of Cardinal Wolsey's – and this radical solution may have been his idea; certainly his was the executive genius which put it into practice. The idea itself somehow bears the stamp of the King's single-minded ruthlessness when it came to getting his own way. At all events, it was an idea which could hardly fail to appeal to him.

In July 1531 he finally separated from Catherine. Henry had gone on a hunting trip, accompanied as usual by Anne, and he sent a message ordering the Queen to leave the court before his return. Catherine replied calmly that she would go wherever her husband commanded, to the stake if need be. Sympathy for her plight among all classes of Englishmen and their wives (especially their wives) was now so strong that Eustace Chapuys thought very little encouragement would be necessary to produce a general uprising against the divorce. Despite government intimidation and bribery, this feeling was reflected in both Houses of Parliament; but, although the members would do nothing directly to assist the King to get his divorce, it was easy to incite them to attack the Church. In May 1532, the clergy, already badly shaken by Wolsey's fall, lacking any effective leadership at home and with little support apparently forthcoming from Rome, abjectly surrendered all their ancient freedom from lay authority. To all intents and purposes, the English Church was Henry's to do what he liked with.

Only one obstacle now remained. William Warham, Archbishop of Canterbury, was an old man, ill and frightened, but there was a point beyond which he would not go. He would not defy the Pope's ban on any reopening of the 'great matter' in England, and the King must have the authority of Canterbury to give his divorce and remarriage even the appearance of legality. In August, Providence came to Henry's aid and death removed the Archbishop from the scene. Cromwell and Anne Boleyn knew the very man to replace him: Thomas Cranmer, once a chaplain in the Boleyn household, an inoffensive creature who could be relied on to do what he was told.

That October Anne, decked in Queen Catherine's jewels, was to accompany the King on a state visit to France, but before the ambiguous couple crossed the Channel an event of considerable significance had taken place. Anne at last surrendered the citadel of her body and gave Henry what he had been waiting for since

1526. Her sense of timing was impeccable. Had she yielded sooner, she might easily have lost everything. Had she insisted on waiting for Cranmer's installation, the King might have had too much time to think. Infatuated though he was, he had not been entirely unresentful of some of her high-handed ways, and serious doubts about her virtue were (not surprisingly) being expressed by a good many people. Now that divorce was within his grasp, Henry might well have reflected that another more tractable, more socially acceptable wife than Anne could also give him the sons he yearned for. But in September 1532 his gratification was complete. Anne had surrendered on her own terms and was accorded full honours of war. She marched out, as it were, with bands playing and colours flying, being created Marquess of Pembroke in her own right on the first of the month. A grant of a thousand pounds a year in land went with her new dignity, and remainder in lands and title to the heirs male of her body – the usual qualifying phrase 'lawfully begotten' being omitted from the Letters Patent. The significance of the omission is clear enough. Anne felt reasonably confident of final victory now, but even at this late stage she was taking no unnecessary chances. In the years to come her daughter was to display the same cautious hard-headedness, the same determination always to leave open a line of retreat.

CHAPTER III

'An Incredible Fierce Desire to Eat Apples'

ON 22 February 1533 a very odd little episode took place at court and was promptly reported to Eustace Chapuys, the Emperor's ambassador, who made it his business always to be well informed of current gossip. It seemed that Anne Boleyn, Marquess of Pembroke, or 'the Lady' as Chapuys usually scornfully referred to her (at other times he used a blunter epithet) had emerged from her private apartments into the hall or gallery, where a large crowd was assembled. Seeing a particular friend among the company, 'one she loves well' – most likely it was Sir Thomas Wyatt – she called out to him in sudden excitement, apparently *à propos* of nothing, that 'for the last three days she had had such an incredible fierce desire to eat apples as she had never felt before, and that the King had said to her that it was a sign that she was with child, and she had said no, it was not so at all'. She then burst out laughing and disappeared abruptly back into her rooms, while the onlookers stared at each other 'abashed and uneasy'.[1] It is not difficult to imagine the scene – the ring of avidly curious faces, the awkward silence broken by that disconcerting shriek of laughter, the shut door and then a rising susurration of voices as the court fell happily on this juicy new titbit of scandal. Anne was, in fact, nearly three months pregnant by the time she made her somewhat unconventional announcement. She did not add that it was now nearly a month since she had been married to the King, or perhaps it would be more accurate to say had gone through a form of marriage with him, since Henry, in spite of everything, was still legally tied to his first wife. The secret had been well kept. Even Thomas Cranmer, Archbishop-elect of Canterbury, was not told, so he said, until a fortnight after the event. Eustace Chapuys, for all his excellent intelligence network, had heard nothing definite; though that devoted friend and tireless champion of Queen Catherine and her daughter was becoming increasingly worried by the way things were going.

Henry must have known that Anne was pregnant by about the middle of January, and from then on that one momentous fact transcended everything else in importance. Whatever happened, whoever had to suffer, no matter what drastic action had to be taken, the child – the longed-for son and heir – must be born in wedlock and there was no more time to lose. Already a Bill setting out the self-sufficiency of the English Church was being drafted for parliamentary approval. In future all spiritual causes, including, of course, the royal divorce, were to be settled within the jurisdiction of the state without appeal to any higher earthly authority, because in future no higher earthly authority would exist. But the breach with Rome was not yet complete. Before it became irreparable, one last vital favour must be wrung from the Pope. In spite of Chapuys's repeated and vehement warnings that Cranmer had the reputation of being 'devoted heart and soul to the Lutheran sect', that he was a servant of Anne's and would do nothing to displease the King, the Pope, astonishingly, allowed himself to be duped into accepting Cranmer's nomination to the see of Canterbury and on 26 March the Bulls authorising his consecration arrived in England. On 30 March the new Archbishop was installed with all the usual pomp of the ancient ceremony. On 11 April, less than a fortnight after he had sworn a solemn oath of allegiance to the Pope before the high altar, Cranmer defied the Pope's solemn decree imposing silence on all parties to the divorce *lite pendente*. In a letter which is almost comic in its crawling servility, he begged the King for licence 'to proceed to the examination, final determination and judgement' of his matrimonial difficulties. Licence was duly granted. It would certainly not have been proper, wrote Henry in reply, for Cranmer, as a subject, to meddle in 'so weighty and great a cause, pertaining to us, being your Prince and Sovereign' without prior permission. The King recognised no superior on earth and was not subject to the laws of any other earthly creature; 'yet', he continued kindly, 'because ye be, under us, by God's calling and ours, the most principal minister of our spiritual jurisdiction, within this our realm, who we think assuredly is so in the fear of God, and love towards the observance of His laws, to the which laws, we, as a Christian King, have always heretofore and shall ever most obediently submit ourself, will not therefore refuse . . . your humble request, offer, and towardness; that is, to mean to make an end, according to the will and pleasure of Almighty God, in our said great cause of matrimony'.[2] The fact that the Archbishop had received his preferment and authority at the hands of the Pope was now conveniently ignored. The unblinking dishonesty of these manœuvres was also ignored. They would achieve the desired result, and that was all that mattered.

Any remaining shreds of reticence about the exact nature of Anne's status were now cast aside. On Easter Saturday, 12 April, she appeared in public for the first time in full royal state; going to Mass with trumpets sounding before her, 'loaded with diamonds and other precious stones' and wearing a gorgeous dress of gold tissue, with the Duke of Norfolk's daughter carrying her train. Henceforth Anne was officially prayed for as Queen, though this caused more than one congregation to walk out in protest, and the nobility, with the King's eye watchfully fixed on them, were required to pay their respects to her. According to Chapuys, now that the moment had come, 'all people here are perfectly astonished, for the whole thing seems a dream, and even those who support her party do not know whether to laugh or cry'.[3]

On the afternoon of 10 May, Cranmer opened his enquiry into 'the great cause of matrimony' at the small Augustinian priory of St Peter at Dunstable, chosen because it was well away from London and near enough to Ampthill, the secluded Bedfordshire manor where she was now living, to enable Catherine to attend without causing any commotion. In fact, the government hoped to get the whole business over and done with before too many people realised what was happening. Catherine, of course, refused to recognise the jurisdiction of Cranmer's court and ignored his summons to appear, no doubt to his enormous relief. On 23 May, to the surprise of no one, the Archbishop pronounced the King's first marriage to have been null and void from the beginning. By 28 May he had faithfully completed his task by finding his master's second marriage good and lawful; 'for', as he wrote, 'the time of the Coronation is so instant, and so near at hand, that the matter requireth good expedition to be had in the same'.[4] Thus the stage was set for the legitimate appearance of the child for whose sake the ancient framework of the canon law had been so ruthlessly manipulated. The King himself might be satisfied but many loyal subjects entertained serious doubts as to whether he did, in fact, have the power to interpret the law of God to suit himself.

When, on 31 May, Anne rode in state through the City to Westminster to be crowned, she is said to have complained that she saw 'a great many caps on heads, and heard but a few tongues'. According to one hostile witness, there were not ten people who greeted her with 'God save you!'[5] Chapuys, of course, thought the whole occasion 'a cold, meagre, and uncomfortable thing, to the great dissatisfaction not only of the common people, but also of the rest'[6] The common people always enjoyed a good show, but the initials H.A. set up everywhere by the city authorities provoked some rude laughter. Ha ha! Ha ha! jeered the cynical Londoners and, in spite of the free drink running in profusion from the conduits all that day, the general reaction was one of obstinate distaste and a conviction that no amount of ceremony would ever make a Queen out of that 'goggle-eyed whore' Nan Bullen.

As for Catherine, still the true Queen to the vast majority of the English people, in loneliness, humiliation and apparent defeat, she was still fighting. That April, before Cranmer had even opened his court at Dunstable, she had been visited by a deputation headed by Anne Boleyn's uncle, the Duke of Norfolk. The substance of their message, reported Chapuys, was that Catherine must renounce her title of Queen and allow her case to be decided in England. By so doing she would not only prevent possible bloodshed, but would be treated 'much better than she could possibly expect'. In any case, Norfolk told her flatly, further resistance was useless, as the King had already married again. In future she was to be known as Princess Dowager and, unless she submitted, would have to manage on a greatly reduced allowance. Catherine's reply was predictable. 'The Queen', Chapuys's report continued, 'resolutely said that as long as she lived she would entitle herself queen; as to keeping house herself, she cared not to begin that duty so late in life.' She hoped her husband would allow her to retain her confessor, a physician, an apothecary and two maids. If even that seemed too much to ask, 'she would willingly go about the world begging alms for the love of God'.[7]

In the opinion of Chapuys, the King, although by nature kind and generously inclined, had been so perverted by Anne's malign influence that he no longer seemed the same man. Henry would listen to none of the ambassador's indignant remonstrances about Catherine's treatment, but when Chapuys was awkward enough to point out that he could not be certain of having children by his new wife the King exclaimed three times running: 'Am I not a man like others?' All the same, it is embarrassing for any man to find himself with two wives. A King with two Queens crowned and anointed in his realm runs a grave risk of looking foolish, or worse. So, in July, yet another attempt was made to bully Catherine into surrender. The King's commissioners found her 'lying on her pallet, because she had pricked her foot with a pin, so that she might not well stand or go, and also sore annoyed with a cough', but she was as indomitable as ever. When Catherine of Aragon had told the two Cardinals, Wolsey and Campeggio, five years earlier that she believed herself to be Henry's lawful wife and would submit to the Pope's judgement in the matter and to no one else's, she had meant just that. Now she restated her position yet once more, yielding not one inch of ground, and was faced with the meanest threat of all; that her obstinacy and 'unkindness' might well provoke the King to 'withdraw his fatherly love' from her daughter, 'which chiefly should move her', thought the commissioners hopefully, 'if none other cause did'. Catherine was grieved but unmoved. Her reply, as quoted in the official report, was a model of dignity and courage.

> As to the Princess, her daughter, she said that she was the King's true begotten child, and as God had given her unto them, so, for her part, she would render her again unto the King, as his daughter, to do with her as shall stand with his pleasure; trusting to God that she will prove an honest woman.[8]

Not for any consideration on earth, not even for her beloved only child, would the daughter of the Catholic Kings of Spain put her immortal soul in danger, or allow her honour to be impugned. Nothing and nobody would ever induce her 'to be a slanderer of herself and confess to have been the King's harlot these four-and-twenty years'.[9] When the commissioners, at her request, brought her the written account of their confrontation, Catherine called for a pen and furiously scratched out the words 'Princess Dowager' wherever they appeared.

The fine summer of 1533 wore on. Anne's time was approaching and preparations for her lying-in had begun. 'The King', wrote Chapuys,

> believing in the report of his physicians and astrologers, that his Lady will certainly give him a male heir, has made up his mind to solemnize the event with a pageant and tournament. . . . The King has likewise caused to be taken out of his treasure room one of the most magnificent and gorgeous beds that could be thought of. . . .

'Very fortunately for the Lady', continued the ambassador rather spitefully,

> the said bed has been in her possession for the last two months; otherwise she would not have it now, for it appears that she being some time ago very jealous of the King, and not without legitimate cause, made use of certain words which he very much disliked, telling her that she must shut her eyes and endure as those who were better than herself had done, and that she ought to know that he could at any time lower her as much as he had raised her.[10]

The coldness following this tiff had lasted several days but Chapuys felt obliged to add that it was only a 'love quarrel' of which 'no great notice should be taken'. Nevertheless it was a red light, a warning that the honeymoon was over.

By early September the court had moved to the delightful riverside palace of Placentia at Greenwich. Originally built as a royal residence by Humphrey, Duke of Gloucester, the same Duke of Gloucester who had once so harried Owen Tudor, it had become a favourite home of Owen's descendants. Henry himself had been born there. It was at Greenwich that he had married Catherine nearly a quarter of a century ago. His daughter Mary had been born and christened there, and at Greenwich on 'the seventh day of September, 1533, being Sunday, Queen Anne was brought to bed of a fair daughter at three of the clock in the afternoon'.[11]

Chapuys, though he said he considered the news of no great

importance, could not conceal his malicious satisfaction. 'The King's mistress', he reported, 'was delivered of a girl, to the great disappointment and sorrow of the King, of the Lady herself, and of others of her party, and to the great shame and confusion of physicians, astrologers, wizards and witches, all of whom affirmed it would be a boy.'[12]

Henry's private feelings can only be guessed at. Throughout the long, bitter struggle for the divorce – in the course of which he had defied the Pope, insulted the Emperor and deeply offended so large a proportion of his subjects that even his apparently unassailable popularity had waned – he had been driven by that most primordial urge: the urge to beget a son and heir. And now he had failed to secure the succession; if anything he had made matters worse by introducing an element of doubt and confusion. The only saving grace was that Anne's useless daughter was at least healthy and gave promise that she might have healthy brothers. All the same, Henry was forty-two now. If and when he did have a son, there was a strong likelihood of another long minority and nobody was under any illusions about the kind of trouble that could lead to. Probably no royal birth in English history was quite such a grievous disappointment as Elizabeth Tudor's.

Still, a good face had to be put on it. A Te Deum for Anne's safe delivery was sung in St Paul's in the presence of the Lord Mayor and the Aldermen, and the christening took place on the afternoon of Wednesday, 10 September in the Friars' Church at Greenwich. The Mayor and Aldermen were there again in force, and the way between the palace and the church was hung with arras and strewn with green rushes. In the church, which was also hung with arras, 'divers gentlemen with aprons and towels about their necks' stood round the font, over which was hung a canopy of crimson satin fringed with gold so that 'no filth should come in', and 'a close place with a pan of fire' was provided 'to make the child ready in'. The procession, headed by eleven selected citizens of London, then formed up at the Palace. The three-day-old baby, wrapped in a mantle of purple velvet with a long train, was carried by the Dowager Duchess of Norfolk, flanked by the Dukes of Norfolk and Suffolk and followed by the Countess of Kent, the Earl of Wiltshire, who must surely have been a pardonably proud grandfather, and the Earl of Derby. 'When

the child was come to the church door', says Edward Hall in his
Chronicle,

> the Bishop of London met it with divers bishops and abbots mitred,
> and began the observances of the Sacrament. The godfather was the
> lord Archbishop of Canterbury: the godmothers were the old
> Duchess of Norfolk and the old Marchioness of Dorset, widows, and
> the child was named Elizabeth.

The baby was then brought to the font and baptised,

> and this done, Garter chief King of Arms cried aloud, God of His
> infinite goodness, send prosperous life and long, to the high and
> mighty Princess of England, Elizabeth: and then the trumpets blew,
> then the child was brought up to the altar, and the Gospel said over
> it: and after that immediately the Archbishop of Canterbury
> confirmed it.[13]

The trumpets sounded again, suitably expensive gifts were presented, and refreshment of wafers, comfits and hippocras was
provided for the company. Then the procession reformed and
trooped back to the palace by torchlight. After the infant Princess
had been safely restored to her mother, the city fathers were
thanked for their attendance and repaired to the cellar to wet the
baby's head in a more sustaining beverage than hippocras before
taking their barges to go home.

The faithful Chapuys duly reported to the Emperor that the
christening of 'the little bastard' – he always referred to Elizabeth
in the flattest terms – had been 'as dull and disagreeable' as the
mother's coronation and that nowhere had there been 'the
bonfires, illuminations, and rejoicings customary on such occasions'. The ambassador was most afraid of the consequences for
the King's elder daughter, now seventeen years old and still
officially heir to the throne. Immediately after Elizabeth's birth it
had been proclaimed that Mary was no longer to be called
Princess of Wales. There was also a rumour going round the
court that her household and allowance were soon to be reduced.
'May God in His infinite mercy', wrote Chapuys, 'prevent a still
worse treatment. Meanwhile', he continued, 'the Princess, prudent and virtuous as she naturally is, has taken all these things
with patience, trusting entirely in God's mercy and goodness. She

has addressed to her mother, the Queen, a most wonderful letter full of consolation and comfort.'[14]

It was two years now since Mary had been allowed to see Catherine and, obliged to stand helplessly by, watching from a distance while her mother's predicament steadily worsened, she not unnaturally harboured thoughts of Anne Boleyn which were far from being either prudent or virtuous. Mary had always ranged herself beside her mother on the domestic battlefront as – quite apart from her strong natural loyalties and deep religious convictions – she was bound to do. For if Mary admitted the nullity of her parents' marriage she also admitted her own illegitimacy and denied her rights of inheritance.

Until the arrival of her half-sister, Mary had been left more or less alone, living quietly in the country chaperoned by her friend and Lady Governess, the Countess of Salisbury. Now all this was to be changed. On 20 September her newly appointed Chamberlain, Lord Hussey, reported to the Council that he had, as commanded, signified to the Princess the King's pleasure 'concerning the diminishing of her high estate of the name and dignity of Princess'. It was the first direct challenge and Mary met it boldly. She was astonished, she told Hussey, at his declaring such a thing 'alone, and without sufficient authorisation by commission or other writing from the King'. She knew herself to be the King's lawful daughter and heir and would not believe that he intended to diminish her estate 'without a writing from him'.[15] On 2 October Hussey received a letter from William Paulet, Comptroller of the King's Household, ordering Mary's removal from her pleasant house at Beaulieu, the manor of Newhall Boreham in Essex, because the King wished to lend it to, of all people, Anne Boleyn's brother George. Mary demanded to be shown Paulet's letter and there saw herself referred to baldly as 'the Lady Mary, the King's daughter'. Her title of Princess had disappeared. Apparently she was now no better than Henry Fitzroy, the King's bastard, or not as good – he at least bore the title of Duke of Richmond. Mary tried sending a letter to her father, hoping perhaps that a personal appeal might still reach him, 'for I doubt not', she wrote pathetically, 'but you take me for your lawful daughter born in true matrimony. If I agreed to the contrary I should offend God; in all other things Your Highness shall find me an obedient daughter.'[16]

Her only answer was an admonitory visit from a commission of three earls and Dr Simpson, Dean of the King's Chapel. They brought with them 'Articles' which were to be shown on the King's behalf to his daughter, the Lady Mary. The King, according to this document, was 'surprised' to be informed that his said daughter had so far forgotten her 'filial duty and allegiance' as to 'arrogantly usurp the title of Princess' and pretend to be heir apparent. The commissioners were 'commanded to declare to her the folly and danger of her conduct' and to point out that she 'worthily deserved the King's high displeasure and punishment by law'. However, if she conformed to his will, he might incline, 'of his fatherly pity', to promote her welfare.[17] Faithfully taking her tune from her mother, Mary would not conform and the battle between father and daughter was joined.

On 3 November, Chapuys wrote to the Emperor with his usual splutter of indignation that, 'not satisfied with having taken away from his own legitimate daughter the name and title of princess', the King was now threatening to send Mary to live as a maid-of-honour to 'his bastard daughter'.[18] The ambassador was genuinely appalled. Not merely would such a step be a brutal humiliation to the proud, sensitive girl accustomed all her life to being treated as the King's heir, but Anne Boleyn had already been heard to express herself with some violence on the subject of Mary and her obstinacy. If the King carried out his threat, she would be alone and unprotected in a household ruled by Anne's relations. There was no knowing what indignities she might be subjected to, or what 'perils and insidious dangers' might lie in wait for her in such a situation. Chapuys continued to remonstrate, to expostulate and to hint darkly at the undesirable consequences likely to result from the 'cruel and strange' treatment being accorded to the Emperor's cousin, but he got little satisfaction. The King was an honourable, virtuous and wise prince, incapable of doing anything not founded on 'justice or reason', Thomas Cromwell assured him blandly.

By the end of November, arrangements for the separate establishment to be set up for the little Princess Elizabeth had been completed. On 2 December it was formally recorded in the Acts of the Council that:

Item, the King's Highness hath appointed that the Lady Princess shall be conveyed from hence toward Hatfield upon Wednesday the next week; and that Wednesday night, to repose and lie at the house of the Earl of Rutland, in Enfield; and the next day to be conveyed to Hertford* and there to remain with such family in household, as the King's Highness hath assigned and established for the same.[19]

This was normal procedure. The court was not regarded as a suitable place for bringing up small children, who needed clean country air, free from plague and other infections, if they were to have an even chance of survival. The new household was put under the general charge of Anne Shelton and Alice Clere, both Anne Boleyn's aunts, while the 'Lady Mistress', with particular responsibility for the baby's health and well-being, was Margaret Bryan, also a connection of Anne's on the Howard side.

So, on or about 12 December, the three-month-old Elizabeth set out on her first 'progress', being carried through the City with some ceremony, in order, according to Chapuys, 'the better to impress upon the people the idea of her being the true Princess of Wales'. Escorting the party was the Duke of Norfolk who, once he had seen his great-niece safely installed at the old bishop's palace at Hatfield, descended on the unfortunate Mary and bundled her off at half-an-hour's notice to join the nursery establishment. When asked, on her arrival, 'if she did not like to see and pay her court to the Princess', Mary replied fiercely that 'she knew of no other princess in England but herself' and that 'the daughter of "Madam of Pembroke" was no princess at all'. If the King acknowledged the baby as his daughter, then Mary would call her 'sister', as she called Henry Fitzroy 'brother', but no more. Before he abandoned her to her hostile surroundings, Norfolk enquired if she had any message for the King. 'None', came the immediate retort, 'except that the Princess of Wales, his daughter, asks for his blessing.' Norfolk told her that he dared not take such a message. 'Then go away', cried Mary, her control snapping, 'and leave me alone.' According to Chapuys, 'she then retired to her chamber to shed tears, as she is now continually doing'.[20]

While one duke was bullying Mary, the other, Suffolk, had gone on a similar errand to Catherine, now at Buckden in Huntingdonshire. His orders were to take her to Somersham, an even more

* Hertford Castle had been the first choice of residence, later altered to Hatfield but not corrected in the document the second time.

remote house situated in the middle of the Fen country and notoriously unhealthy. Catherine flatly refused to go, unless 'bound with ropes'. To agree to such a move, she said, would be tantamount to conniving at her own suicide. After a furious scene with Suffolk who, to do him justice, had little enthusiasm for his task, Catherine locked herself in her bedroom and refused to budge. 'If you wish to take me with you,' she told the harassed Suffolk through a hole in the wall, 'you must first break down the door.' The idea of the move to Somersham was quietly dropped, but not long afterwards Catherine was taken to Kimbolton Castle, a gloomy, semi-fortified, moated house half-a-day's ride from Buckden. There, refusing to acknowledge the existence of those newly appointed household officers who had been sworn to her as Princess Dowager, and whom she frankly regarded as jailers, she confined herself entirely to her own rooms, waited on by the few faithful Spaniards who still remained with her, and having her food cooked before her eyes as a precaution against poison.

At Hatfield, Mary was forced to eat all her meals in the crowded Great Hall without even the customary safeguard of a servant ordered to taste her food. She was made to yield precedence to her baby sister, and was not allowed out even to hear Mass. When Henry came to visit Elizabeth in January, Mary was kept out of sight. Chapuys believed this to be Anne's doing – that she was afraid the King's resolution might weaken if he were to see his elder daughter. Chapuys also heard that Anne had sent a message to Lady Shelton telling her to give Mary a box on the ears now and then 'for the cursed bastard she is'.

It is not easy to find any justification in human terms for Henry's protracted persecution of his discarded wife and elder daughter, whose only crime was their stubborn refusal to accept their relegation. All the same, it must in fairness be said that there was some political justification for the King's attitude. Catherine and Mary were fighting for what they believed to be their basic human rights, against what they believed to be the powers of darkness, and they were both the objects of very considerable popular sympathy. As long as they continued to resist, they would provide a natural rallying-point for the growing disaffection in the country. This applied especially to Mary – still the rightful heiress to the great majority of Englishmen. Her submission would be the most valuable and the heaviest pressure was now directed against her. For the next two and a half years Mary endured insult and neglect, personal sorrow and physical fear, the effects of which permanently ruined her health and spoilt her disposition, and turned a gentle, affectionate child into a bigoted, neurotic and bitterly unhappy woman.

In March 1534 the Pope at long last gave judgement on the King's divorce, and gave it in Catherine's favour. Almost simultaneously Parliament passed the Act of Succession, which finally ratified Anne's marriage and entailed the crown on her children. It was now high treason to question the legality of the divorce by deed or writing. In order to drive the lesson home, every member of Parliament, 'all the curates and priests in London and throughout England', and indeed 'every man in the shires and towns where they dwelled' were required to swear a solemn oath 'to be true to Queen Anne and to believe and take her for lawful wife of the King and rightful Queen of England, and utterly to think the Lady Mary . . . but as a bastard, and thus to do without any scrupulosity of conscience'.[21] Anyone who refused the oath could be held guilty of misprision of treason.

Meanwhile the new heiress of England, in her cradle trimmed with crimson satin and fringe, grew and throve – untouched as yet by the storms brewing round her. The nursery was on the move again in the spring and William Kingston wrote to Lord Lisle on 18 April: 'Today the King and Queen were at Eltham and saw my Lady Princess – as goodly a child as hath been seen. Her Grace is much in the King's favour, as goodly child should be, God save her.'[22] But while Henry fondled and played with the six-month-old Elizabeth at Eltham Palace, there were definite indications that the baby's mother was no longer in a similarly favoured position. A rumour had been circulating that she was pregnant again, but it proved a false hope and by midsummer it was noticed that the King was paying quite marked attentions to one of the maids-of-honour. Her name is not mentioned but it was probably Jane Seymour. When Anne, in a rage, tried to dismiss the girl from her service, Henry told her brusquely that 'she ought to be satisfied with what he had done for her; for, were he to begin again, he would certainly not do as much; she ought to consider where she came from, and many other things of the same kind'.[23] All these scraps of gossip, lovingly collected and passed on by Chapuys, did not amount to very much in themselves, but before the end of the year the situation was clear enough to any interested observer. Henry's passion had burnt itself out, leaving nothing but cold, sour ashes behind it, while Anne's growing sense of insecurity drove her on into making scenes which only exacerbated his irritation and distaste. She had developed an almost insane hatred of Catherine and Mary, especially Mary, and the elegant, fascinating, dark-eyed girl who had once so enslaved the King was becoming a shrill, nervous virago who could not always control her hysterical outbursts, even on public occasions. She once deeply offended a French ambassador who thought she was laughing at him.

Potentially serious though they were, Henry had more on his mind than his domestic disappointments during the autumn and winter of 1534. In November, he and Thomas Cromwell set the capstone on their programme of legislation codifying the breach with Rome, when the Act of Supremacy, declaring the King to be officially, explicitly and unconditionally Head of the Church in England came before Parliament. As from the following February it would be high treason 'maliciously' to deny this addition to the royal style. The Act was, as Sir Thomas More put it, 'like a sword with two edges, for if a man answer one way it will destroy the soul, and if he answer another it will destroy the body'. In the summer of 1535 John Fisher, Bishop of Rochester, and Thomas More, once Lord Chancellor of England – neither of whom shared the King's splendid confidence in his special relationship with the Almighty, and whose consciences could not allow them to accept Henry Tudor as their supreme earthly authority on spiritual matters – suffered the penalty of that treason. Although the most illustrious, they were by no means the only victims who considered the soul of more importance than the body. As he stood on the scaffold, Thomas More once again put the matter in a nutshell for them all. 'I die the King's good servant,' he said, 'but God's first.' The deaths of Fisher, a prince of the Church, and More, a scholar renowned and respected throughout the civilised world, sent a shockwave of revulsion round Europe. But Henry had learnt his own strength now (not long before, Thomas More had warned Cromwell, ' . . . if a lion knew his own strength, hard were it for any man to rule him') and in future it would be impossible to rule him. Chapuys was seriously afraid that Catherine and Mary might be his next victims. Both, needless to say, had refused to take the Oath of Succession and neither was prepared to recognise the King as Head of the Church. Chapuys also continued to fear Anne's influence. Earlier in the year an ugly little story had been going round that Anne had bribed a soothsayer to tell the King that she would never conceive a son while Catherine and Mary lived.

In the second half of the summer Henry went on a progress through the south-western counties and the court paid a visit to the home of Jane Seymour's father in Wiltshire. The household of the Princess Elizabeth followed its usual routine, keeping regularly on the move on the circuit of royal manors round London – Hunsdon, Hatfield and Hertford, the More near Rickmansworth, on to Richmond, down-river to Greenwich or neighbouring Eltham on its windy hill. Sometimes the baby was visited by her parents – sometimes she was brought to visit them, decked out perhaps in one of the elaborate white or purple satin caps 'laid with a rich caul of gold' which her mother had ordered to be made for her. An important stage in her development was now felt to have been reached: a decision solemnly conveyed to Thomas Cromwell, chief Secretary of State, by William Paulet on 9 October. 'The King's Highness,' wrote Paulet, 'well considering the letter directed to you from my Lady Bryan and other my Lady Princess' officers, His Grace, with the assent of the Queen's Grace, hath fully determined the weaning of my Lady Princess to be done with all diligence.'[24]

The winter closed in. Chapuys could get no access to Mary and he heard rumours that the Oath of Succession was soon to be put to her again. There was also a whisper that Acts of Attainder, the same weapon which had been used against More and Fisher, would be prepared against both Catherine and Mary if they continued to refuse the Oath. Chapuys continued to hint at the reprisals which would be taken by his master should 'anything untoward happen to either of the ladies'; but the Emperor, though sympathetic, could do little in practical terms to alleviate the plight of his aunt and cousin. Over-burdened as he already was by the weight of his unwieldy territories, he would not add a war with England to his problems if he could help it. He sent a message from Naples on 29 December that, although 'the good ladies must be advised not to take the oath except at the last extremity', nevertheless if the danger seemed really imminent, rather than lose their lives, they should submit.

Catherine was not called upon to face such a decision. Her troubles were resolved by death in the first week of January 1536, but she died in her bed at Kimbolton – her spirit and her will unbroken. Henry did not attempt to conceal his relief. 'Thank God, we are now free from any fear of war!' he exclaimed. The day after the news reached the court, which was a Sunday, Chapuys reported:

> the King dressed entirely in yellow from head to foot, with the single exception of a white feather in his cap. His bastard daughter Elizabeth was triumphantly taken to church to the sound of trumpets and with great display. Then, after dinner, the King went to the hall where the ladies were dancing, and there made great demonstrations of joy, and at last went to his own apartments, took the little bastard in his arms, and began to show her first to one, then to another, and did the same on the following days.[25]

The temptation to speculate on whether this was Elizabeth's first conscious memory is irresistible. She was nearly two and a half now and a bright, 'noticing' child. It seems just possible that she would be able to recall the events of that Sunday as one remembers a vague, bright dream of long ago. Certainly the occasion must have been indelibly printed on the retina of her unconscious mind: the braying of the trumpets; the smells of sweat and incense and hot wax; the bright lights and colours; the pale blur of upturned, admiring faces and the half-pleasurable, half-terrifying sensation of being swung up in her father's arms and carried in triumph round the room by that tremendous, god-like being.

It would be more than twenty years before Elizabeth Tudor rode in triumph again.

CHAPTER IV

'Anne Sans Tête'

CATHERINE OF ARAGON was buried in the Benedictine Abbey at Peterborough on Saturday, 29 January 1536, and by a curious irony of fate, on the very day of the funeral, 'Queen Anne was brought abed and delivered of a man child before her time, for she said that she had reckoned herself but fifteen weeks gone with child. It was said she took a fright, for the King ran that time at the ring and had a fall from his horse. . . .'[1] Anne tried, rather desperately, to put the blame on her uncle, the Duke of Norfolk, who, she said, had upset her by tactlessly breaking the news of the King's accident. This was held to be a lame excuse. According to gossip, it was not so much concern for her husband's safety as jealous rage over his continuing and marked attentions to Jane Seymour which had been the cause of the Queen's unlucky miscarriage – either that, or her own 'defective constitution'. Whatever the reason, it was a personal disaster for Anne, whose position was becoming increasingly precarious. Eustace Chapuys heard that the King had not spoken to 'his concubine' more than a dozen times in the past three months. Henry was also telling certain close friends, in the strictest confidence of course, that he had been tricked into his second marriage by charms and witchcraft, and therefore considered it to be null and void. Even more ominously, he was again referring to the evident signs of God's displeasure. If this was repeated to Anne, she would have known what it meant to be afraid. That she was aware, in part at least, of her danger is evident by the fact that she had been making overtures of friendship to Mary – overtures which were scornfully rejected.

When the King was told that Anne had miscarried of a son, he said, simply and terribly, 'I see that God will not give me male children.' He showed his wife no sympathy, saying only as he left her bedside, 'When you are up I will come and speak to you.'[2] By a certain rough justice Anne was now experiencing something of

what her predecessor had suffered, but with none of Catherine's
iron capacity for endurance to support her. During the pre-
Lenten festivities, Henry left her behind at Greenwich while he
went off to disport himself in London; 'whereas', as Chapuys
noted, 'in former times he could hardly be one hour without her'.
On 31 March the ambassador had an illuminating conversation
with Thomas Cromwell, who remarked, with an ill-concealed
smirk, that although the King was still inclined to sport with
ladies he thought he would continue to live chastely in his present
marriage. Chapuys was not deceived. It was obvious to any
interested observer that the pale, prim Jane Seymour, carefully
chaperoned and coached by her brother Edward, was being
groomed for the role of third wife. It was also clear that Cromwell
did not intend to lift a finger for Anne. All the same, Chapuys,
who never missed an opportunity of doing anything that might
even indirectly be of advantage to Mary, still thought it worth his
while to present the Queen with two candles in church on Easter
Tuesday. As he remarked in a letter to a friend, if he had seen any
hope of the King's answer he would have offered not two but
a hundred candles to the she-devil.[3]

But the sands were running out. Henry was already making
definite enquiries about the possibility of a second divorce, but
Chapuys heard that the Bishop of London, on being approached
(and evidently considering discretion to be the better part of
valour), had refused to commit himself. It was hardly likely,
though, that Anne would be allowed to escape so lightly. Even
divorced she would still be Marquess of Pembroke with a considerable income in her own right. She was not entirely without
friends or influence and, with her child having once been officially
recognised as the King's heiress, she would constitute a serious
embarrassment to the government. Obviously a more final solution to the problem would have to be found. Henry would not
initiate the necessary action himself, that was not his way, but
Thomas Cromwell knew what was expected of him and his path
proved a good deal smoother than Wolsey's had been. A word of
warning in a receptive royal ear that treason was brewing and
that it might be wise to hold a thorough investigation, and the
matter was as good as settled. By 24 April, a special commission
consisting of Cromwell himself, the Dukes of Norfolk and Suffolk,
the Lord Chancellor Thomas Audeley, several earls (including the

Earl of Wiltshire) and various assorted judges and officials had been set up, empowered to enquire as to every kind of treason by whomsoever committed. The commission wasted no time.

'On May Day', recorded Edward Hall in his Chronicle, 'were a solemn jousts kept at Greenwich, and suddenly from the jousts the King departed having not above six persons with him, and came in the evening from Greenwich into his place at Westminster. Of this sudden departing many men mused, but most chiefly the Queen. . . .'⁴ Henry's abrupt retreat to Westminster was the signal and that night, alone at Greenwich – a place of ill-omen for her – cut off from any hope of escape or possibility of appeal, Anne could only wait. Next day she was arrested on a charge of adultery and 'about five of the clock at night' was brought up-river to the Tower – that same journey which she had made in triumph on the way to her coronation. This time her escort was a grim quartet, comprised of the Lord Chancellor, the Duke of Norfolk, Thomas Cromwell and William Kingston, Constable of the Tower; 'and when she came to the court gate, entering in, she fell down on her knees before the said lords, beseeching God to help her as she was not guilty of her accusement, and also desired the said lords to beseech the King's grace to be good unto her, and so they left her their prisoner'.⁵

In fact William Kingston was left to cope with the prisoner, by now in a state of near collapse. She asked if she was to go into a dungeon and on being told, 'no, madam, you shall go into the lodging you lay in at your coronation', exclaimed, 'it is too good for me, Jesu have mercy on me'. She then, Kingston's report continued,

kneeled down, weeping a good space, and in the same sorrow fell into a great laughing, as she has done many times since. . . . And then she said, Mr Kingston, do you know wherefore I am here? and I said nay. And then she asked me, when saw you the King? and I said I saw him not since I saw him in the tilt yard. And then, Mr Kingston, I pray you to tell me where my lord father is? And I told her I saw him afore dinner in the Court. O where is my sweet brother? I said I left him at York Place; and so I did. I hear say, said she, that I should be accused with three men; and I can say no more but nay, without I should open my body. And therewith opened her gown. O Norris, hast thou accused me? Thou art in the Tower with

me, and thou and I shall die together; and, Mark, thou art here too. . . .
And then she said, Mr Kingston, shall I die without justice? And I
said, the poorest subject the King hath, hath justice. And therewith
she laughed. . . .[6]

Anne had evidently been told that Henry Norris, one of the
gentlemen of the Privy Chamber, and Mark Smeaton, the lute
player, had been arrested; but Kingston did not have the courage,
it seems, to tell her that her 'sweet brother' George, Viscount
Rochford, was also a prisoner. Two days later Sir Francis Weston
and William Brereton were brought to join the others. All five
were accused of 'using fornication' with the Queen and of
conspiring the King's death. On 5 May Sir Richard Page and
Thomas Wyatt the poet completed the list.

Indictments were now drawn up charging the Queen, Rochford,
Norris, Smeaton, Weston and Brereton. It was alleged that Anne,
'despising her marriage, and entertaining malice against the King,
and following daily her frail and carnal lust, did falsely and
traitorously procure . . . divers of the King's daily and familiar
servants to be her adulterers and concubines'. She was also
charged with having 'procured and incited her own natural
brother' to violate her; and of having conspired with her lovers
'the death and destruction of the King . . . often saying she would
marry one of them after the King died, and affirming that she
would never love the King in her heart'.[7] According to the
indictment, all these 'abominable crimes and treasons' had begun
within a month of her daughter's birth.

A true Bill was duly returned by two juries, and on 12 May the
four commoners were tried before a special Commission of Oyer
and Terminer in Westminster Hall. They all pleaded not guilty,
with the exception of poor, terrified Mark Smeaton. He was the
only one who had confessed having intercourse with the Queen,
but this admission had apparently been extorted from him by
torture or the threat of it, and he was – it was generally agreed –
not a gentleman. The proceedings were little more than a formality
and all four were convicted and condemned to death.

The Queen herself and her brother were to be tried within the
precincts of the Tower on the following Monday, 15 May, before
a commission of the House of Lords, headed by the Duke of
Norfolk. During the fortnight she had been in prison Anne's

moods had fluctuated wildly. She had asked to have the sacrament in her closet so that she might pray for mercy, and, according to one of William Kingston's painstaking reports to Cromwell, 'one hour she is determined to die and the next hour much contrary to that'. She told Kingston that she had been 'cruelly handled as was never seen', but added 'I think the King does it to prove me; – and did laugh withal and was very merry'.[8] But when she appeared before her judges, she was controlled and dignified. She denied all the charges absolutely and, according to Chapuys, gave a plausible answer to each. Even after she had been convicted and heard the sentence, to be burnt or beheaded at the King's pleasure, pronounced by her uncle Norfolk 'she preserved her composure', saying she was ready for death and regretted only that the other prisoners, who were innocent and loyal to the King, were to die for her sake. She may have been trying to help her brother, whose own trial followed immediately. George indeed defended himself so ably that Chapuys heard that several of those present wagered ten to one he would be acquitted. They lost their money.

Was there, in fact, any substance in the charges? Anne had been in regular daily contact with the five men accused of being her lovers. She *could* have slept with any or all of them, but, apart from Smeaton's dubious confession, not a shred of direct evidence was ever produced to show that she did. It is hardly credible that she, who had been 'so cunning in her chastity' would have deliberately put at risk everything she had so laboriously gained. She may well have been indiscreet, even recklessly so. The date, October 1533, assigned to her first misconduct is significant. Anne's vanity craved attention and admiration. She throve on excitement and basked in the limelight. When, after those six heady years of royal courtship, she found herself being relegated to the role of brood mare, it was quite in character that she should have turned more and more to the company of the professional gallants about the court. She undoubtedly enjoyed and encouraged the sort of stylised love-play fashionable among young people in high society at the time – the heavy sighs and meaning glances, the exchange of tokens, extravagant compliments and flirtatious chatter. Anne seems, too, to have taken a perverse pleasure in egging her admirers on. She had asked Norris why he delayed his marriage and when he replied that 'he would tarry a time' she said, 'You look for dead men's shoes, for if aught came to the King but good, you would look to have me.' Norris did not respond as she apparently expected and she turned on him, saying 'she could undo him if she would'.⁹ She certainly encouraged the wretched Smeaton to make sheep's eyes at her, and did much the same with Francis Weston. As for the charge of incest, this would appear to be merely frivolous and was based, according to Chapuys, on nothing more than the fact that Rochford had once been a long time in Anne's room with her. Brother and sister were known to be fond of each other, and most likely the accusation was simply used as a convenient pretext for getting rid of George who might otherwise have made a nuisance of himself.

The government, of course, was playing up the horrid scandal of the Queen's behaviour for all it was worth – and more. Cromwell told Stephen Gardiner that 'the Queen's incontinent living was so rank and common that the ladies of her privy chamber could not conceal it'. He added solemnly that 'besides that crime there brake out a certain conspiracy of the King's death, which extended so far that all we that had the examination of it quaked at the danger his Grace was in'.¹⁰ John Hussey, in a letter to Lady Lisle dated 13 May, gave it as his opinion that anything which had ever been 'penned, contrived, and written' against women since Adam and Eve was 'verily nothing in comparison of that which hath been done and committed by Anne the Queen'. Hussey was ashamed, he said, that any good woman should give ear to it, although, he added honestly, he could not believe that all the rumours going about were true.¹¹

The King, who was taking an active interest in the proceedings, believed them all – or said he did. Indeed, he said he believed that Anne had had to do with more than a hundred men. He had long been expecting something of this kind to happen and had written a tragedy on the subject which he carried about with him in his bosom, so the Bishop of Carlisle told Chapuys. One of the counts in the indictment against Anne had been that when the King became aware of her misdeeds, he 'took such inward displeasure and heaviness' that certain harms and perils had befallen his royal body; but Chapuys remarked that he had never seen 'prince nor man who made greater show of his horns or bore them more pleasantly'. The court, in fact, had seldom been gayer. Henry was seeing a lot of Jane Seymour, dining with her and sometimes staying until after midnight. Chapuys heard that on one such occasion, returning by river to Greenwich, the King's barge was filled with minstrels and musicians, playing and singing; 'which state of things', wrote the ambassador, 'was by many a one compared to the joy and pleasure a man feels in getting rid of a thin, old and vicious hack in the hope of getting soon a fine horse to ride.'[12] Although Anne had never been popular and few people felt any sympathy for her personally, it was generally considered that the King's behaviour was not quite in the best of taste.

Rochford, Norris, Smeaton, Weston and Brereton were executed on 17 May. The charges against Richard Page and Thomas Wyatt had been quietly allowed to drop and they were presently released. Two things had to be done before the Queen went to her death. The executioner from Calais, the only one of the King's subjects who knew how to behead with a sword, had to be summoned and Anne's marriage had to be annulled. This last office was performed by the ever-useful Thomas Cranmer. Cromwell had tried to find grounds for annulment by proving a pre-contract between Anne and young Percy, but received such a categorical denial from the now Earl of Northumberland that he was obliged it seems to fall back on – of all things – the King's previous adultery with his sister-in-law, Mary Boleyn. Why did Henry feel it necessary to divorce Anne as well as kill her? One of the reasons was apparently to bastardise her daughter. For one so set on establishing the succession, the King was prodigal in disposing of possible heirs. Chapuys heard it was to be declared that Elizabeth was not even the King's daughter, but begotten by Norris; however, Henry would not allow that. Elizabeth might be a bastard, but she was unquestionably his bastard and her paternity cannot be doubted. Cranmer pronounced his sentence of nullity on the seventeenth, and on 18 May Anne was to die for adultery, having never been a wife.

At the last moment there was a hitch, possibly due to the late arrival of the executioner. His importation seems to have been in the nature of a special favour and cost the Treasury £23 6s 8d. Although two days earlier Kingston had reported that 'at dinner the Queen said she would go to a nunnery and is in hope of life', she was now anxious to end it. She chafed at the delay and complained to Kingston, 'I thought to be dead by this time and past my pain'. He told her there would be no pain, it was so little. 'And then she said,' continued a puzzled Kingston, ' "I heard say the executioner was very good, and I have a little neck", and put her hands about it, laughing heartily. I have seen many men and also women executed, and all they have been in great sorrow, and to my knowledge this lady has much joy and pleasure in death.'[13] Chapuys, too, heard that Anne was in high spirits that night and had said it would not be hard to find a nickname for her – she would be called 'la Royne Anne sans teste'.

Next day, Friday, 19 May, all was ready and 'at eight of the clock in the morning, Anne Boleyn, Queen, was brought to execution on the green within the Tower of London' where a select band of spectators was waiting. In spite of official instructions that all foreigners were to be excluded, by far the most vivid account of Anne's last moments is to be found in the Chronicle of Henry VIII, written by an anonymous Spaniard living in London. His chronicle is not always a reliable source, but on this occasion it has the unmistakable flavour of an eye-witness report. The Queen was wearing a night robe of damask with a red damask skirt and a netted coif over her hair, and 'was as gay as if she was not going to die'. According to established etiquette, the executioner asked forgiveness for what he had to do and then begged her to kneel and say her prayers.

So Anne knelt, but the poor lady only kept looking about her. The headsman, being still in front of her, said in French, 'Madam, do not fear, I will wait till you tell me.' Then she said, 'you will have to take this coif off', and she pointed to it with her left hand. The sword was hidden under a heap of straw, and the man who was to give it to the headsman was told beforehand what to do; so, in order that she should not suspect, the headsman turned to the steps by which they had mounted, and called out, 'bring me the sword'. The lady looked towards the steps to watch for the coming of the sword, still with her hand on her coif; and the headsman made a sign with his right hand for them to give him the sword, and then, without being noticed by the lady, he struck off her head to the ground.[14]

Head and trunk were hastily stowed in a plain coffin – according to one report, a chest used for storing arrows – and buried with little ceremony in the choir of St Peter-ad-Vincula within the Tower. And so she was gone. She was twenty-nine years old and 'had reigned as Queen three years, lacking fourteen days, from her coronation to her death'.

Some people remarked disapprovingly that the Queen had died 'very boldly' but Chapuys, who knew how to give credit when it was due, praised her courage and great readiness to meet death. In his despatch to the Emperor dated 19 May, he added: 'The lady who had charge of her has sent to tell me in great secrecy that the Concubine, before and after receiving the sacrament, affirmed to her, on the damnation of her soul, that she had never been unfaithful to the King.'[15]

'Who so list to hunt, I know where is an hind' Thomas Wyatt had once written, in a thinly veiled reference to Anne Boleyn, but:

> Who list her hunt, I put him out of doubt
> As well as I may spend his time in vain:
> And graven with diamonds, in letters plain
> There is written her fair neck round about:
> *Noli me tangere,* for Caesar's I am;
> And wild for to hold, though I seem tame.

This image of a deer appears more than once in Wyatt's poetry. Perhaps there was something doe-like about Anne, with her great dark eyes and swift, nervous movements. And Caesar had hunted her down the years, with cheerfully amorous enthusiasm, with obsession, with cold, revengeful fury, until he brought her to bay on a May morning on Tower Green, and his lust at last was sated, his guilt was purged and his vengeance complete. She was gone, that wild, strangely disturbing creature, her only legacy a red-headed little girl, now two years and eight months old.

There were several consequences of Anne's death. The most immediate being that

> on the 20th day of May the King was married* secretly at Chelsea, in Middlesex, to one Jane Seymour, daughter to Sir John Seymour, knight, in the county of Wiltshire . . . which Jane was first a waiting gentlewoman to Queen Katherine, and after to Anne Boleyn, late Queen, also; and she was brought to White Hall, by Westminster, the 30th day of May, and there set in the Queen's seat under the canopy of estate royal.[16]

* This was the betrothal ceremony. The wedding took place at Whitehall on the thirtieth.

Chapuys was hoping for great things from the new Queen's influence. She was thought to have remained faithful to the memory of her first mistress and had already shown herself friendly to Catherine's daughter. As for Mary, she clearly believed that things would be different now. On 26 May, a week after Anne's death, she wrote to Cromwell:

> Master Secretary, I would have been a suitor to you before this time, to have been a mean for me to the King's grace, my father, to have obtained his Grace's blessing and favour; but I perceived that nobody durst speak for me, as long as that woman lived, which now is gone, whom I pray our Lord of his great mercy to forgive. Wherefore, now she is gone, I am the bolder to write to you. . . .[17]

As her mother had done before her, Mary clung desperately to the belief that all her troubles were due to the malignity of 'that woman'. She totally failed to appreciate that her father's unlovable behaviour, for which Anne had so long been a convenient scapegoat, in fact had its origin in traits inherent in his own nature.

Guided by Thomas Cromwell, Mary now submitted abjectly enough. She made two copies of a letter sent to her by the Secretary in which she was prostrate before the King's most noble feet, his most obedient subject and humble child, who not only repented her previous offences but was ready henceforward to put her 'state, continuance, and living' in his gracious mercy. The copies, one sealed for the King and another open, were returned to Cromwell, together with a covering letter from Mary telling him that she had done the uttermost her conscience would suffer her. But when Cromwell read his copy he found a fatal reservation added to his draft. Mary was ready to submit to the King 'next to Almighty God'. This would not do. Another draft was sent down to her at Hunsdon and this time, tormented by neuralgia which gave her 'small rest day or night', Mary copied 'without adding or minishing'. Only one copy this time, because she 'cannot endure to write another'. Still it was not enough, and a commission – headed by that bird of ill-omen the Duke of Norfolk – was sent to visit her. They brought with them a document for her signature which explicitly acknowledged the King as Supreme Head of the Church and the nullity of her mother's marriage. When Mary refused to sign, the behaviour of the commissioners finally extinguished any lingering hopes she may have had of an honourable reconciliation with her father. She was such an unnatural daughter, said one, that he doubted whether she was even the King's bastard. Another added pleasantly that if she was *his* daughter, he would beat her to death or strike her head against a wall until it was as soft as a boiled apple. They told her she was a traitress and would be punished as such. Finally they said she might have four days to think the matter over and ordered Lady Shelton to see that she spoke to no one, and was not left alone for a moment, day or night. In spite of this, Mary contrived to make two last frantic appeals for help, to Chapuys and to Thomas Cromwell.

But the ambassador, for so long her faithful friend and ally, saw that the time had come for surrender and advised her to yield. Trying to comfort her, he wrote that God looked more at the intentions than the deeds of men. As for Cromwell, he was badly frightened and told Chapuys that for several days he had considered himself a dead man. When the commissioners reported their failure with Mary, Henry flew into a towering rage, directed not only at his daughter but anyone who could be suspected of showing her any sympathy, or of encouraging her resistance. The Privy Council was in session from morning till night and the King forced the judges to agree that if Mary continued to defy him she could be proceeded against in law.

Cromwell made his feelings perfectly clear in his reply to Mary's appeal. 'How great so ever your discomfort is', he wrote, 'it can be no greater than mine, who hath upon your letters spoken so much of your repentance . . . and of your humble submission in all things, without exception and qualification.' He enclosed 'a certain book of articles' which she was to sign, and added,

if you will not with speed leave all your sinister counsels, which have brought you to the point of utter undoing . . . and herein follow mine advice, I take my leave of you for ever, and desire you never to write or make means to me hereafter. For I will never think you other than the most ungrate, unnatural, and most obstinate person living both to God and your most dear and benign father.[18]

When Cromwell's letter reached her, Mary knew that she was beaten. For nearly three years she had fought gallantly to defend her principles and her good name – now, ill, alone and exhausted, she gave in. At eleven o'clock at night on a Thursday about the middle of June, she signed the 'book of articles' acknowledging 'the King's Highness to be supreme head in earth under Christ of the Church of England' and utterly refusing 'the Bishop of Rome's pretended authority'. She also acknowledged that her parents' marriage had been 'by God's law and Man's law incestuous and unlawful'.[19]

Her reward came on 6 July, when she was 'brought riding from Hunsdon secretly in the night to Hackney, and that afternoon the King and the Queen came thither, and there the King spake with his dear and well-beloved daughter Mary, which had not spoken with the King her father in five year afore'.[20] Two days later Chapuys wrote of this encounter:

> It is impossible to describe the King's kind and affectionate behaviour towards the Princess, his daughter, and the deep regret he said he felt at his having kept her so long away from him. . . . There was nothing but conversing with the Princess in private and with such love and affection, and such brilliant promises for the future, that no father could have behaved better towards his daughter.[21]

Henry's attitude showed his unbounded relief at Mary's surrender. It is easy to dismiss him as a monster for his undeniably brutal treatment of her, but the political implications of the situation have to be remembered. There was serious unrest over the King's revolutionary religious policy, especially in the more backward and rural parts of the country, as the Pilgrimage of Grace was presently to demonstrate. Mary represented the old, familiar ways and had a considerable popular following. Until she herself had renounced her birthright, there was a strong possibility that she might have been used as a lever in an attempt to force Henry back to the paths of righteousness.

Mary rode back to Hunsdon with 'a very fine diamond ring' given her by Queen Jane and 'a check for about 1,000 crowns' from her father, but nothing could help her in the bitterness of her remorse. She begged Chapuys to ask the Pope to give a secret absolution for what she had done, but for one of her stubborn rectitude not even that could alter the fact that she had knowingly betrayed her religious faith and her mother's memory – the two things which meant most in the world to her. The memory of that betrayal, made by a frightened girl of twenty, was to haunt her for the rest of her life.

Meanwhile, the King's younger daughter was being bastardised and disinherited in her turn. Parliament had met in June and passed a second Act of Succession, ratifying the annulment of Henry's marriage to Anne Boleyn and officially declaring the issue of that marriage to be illegitimate. The succession was now vested in the offspring of Henry and Jane Seymour. Failing this, the King was given full powers to appoint any heir or heiress he chose at any time by Will or by Letters Patent. This unprecedented step shows how acute the problem of the succession was becoming. There was some talk of naming the Duke of Richmond. As the Earl of Sussex remarked, reasonably enough, if all the King's children were bastards, why not choose the boy? If Henry had any such plans they were frustrated, for young Richmond died on 22 July 1536, at the age of seventeen, 'having pined inwardly in his body long before he died', a victim of the tuberculosis to which the young Tudor males were so fatally susceptible. If the downfall of the House of Plantagenet had been too many sons, the likely cause of the downfall of the House of Tudor was by now all too apparent.

None of this, of course, not even the abrupt diminution of her own social status, as yet troubled the small Elizabeth overmuch. There is a story that Sir John Shelton, husband of Lady Shelton and steward or governor of the household at Hunsdon, made a formal announcement to the child regarding her new style. Elizabeth is supposed to have replied sharply: 'How haps it, Governor, yesterday my lady Princess, today but my lady Elizabeth?' Sir John, who seems to have been a rather tiresome individual, may well have made the announcement. The retort, even allowing for the unnerving precocity of sixteenth-century royal children, is a little difficult to credit. A far more convincing portrait is drawn by Margaret Bryan, the Lady Mistress, in her famous letter to Thomas Cromwell, written in August 1536. It also reflects the confusion currently reigning in the nursery. 'Now,' wrote Lady Bryan distractedly, 'as my lady Elizabeth is put from that degree she was in, and what degree she is at now I know not but by hearsay, I know not how to order her or myself, or her women or grooms.' The little girl was evidently growing fast, for 'she has neither gown nor kirtle nor petticoat, nor linen for smocks', not to mention such other necessities as nightgowns, nightcaps, 'body-stychets' and handkerchiefs. 'All these her Grace must take. I have driven off as long as I can, that, by my troth, I cannot drive it no longer.' Lady Bryan had been having trouble with the interfering John Shelton, who 'saith he be master of this house. What fashion that shall be', continued her ladyship tartly,

> I cannot tell, for I have not seen it afore. . . . Mr Shelton would have my lady Elizabeth to dine and sup every day at the board of estate. It is not meet for a child of her age to keep such rule yet. If she do, I dare not take it upon me to keep her Grace in health; for there she shall see divers meats, and fruits, and wine, which it would be hard for me to restrain her Grace from.

Lady Bryan sensibly wanted her charge to have 'a good mess of meat to her own lodging, with a good dish or two meet for her to eat of'. There were other problems, too, equally familiar to anyone who has ever looked after a small child. 'My lady hath great pain with her great teeth, and they come very slowly forth, which causeth me to suffer her Grace to have her will more than I would.' However, the Lady Mistress means to put this right as soon as possible. 'I trust to God and her teeth were well graft, to have her Grace after another fashion than she is yet, so as I trust the King's grace shall have great comfort in her Grace. For she is as toward a child and as gentle of conditions, as ever I knew any in my life, Jesu preserve her Grace.' Lady Bryan will guarantee Elizabeth's good behaviour at any time when 'it shall please the King's grace to have her set abroad' but afterwards she must be allowed 'to take her ease again'.[22] Lady Bryan got her way about meal times, for on 16 August John Shelton was writing to Cromwell: 'I perceive by your letter the King's pleasure that my lady Elizabeth shall keep her chamber and not come abroad.' But Sir John had his problems, too, and told Cromwell that unless he received the King's warrant for money for the household he would not be able to continue it. Especially as 'within seven or eight days provision must be made at the seaside for Lent store (presumably salt fish) and other necessaries'.[23]

All the same, there is nothing to suggest that Elizabeth was ever deliberately made to suffer for her mother's disgrace, and no evidence that her household was reduced. The unfortunate state of her wardrobe was more likely due to oversight than any fixed policy of neglect. Also, of course, since Anne's death there was no longer anyone at court with a special interest in her welfare, or who would even think to remember that the child must be growing out of her clothes.

There is nothing to indicate either when or how Elizabeth heard what had happened to her mother. Most probably she was never officially told, but it would be very odd if, in the cheerfully crowded conditions which prevailed in manor-houses like Hunsdon and others where she spent so much of her early life, such an intelligent child did not overhear a good deal of talk not meant for her ears – talk that would be the more disturbing for being only dimly understood. All those fascinating tales of Anne's scandalous behaviour would lose nothing in the retelling, and as Elizabeth grew up she would never be able to remember a time when she had not known that her mother was a bad woman, an adulteress, perhaps worse, for it was freely rumoured that Anne had hastened good Queen Catherine's death by giving her poison. In May Chapuys was reporting that the King, with tears in his eyes, had told his bastard son that he and his sister, meaning Mary, had had a narrow escape from the hands of 'that woman, who had planned their deaths by poison'. When Richmond died in July, it was said that Anne had indeed been poisoning him by some unspecified and diabolical means.

Elizabeth would also never be able to remember a time when she had not known that her mother had died because her father ordered it. There is no record that she ever mentioned Anne's name during her childhood, or ever asked any questions about her; but the necessary information was there, filed away in that acutely receptive brain – its implications registered long before the conscious mind could comprehend and deal with it.

CHAPTER V

The King's Daughter

T HE two disinherited princesses continued, for the most part, to share an establishment over the next few years. No doubt it was a convenient and economical arrangement. The sisters now stood on equal terms socially but Mary, as the elder, had regained a natural precedence. Several of her old friends and servants were being allowed to rejoin her and early in August Chapuys reported that 'the treatment of the Princess is every day improving. She never did enjoy so much liberty as she does now, nor was she ever served with such solemnity and honour as she is at present.' Although nothing had yet been formally settled, the ambassador was hoping that soon there would be a complete reversal of fortune with 'the little bastard' having to pay her court to the Princess of Wales.[1] Contrary to many people's expectations, however, Mary's title was not restored and her position, like Elizabeth's, remained in a state of ambiguity. Both were the King's daughters and were treated as such, and yet both were and continued to be bastards by Act of Parliament.

There is no reason to suppose that at this time Mary harboured any resentment towards the little girl who had been the cause of so much of her unhappiness – rather the contrary. She wrote to the King: 'My sister Elizabeth is in good health, thanks be to our Lord, and such a child toward, as I doubt not but your Highness shall have cause to rejoice of in time coming.'[2] All her life Mary was pathetically fond of children and her privy-purse accounts contain a number of entries relating to presents of pocket-money and other things for her small sister.

In October 1536, at the time of the ill-fated rising in the North known as the Pilgrimage of Grace, both sisters were summoned to court. According to an anonymous correspondent writing to Cardinal du Bellay, the Bishop of Paris, this was intended to 'soften the temper of the people'. More probably Henry wanted his daughters safely under his eye during a time of potential danger. Cardinal du Bellay's informant continued: 'Madame Marie is now the first after the Queen, and sits at table opposite her, a little lower down, after having first given the napkin for washing to the King and Queen . . . Madame Isabeau [Elizabeth] is not at that table, though the King is very affectionate to her. It is said he loves her much.'[3] Despite indications to the contrary, it is undoubtedly true that Henry *was* fond and proud of all his children and, provided of course they never showed any sign of having wills of their own, he was an affectionate even an indulgent father. As for his children, they were none of them – not even Mary with her first-hand experience of the dark side of his nature – immune from the astonishing force of his personality or the irresistible simplicity of his charm, and they repaid him with a genuine, if fearful, devotion, taking enormous pride in their remarkable parent.

In 1537 came the event for which Henry had been striving throughout the whole of the previous decade. At two o'clock in the morning of Friday, 12 October, Jane Seymour gave birth to a healthy son at Hampton Court Palace. Later that morning a solemn Te Deum was sung in St Paul's Cathedral and every parish church in London. The bells rang out, toasts were drunk and bonfires lit all over the City.

> Also the same night, at five of the clock, there was new fires made in every street and lane, people sitting at them banquetting with fruits and wine, the shalmes* and waits playing in Chepeside, and hogsheads of wine set in divers places of the City for poor people to drink as long as they listed; the mayor and aldermen riding about the city thanking the people, and praying them to give laud and praise to God for our prince; also there was shot at the Tower that night above two thousand guns, and all the bells ringing in every parish church till it was ten at the clock at night.[4]

Everyone joined in the party. Even the foreign merchants of the Steelyard lit bonfires and torches, 'and gave a hogshead of wine to poor people, and two barrels of beer also'. There must have been some notable hangovers in London on 13 October. Messengers rode out to 'all the estates and cities of the realm' spreading the glad news, and the whole country went hysterical

* A reed instrument.

with joy. After very nearly thirty years there was an indisputable male heir born in unquestionably lawful wedlock. It was certainly high time. Henry was forty-six now. He had put on a lot of weight and there were signs that even his magnificent physique was beginning to rebel against the demands he made on it.

The infant prince was christened Edward, in the chapel at Hampton Court on Monday, 15 October, and in the ceremonial procession to the font his four-year-old sister Elizabeth carried out her first official duty, bearing the chrisom (the heavily jewelled and embroidered baptismal robe) on her breast; although 'the same lady for her tender age was borne by the Viscount Beauchamp'. Viscount Beauchamp was the recently ennobled Edward Seymour, brother of Queen Jane. Another Seymour, Thomas, was also present – one of six gentlemen supporting the canopy carried over the Prince. Elizabeth would know both brothers all too well in later years. Her grandfather, the Earl of Wiltshire, was there too, still gamely hanging on, with a towel round his neck bearing the taper of virgin wax.

Thanks, no doubt, to Lady Bryan's careful training, the little princess apparently conducted herself with suitable decorum and in the return procession, relieved of her burden, she walked with her sister Mary, Lady Herbert of Troy bearing her train. Lady Herbert was the sister of a future step-mother, Katherine Parr. The Tudor children lived in a small, close-knit world.

Mary had officiated as godmother to the baby, the other sponsors being Archbishop Cranmer and the Duke of Norfolk – a more curiously assorted trio is hard to imagine.

Jane Seymour died on 24 October. According to Thomas Cromwell, her death was due to 'the neglect of those about her who suffered her to take cold and eat such things as her fantasy in sickness called for'.[5] A more likely cause is puerperal sepsis, which carried off so many women after childbirth. Her funeral took place at Windsor on 12 November, with Princess Mary as chief mourner. Jane was the first, in fact the only one, of Henry's wives to be buried as Queen. Perhaps this was fair. She was, after all, the only one who had fulfilled her side of the bargain to his satisfaction.

After the birth of his son, 'England's Treasure', Henry naturally had less attention to spare for his daughters. They were now little more than potentially useful assets on the international marriage-market; but, although their names occur from time to time in ambassadors' despatches in connexion with various rather half-hearted matrimonial projects, their value was considerably reduced by the King's obstinate insistence on their bastard state.

Elizabeth's life continued to follow much the same course as before, moving with her household round the same circuit of royal manors, sharing with either her sister or brother. There were sound practical reasons for this restless existence. In such large establishments, crowded with hangers-on and with only the most primitive sanitary arrangements, it was obviously a sensible precaution to vacate the premises at regular intervals to allow for a general 'sweetening' and cleaning up. Also, in days of slow and difficult transport, once the royal households had eaten up all the locally available provisions, it was tactful as well as necessary to move on to pastures new. Another reason, of course, was to avoid contact with outbreaks of infectious disease, or to seek a healthy situation according to the time of year.

These were quiet and (to the best of anybody's knowledge) happy childhood years for Elizabeth, spent in pleasant places with affectionate friends around her. Although Margaret Bryan's time was now fully occupied supervising Prince Edward's nursery, Elizabeth was not neglected. There was Blanche Parry, the Welshwoman, who had seen her rocked in her cradle. There was Katherine Champernowne, who had been appointed a waiting gentlewoman in her household in June 1536, on the recommendation of Thomas Cromwell. Katherine was a Devonshire woman of good education and good, though impoverished, family. Four months after her appointment she was obliged to write rather plaintively to Cromwell, pointing out that she could not maintain her position to the King's honour without some yearly stipend and adding that she would be loath to charge her father, 'who has as much to do with the little living he has as any man'.[6] Presumably Mistress Champernowne got her stipend, for she was soon promoted to become Elizabeth's governess. In 1545 she married John Ashley or Astley, a first cousin of Anne Boleyn's, but she remained in the service of her princess, and the two were devoted to one another. And then, throughout these early years, there was always Mary, the kind grown-up sister and nearest substitute for a natural mother that the small Elizabeth was to know.

She was undoubtedly a most attractive child physically. Even Eustace Chapuys, who saw her with Edward in March 1538, and was hardly likely to be prejudiced in her favour, felt bound to admit that she was 'certainly very pretty'. Her other qualities, too, were becoming apparent. Her New Year's gift to her brother in 1539 was 'a shirt of cambric of her own working'. In December of that year, Thomas Wriothesley paid a visit to Mary at Hertford Castle, where both sisters were then in residence. He reported to Cromwell:

When I had done with her Grace, I went then to my Lady Elizabeth's Grace, and to the same made the King's Majesty's most hearty commendations, declaring that his Highness desired to hear of her health and sent her his blessing. She gave humble thanks, enquiring again of his Majesty's welfare, and that with as great a gravity as she had been forty years old. If she be no worse educated than she now appeareth to me, she will prove of no less honour to womanhood than shall beseem her father's daughter.[7]

At six years old Elizabeth was evidently already well schooled in the elaborate code of politeness and subservience to her elders that all properly brought-up children were expected to observe. Her formal education would, of course, have been progressing for at least a year by this time, although little or nothing is known of its beginnings. Presumably she learnt to read and write under the supervision of Katherine Champernowne, and as her later achievements testify she was certainly well grounded in Latin at an early age. Perhaps Mary had some hand in this, for despite the fact that she never showed anything like the formidable intellectual capacities of her younger brother and sister she had received a thorough classical training in the best Renaissance tradition.

Elizabeth's education was progressing in other directions too, as she began to become aware of the world around her – the world outside the nursery and the schoolroom. Travelling in her litter to or from Hertford or Enfield, Ashridge or Hatfield, Hunsdon or Havering Bower, or to visit her father at Greenwich or Hampton Court, through the green, well-wooded countryside as yet barely scarred by man, the horses throwing up clouds of white dust in summertime, slipping and straining in the mired ruts of winter, she was learning to return the greetings of country-

folk, who left their work in fields and gardens to watch the King's
daughter and her company ride by. Passing through the little
towns and villages round London she would see the housewives
and schoolchildren, the tradesmen and their apprentices who
came to their doors and windows to wave and cry 'God save
you'. These were the English people, tough, vigorous, quarrel-
some, independent, irrepressibly free-spoken, whose goodwill was
to be the breath of life to Elizabeth all her life. A people, roughly
three million of them, whose existences, despite their idyllic surroundings, were for the most part unimaginably hard, narrow and
precarious in a world where only the fittest, and the luckiest,
survived and where life was always balanced on a knife-edge with
death. There were plenty of reminders of this for an observant
child. A funeral procession or a blackened corpse rotting on a
wayside gallows were familiar sights, and death, as Elizabeth
already knew, was no respecter of rank or dignity.

On the road she would meet a fair cross-section of other
traffic: drovers with their herds of cattle going to market at
Smithfield and farmers with wagons piled high with produce,
rumbling in to feed the ever-hungry capital; trains of pack-horses
carrying grain or wool or finished cloth; a prosperous merchant
on a buying trip; some great lord's steward on business for his
master; a band of strolling players or tumblers; a laden packman
trudging to the next village. Sometimes her escort would quicken
to attention, forming a close hedge about her and her ladies, and
then there would be the fearful thrill of catching a glimpse of a
troop of 'sturdy beggars' on their way to terrorise some isolated
hamlet or lonely farmhouse. The fact that in this 'fair field full of
folk' there might be a number of dispossessed monks, and nuns
too, turned out of their convents to seek a living as best they
could; or that one no longer saw the black or grey habited figures
of the itinerant preaching friars, or the cheerful, jingling parties
of pilgrims travelling to one of the world-famous shrines – Our
Lady of Walsingham or the Holy Blissful Martyr of Canterbury
himself – would mean little to Elizabeth. She would never be able
fully to understand the anguished distress which the dissolution
of the monasteries and desecration of the shrines, now proceeding
briskly under the aegis of Thomas Cromwell, caused to people
like her sister Mary, who clung to the old ways. Very much a
child – if not, in fact, *the* child – of the English Reformation,

Elizabeth was little affected by these early manifestations of the social revolution going on around her.

This is not the place for any sort of detailed survey of the niceties of doctrinal change resulting from the break with Rome; but it should perhaps be remembered that the Henrician Reformation was essentially a movement initiated and controlled from above – as opposed to the progressive movement from below, which began to gather strength after the King's death and to work its way steadily to the surface throughout the remainder of the century. Henry was never really a Lutheran: he was far too much of a natural conservative and a natural autocrat. Indeed, there was a certain amount of truth in Martin Luther's scornful remark that 'Squire Harry wishes to be God and to do as he pleases.' Henry's Church was very much his own creation and bears the unmistakable stamp of his own idiosyncratic personality.

It has been said that during his reign England remained Catholic without the Pope, but this is an oversimplification. Changes – apart from that first fundamental one – were made, new ideas considered and experimented with. An English Bible was provided in every church. A simple, vernacular prayer book, the first official English Primer, was published and Cranmer was given royal permission to embark on a programme of major liturgical reform. Even the education of Prince Edward was entrusted to those whose opinions were distinctly left of centre. On the other hand it is true that Henry upheld, and (by means of the Act of Six Articles) saw to it that his subjects also upheld, belief in such basic tenets of Catholicism as transubstantiation, the celibacy of the clergy, the existence of purgatory and the need for auricular confession. Consistency was never a strong point of the Supreme Head of the new Church of England. He could (and did) prosecute both Lutherans and Catholics for their faith; but, in an age when religion and politics were for all practical purposes indivisible, the King found it useful to hold a balance between the parties of progress and reaction. He was well aware of the dangers that could result if either side became too powerful, and had no intention of allowing control to slip out of his own hands.

By the end of 1539 Henry had been a widower for two years and was about to embark on the second half of his matrimonial marathon. After an intensive search for a bride through the courts of Europe – during which Hans Holbein the Younger had been kept busily employed providing portraits of no fewer than five princesses – the King's choice had fallen on a German girl, Anne, sister of the Duke of Cleves. A rather surprising choice, in view of the report from Nicholas Wotton that Anne occupied most of her time in needlework, could speak no language but her own, and neither sang nor played any instrument, 'for they take it here in Germany for a rebuke and an occasion of lightness that great ladies should be learned or have any knowledge of music'. Wotton added, 'I could never hear that she is inclined to the good cheer of this country.'[8] None of this makes her sound a particularly suitable bride for Henry VIII; and, contrary to the legend, Holbein's portrait did not depict a ravishing beauty. However, other reports were more encouraging and Anne of Cleves landed at Dover on 27 December 1539. The moment Henry set eyes on her he was grievously disappointed. This dull, shy, rather cow-like creature bore no resemblance to the paragon he had apparently been expecting. 'Alas,' he grumbled, 'whom should men trust?' He felt he had been shamefully deceived by his ambassadors – it is always convenient to be able to blame someone else. To Thomas Cromwell he said: 'Is there none other remedy but that I must needs, against my will, put my neck in the yoke?' None immediately suggested itself. England needed friends abroad and Henry did not quite have the courage to send Anne back to her brother as substandard goods. The wedding took place on 6 January, the bridegroom still dragging his feet and complaining piteously to Cromwell that 'if it were not to satisfy the world and my realm, I would not do that I must do this day for none earthly thing'.[9] Not even for his realm, though, could he bring himself to consummate the marriage and some remedy had to be found. Especially as the royal eye had now been caught by one of the new Queen's maids of honour – pretty, vivacious Katherine Howard who, by a curious coincidence, was Anne Boleyn's cousin. In fact there is an element of farce in the way the King's second divorce parodied his first. Henry's conscience quickly got to work on the fact that Anne had once been tentatively betrothed to the Duke of Lorraine's son, and by midsummer enough legal confusion had been created to enable a nullity case to be got up. On 9 July 1540, Convocation duly pronounced the marriage to be null and void, and four days later an obedient Parliament confirmed the judgement of the clergy. Divorce was a good deal easier now and Anne accepted her relegation with a docility, an alacrity even, which quite surprised the King. She settled down to spend the remainder of her life in comfortable retirement in England, always sure of a good place in royal processions and becoming quite a friend of the family, particularly of Princess Mary.

On 28 July Henry married Katherine Howard, and that same day Thomas Cromwell was executed for high treason. Cromwell's fall bore a close resemblance to that of his former master, Cardinal Wolsey. Like Wolsey, his position had depended entirely on the King's favour. Like Wolsey, he had made enemies and, like Wolsey, his downfall was engineered from below by, among others, the Duke of Norfolk, who was fortunately able to provide another niece to dazzle the King and temporarily distract his attention from the bitter in-fighting going on in the Council.

To the King's small daughter it must sometimes have seemed as if step-mothers came and went with the seasons, but she would soon have learnt that it was not tactful to comment on this interesting phenomenon. According to Gregorio Leti (a not very reliable seventeenth-century biographer of Elizabeth) Katherine Howard made quite a pet of her young kinswoman, and on the day she first dined publicly as Queen under the Cloth of Estate, gave Elizabeth the place of honour opposite her at table, saying she was her cousin and of the same blood and lineage. Leti has been largely discredited as an authority, but on this occasion he may well have been telling the truth. Katherine's rise had been a dizzy one. From being a neglected orphan, dragged up by servants in her grandmother's house, she suddenly found herself, at the age of about nineteen, with the King, and the world, at her feet. A kind-hearted girl (all too kind-hearted as it turned out), she was revelling in her astonishing good fortune and ability to dispense treats.

Henry was entranced by her. He forgot his increasing age and girth and the painful ulcers on his legs, and enjoyed a brief Indian summer of renewed youth and vigour with his 'rose without a thorn'. Unluckily it quickly transpired that Katherine had been unchaste before her marriage and had begun to commit adultery soon after it. When the news was first broken to Henry by Cranmer on 1 November 1541, he refused to believe it. But the evidence was damning and the French ambassador reported in

December that the King 'has changed his love for the Queen into hatred, and taken such grief at being deceived that of late it was thought he had gone mad, for he called for a sword to slay her he had loved so much'. When his rage wore off, 'he took to tears regretting his ill luck in meeting with such ill-conditioned wives'.[10] The wretched Katherine, too, was in a sorry state. Cranmer, who had been sent to try and get a confession out of her, found her in hysterics and approaching such a 'franzy' of remorse and terror that the kindly Archbishop was moved to pity and to fear for her reason. Although for a time Henry seems to have wavered, there was no mercy for Katherine Howard. She was not even accorded the courtesy of a trial. An Act of Attainder was passed against her and on 13 February 1542 she was beheaded on Tower Green and went to join her cousin Anne in the chapel of St Peter-ad-Vincula. Elizabeth was eight years old at the time of Katherine's disgrace. It was another object lesson for the child in the recurring connexion between royal marriage and sudden death.

After his last two unfortunate experiences, the King temporarily abandoned matrimony and turned his attention to more congenial matters, such as harrying the Scots and planning an invasion of France. His children continued to live quietly in the country. Elizabeth was now spending a good deal of her time in the company of her little brother, and according to the dramatist Thomas Heywood: 'Cordial and entire grew the affection betwixt this brother and sister; insomuch that he no sooner began to know her, but he seemed to acknowledge her, and she being of more maturity, as deeply loved him.'[11] Edward's education had now begun under the direction of Dr Cox, Provost of Eton, and Elizabeth apparently shared the services of her brother's tutors. Heywood, writing early in the next century, draws this rather charmingly artless picture of their routine when they were together.

So pregnant and ingenious were either, that they desired to look upon books as soon as the day began to break. Their *horae matutinae* were so welcome, that they seemed to prevent the night's sleeping for the entertainment of the morrow's schooling. Besides, such were the hopeful inclinations of this princely youth and pious virgin, that their first hours were spent in prayers and other religious exercises. ... The rest of the forenoon (breakfast-time excepted) they were doctrinated and instructed, either in language, or some of the liberal sciences; in moral learning, or other collected out of such authors as did best conduce to the instruction of princes. And when he was called out to any youthful exercise, becoming a child of his age, (for study without action breeds dullness) she in her private chamber betook herself to her lute or viol, and (wearied with that) to practise with her needle.[12]

The superhuman attainments of the princely youth and pious virgin (Edward was producing Latin prose by the time he was seven) become rather more understandable if one remembers that to these children Latin was not a dead thing confined within the pages of a grammar, but a living language for everyday writing and speaking, which they began to learn very soon after learning English, and which in its early stages was taught in a way not far removed from the latest 'direct' methods of teaching modern languages. Also, of course, they had the benefit of individual tuition by the cream of the available teaching talent, at a time when some of the best minds in the country were taking a special interest in the education of the young. All the same, there is no doubt that both Edward and Elizabeth were well above average intelligence, eager to learn and with enormous capacities for sheer, concentrated hard work.

On 12 July 1543, the King made his last and, in some ways, his most successful marriage. Katherine Parr was thirty-one, the daughter of a Northamptonshire knight who had already been twice married to men much older than herself, and been twice widowed. She was a pretty woman, mature, cultured and sensible – and far from overjoyed at the honour done to her. Henry was no longer a very attractive proposition physically. Now in his early fifties, he had aged rapidly since the Katherine Howard *débâcle* and was becoming grossly fat, with suppurating, foul-smelling ulcers on both legs. His brain was still razor sharp but he was increasingly moody and suspicious, often morose and unpredictably bad-tempered. It is not surprising that Katherine Parr quailed at the prospect before her – especially as she was already more than half in love with Henry's brother-in-law, the dashing Thomas Seymour. But Tom Seymour knew better than to enter into amatory competition with his sovereign lord. As soon as the King's interest became clear, he melted rapidly into the background, leaving Katherine to shoulder the burden of yet another elderly husband. It is entirely to her credit that she shouldered it cheerfully, and gave Henry loyal and sympathetic companionship during the last years of his life.

In addition to being a good wife, Katherine Parr made an excellent step-mother, taking a serious and constructive interest in the welfare of the King's oddly assorted brood. She became very friendly with Mary – there was only four years difference in their ages – and the two younger children were soon devoted to her. But it was probably Elizabeth who benefited most from her influence. The princess had her tenth birthday that September and was growing up fast; a rather rootless little girl, who badly needed the affection and guidance of an older woman she could respect and admire. She still had Katherine Champernowne (soon to become Katherine Ashley) of course; but Kat, as Elizabeth called her, was always associated with nursery days and her charge was beginning to outstrip her intellectually. There was still Mary but, although the sisters remained on perfectly amicable terms, an invisible barrier was growing up between them as Elizabeth left babyhood behind her, a barrier rooted in the unhappy past. Elizabeth could never enter Mary's private territory and they would never be able to enjoy true intimacy. Also, as the pattern of the younger girl's education developed, the gulf inevitably widened. Edward and Elizabeth were beginning, inevitably, to represent the future, just as Mary must always be identified with the past. In Katherine Parr, Elizabeth was fortunate to find just the friend she needed, at a time when she most needed her.

The new Queen – always a lively patron of intellectual Protestantism – played an active part in the reorganisation of the royal schoolrooms which took place during the first half of 1544, not long after Edward's sixth birthday. In July, Sir John Cheke, Regius Professor of Greek at Cambridge and a leader of progressive religious opinion, was brought in to take over from Dr Cox, assisted by such other luminaries as Roger Ascham and Anthony Cooke (whose daughter later married William Cecil). A few months later, William Grindal, also a Cambridge man and a notable Greek scholar who had been Ascham's pupil, was appointed tutor to Elizabeth. Thus, from the age of eleven, her education became closely associated with the Cambridge humanists and her classical studies now began in earnest. She was

learning French too by this time, and Italian. Her earliest surviving letter, dated 31 July 1544, was written to Katherine Parr in
Italian – probably as an exercise, it certainly reads like one.
'Inimical fortune,' the ten-year-old princess complains to her step-
mother,

> envious of all good and ever revolving human affairs, has deprived
> me for a whole year of your most illustrious presence, and, not thus
> content, has yet again robbed me of the same good; which thing
> would be intolerable to me, did I not hope to enjoy it very soon.
> And in this my exile, I well know that the clemency of your Highness
> has had as much care and solicitude for my health as the King's
> Majesty himself. By which thing I am not only bound to serve you,
> but also to revere you with filial love, since I understand that your
> most Illustrious Highness has not forgotten me every time you have
> written to the King's Majesty, which, indeed, it was my duty to have
> requested from you. For heretofore I have not dared to write to him.
> Wherefore I humbly pray your most Excellent Highness, that, when
> you write to his Majesty, you will condescend to recommend me to
> him, praying ever for his sweet benediction, and similarly entreating
> our Lord God to send him best success, and the obtaining of victory
> over his enemies, so that your Highness and I may, as soon as
> possible, rejoice together with him on his happy return.[13]

This letter has been held to mean that Elizabeth was for some
reason in disgrace with her father at the time, but the evidence
seems extremely slender. Henry had gone over to France on
14 July to superintend the siege of Boulogne and Katherine had
been made Regent in his absence (an honour not accorded to a
Queen Consort since the days of Catherine of Aragon), so she
would have been fully occupied. Elizabeth, bemoaning her
'exile', must mean, if anything, that she has not seen the Queen
during the current year, for she was certainly at court the previous
December with Mary and Edward. Most probably she has only
'not dared' to trouble the King with letters while he is busy on
such important matters abroad. At any rate, Henry, writing to his
wife on 8 September, sends his 'hearty blessings' to all his
children.

Family relations apparently continued to be entirely cordial,
and on New Year's Day 1545 Elizabeth presented her step-mother
with a translation into English prose of a very long and very dull

poem by Margaret of Navarre, entitled *The Mirror of the Sinful Soul*. This laborious effort was accompanied by a letter declaring that since 'pusillanimity and idleness are most repugnant unto a reasonable creature' the writer has undertaken her task to the best of her 'small wit and simple learning' and hopes that the Queen will not find anything in it 'worthy of reprehension'. The whole was enclosed in an embroidered cover worked by the translator. Elizabeth seems to have developed the economical habit of making her own presents at an early age, but no doubt Katherine received it with suitable enthusiasm.

Elizabeth spent most of the closing years of her father's reign with Edward, working quietly at her lessons in such familiar surroundings as Ashridge and Hatfield. By the terms of the third and last Henrician Act of Succession, passed in 1544, she and Mary had been restored to their places in line for the throne, should Edward fail to produce heirs, or failing any new heirs by the latest royal marriage, and subject to certain conditions to be laid down by Henry in his Will or by Letters Patent. Neither princess was legitimised by the new Act, but something had been done to regularise their peculiar position.

The King's health was failing now. He had probably overtaxed himself riding a great courser at the siege of Boulogne and he certainly began to deteriorate visibly after his return from France in October 1544. His vast bulk had to be carried about indoors in a chair and he was subject to frequently recurring attacks of fever, deriving from the ulcers on his legs which caused him intense pain. Henry had suffered from a 'sorre legge' on and off ever since 1528 and it used to be thought that this trouble was of syphilitic origin. However, as there is no record that the King ever received the recognised treatment for venereal disease – a titbit which would hardly have escaped the notice of some sharp-eyed ambassador – and as no other symptoms ever appeared, either in himself or his children, the general consensus of medical opinion now is that the ulcers were varicose, resulting from varicose veins. In a heavy man, addicted to violent physical exercise, who refused to rest and was subjected to the savage therapeutics of his day, such a condition would naturally be exacerbated. Another, more recent, theory is that Henry may have been suffering from osteomyelitis, a chronic septic infection of the bone, following an injury received in one of his mishaps in the tiltyard.[14]

At the end of November 1546 Edward and Elizabeth were separated, he and his entourage going to Hertford Castle and she to Enfield. The parting seems to have been a sorrowful one and prompted a rather pathetic note (written, needless to say, in Latin) from the nine-year-old Prince.

> The change of place, in fact, did not vex me so much, dearest sister, as your going from me. Now, however, nothing can happen more agreeable to me than a letter from you; and especially as you were the first to send a letter to me, and have challenged me to write. Wherefore I thank you both for your good-will and despatch. . . . But this is some comfort to my grief, that I hope to visit you shortly (if no accident intervene with either me or you), as my chamberlain has reported to me.[15]

The visit did indeed take place and, although accident had intervened, it was not with either Edward or Elizabeth.

As the year wore away, it became obvious that the King was seriously ill. Katherine Parr was sent to keep Christmas at Greenwich, but Henry stayed at Westminster. He, who had once been the handsomest prince in Christendom, was now a swollen, rotting hulk, often in such pain that the Imperial ambassador reported he grew black in the face and speechless. But still his mind remained clear, and his indomitable will held on to life while he worked to perfect the safeguards he had devised for Edward's minority. It was less than seventy years since the little princes had disappeared in the Tower and Henry was under no illusions about the dangers that might lie in wait for his son. Towards midnight on Thursday, 27 January he lapsed into merciful semi-consciousness and in the early hours of Friday, the twenty-eighth, he died – his task completed to the best of his ability. He had ruled England for thirty-eight years and had grown from a young god into a father-figure of overwhelming proportions. He had done things which no English king before him had dared to do and had, incredibly, got away with them. Beneath his monstrous, sometimes preposterous, egotism, he had loved England and its people, and the people, although they had not always approved of him, had loved him in return. Indeed, his tremendous personality impressed itself so deeply on the national consciousness that it has passed into folk-memory, and to this day Bluff King Hal is one of the very few English monarchs who is still instantly recognisable.

Almost before the breath had left his body, many of his carefully-thought-out arrangements were being disregarded, as Edward Seymour, now Earl of Hertford, rode out to gain possession of the little King. Hertford brought Edward to Enfield to Elizabeth and there broke the news to brother and sister together. Both wept, clinging together in such a passion of tears that the onlookers watched in some awe, and presently joined in. Whether the children cried from genuine grief, from shock, or just in sympathy with each other it is impossible to say. Probably it was a mixture of all three. Edward, of course, had always been the apple of the King's eye and Elizabeth had never known direct experience of his wrath. He had been a remote figure, a god to be worshipped and propitiated from a distance, but at least he was the one person she could trust implicitly never to let anyone else harm her. For Edward and Elizabeth the sheet anchor had gone, and their world could be a hard place for fatherless children, even, perhaps especially, for royal children. This was the end of childhood for them both, and both knew it. Edward, the fair, pretty, clever boy, who already carried the seeds of the disease which was to kill him, must step into his father's enormous shoes. Elizabeth, she was thirteen and a half now, must begin a hard, lonely apprenticeship in which, she was soon to learn, she would have no one but herself to trust.

CHAPTER VI

Elizabeth's Admiral

IN drawing up his will, Henry VIII had named sixteen executors who were to form a Council of Regency during Edward's minority. There was no mention of a Protector or Governor of the Realm, Henry being apparently reluctant to trust any one man with supreme power, and each member of the Council was to have equal precedence. This inner Cabinet was to be supplemented by a secondary body of assistant executors who could offer guidance and advice, but whose exact powers and status were not defined.

During his lifetime Henry had always been careful to maintain a balance between those members of the Privy Council who favoured his own peculiar brand of Catholicism, and those who urged further reform. After Cromwell's fall, some five years previously, the conservatives had, on the surface at any rate, seemed to gain the edge over the progressives – although the fact that the heir to the throne was being educated as a Protestant did not promise well for their future. Then, in the last months of the old King's life, the conservative party had suffered a virtual death-blow in the loss of its two most influential leaders: the Duke of Norfolk, that eminently dislikeable old man who had, nevertheless, always served King Henry with the grim loyalty of a savage watchdog; and Stephen Gardiner, Bishop of Winchester, a brilliant but tricky lawyer and diplomat.

The ruin of the Howard family seemed complete. Norfolk's arrogant soldier-poet son, the Earl of Surrey, was executed for treason on 19 January 1547, and Norfolk himself escaped a similar fate by a hair's breadth – he had been due to meet the headsman only a few hours after Henry's own death. Stephen Gardiner had fallen out of favour during the autumn of 1546, and when Henry was drafting the final version of his Will in December he struck the Bishop off the list of executors saying that 'he was a wilful man and not meet to be about his son'.

The reasoning which lay behind the assault on the Howards and the removal of Gardiner is by no means clear, but in each case the initiative came directly from the King. Henry may have doubted whether either Norfolk or Gardiner was entirely sound on the question of the Royal Supremacy. He may have feared a Roman counter-attack once his own strong hand had gone, possibly even open violence between the opposing factions. He was also, surely, too much of a realist not to have known that the progressives could not be restrained indefinitely and that with them, in the last resort, must lie the future greatness of the English nation. Henry's motives were frequently either obscure or obscured, but one thing is plain enough: before his death he himself had ensured that in his son's reign the balance of power would be decisively tilted in favour of the Protestants.

The sixteen members of the Council of Regency were all 'new' men, in the sense that none of them bore a title more than ten years old. They were all men who had risen to wealth and influence by their loyalty and service to the Tudor monarchy, and their unquestioning acceptance of the doctrine of Royal Supremacy. Only four of their number could be regarded as having any sympathies with Catholicism. The remainder either had no strong convictions or were declared Protestants. The outstanding figure among them was Edward Seymour, Earl of Hertford, the new King's maternal uncle and a rising star in the political firmament.

Edward Seymour not unnaturally saw himself as the obvious choice for Regent, and while Henry was still alive, speechless and barely conscious in his great bed at Whitehall, Seymour and his friend and ally, that experienced tactician, Secretary of State William Paget, paced the long gallery outside the royal bed-chamber, waiting for the end and discussing future arrangements. During their vigil several important matters were settled. It was agreed that Seymour should go at once to Hertford Castle to fetch the new King and bring him to London. In the meantime, Paget would keep Henry's Will in his own hands (temporarily suppressing any inconvenient portions of it) and would use his considerable authority and prestige to persuade the other executors that Seymour should be made Protector during his nephew's minority. In return, it was understood that Paget should act as Seymour's principal adviser in the new government. It was also agreed that until such time as the transference of power had been completed, the fact of Henry's death should be concealed.

This plan went smoothly into action, the only hitch occurring when Seymour, in his haste to set out to fetch Edward, inadvertently took with him the key of the chest containing the Will and was obliged to send it back to Paget from Hertford Castle, with a hurried note written 'between three and four o'clock in the morning' of 29 January.[1] Such indeed was the speed and efficiency of the whole operation that there was no time for opposition to form.

The executors – or the twelve of them who were in London – met together formally for the first time on Monday, 31 January, and Paget had little difficulty in getting them to disregard both the spirit and the letter of their late master's Will. They agreed

> that being a great number appointed to be executors with like and equal charge, it should be more than necessary, as well for the honour, surety and government of the most royal person of the King our sovereign lord that now is, as for the more certain and assured order and direction of his affairs, that some special man of the number and company aforesaid should be preferred in name and place before others.

After this, by unanimous consent and 'upon mature consideration of the tenderness and proximity of blood' between the new King and the Earl of Hertford, the executors proceeded to bestow on Hertford 'the first and chief place among us, and also the name and title of the Protector of all the realms and dominions of the King's majesty that now is, and of the Governor of his most royal person'.[2]

The news of Henry VIII's death was now officially released and later that same day, 31 January, King Edward arrived in the capital, escorted by his uncle, and was lodged, according to established custom, in the Tower. The *coup d'état* had been a brilliant and painless success, though in fairness to the new Protector it should be said that he did have strong claims to an office normally considered essential during a royal minority. Edward Seymour was an able, sincere and well-meaning man. Whether he possessed the necessary strength and ruthlessness to defend his position against the competitors who would inevitably rise to assail it remained to be seen.

Katherine Parr had been left no say in the guardianship of her stepson, but it was agreed that the Princess Elizabeth should be placed in the Queen Dowager's care while she finished her education. This seemed an eminently suitable arrangement, and shortly after her father's death Elizabeth moved with her household to join the Queen, now installed at Chelsea, part of her jointure property.

Henry VIII had acquired the manor of Chelsea from Lord Sandys in 1536, and had built a new house there, on the site of the present Cheyne Walk, just to the east of the Albert Bridge. Completed about 1540 and supplied with water from a spring in Kensington, it was apparently intended as an extra nursery for the royal children. Elizabeth had been there in May 1541, when an item occurs in the account presented by Robert Kyrton, Master of the Barge, 'for serving my Lady Elizabeth from Suffolk Place to Chelsea'.[3] In 1547, this pleasant red-brick mansion overlooking the Thames at Chelsea Reach, was to see the beginning of the first, and in some ways the most momentous crisis of her life.

Whatever resentment Katherine Parr may have felt at being excluded from any further share in Edward's upbringing was soon forgotten in the excitement of a promising development in her private life. Her old suitor, Thomas Seymour, was renewing his attentions, and now all of a sudden it seemed to Katherine that 'the time is well abbreviated, by what means I know not, except the weeks be shorter at Chelsey than in other places'.[4]

The well-known, near-contemporary description of Thomas Seymour – 'fierce in courage, courtly in fashion; in personage stately, in voice magnificent, but somewhat empty of matter' – is accurate, as far as it goes. It does not add that he was also vain, greedy, selfish and dangerous. Utterly unscrupulous in his use of man, woman or child – especially woman or child – in any scheme which would further his own ends, Tom Seymour, the classic confidence-trickster, possessed just the kind of charm calculated to make him irresistible to his victims.

On 17 February, Edward Seymour had been created Duke of Somerset to match his new dignity, and in the general sharing-out of honours which took place before the coronation Thomas became Baron Seymour of Sudeley and was given the office of Lord High Admiral. He had been named as one of the assistant executors in Henry VIII's Will, which now ensured him a place on the Privy Council, but he was far from satisfied – regarding his elder brother's semi-regal state with savage envy. It seemed the height of injustice to Thomas Seymour that one of the King's uncles should enjoy all the fruits of their valuable relationship, while the other was apparently to be fobbed off with mere consolation prizes.

Labouring under an acute sense of grievance, therefore, the Lord Admiral set about considering ways and means of altering this distressing state of affairs. As an eligible bachelor in his late thirties, his obvious first step was to choose a wife whose position would improve his own status, and with astonishing effrontery he considered the Princesses Mary and Elizabeth in turn. As Henry's daughters had been restored to the Succession with the explicit proviso that any marriages they might make must first be fully approved by the King and Council, Tom Seymour cautiously sounded some of his fellow councillors on the subject and was, not surprisingly, rebuffed. It was only after this that he turned back to the Queen Dowager whose feelings towards him, he was confident, had not changed.

He was perfectly correct in this assumption and Katherine, unaware of her lover's treacherous behaviour, was transparent with happiness. 'I would not have you to think that this mine honest good will toward you to proceed of any sudden motion of passion,' she wrote to him earnestly from Chelsea. 'For as truly as God is God, my mind was fully bent the other time I was at liberty to marry you before any man I knew.'[5] The Almighty, it seemed, had withstood her will 'most vehemently' on that occasion, but now she was to have her reward for self-abnegation and could only say, with heartfelt sincerity, that 'God is a marvellous man.'

Katherine was thirty-four now but, not having been worn out with child-bearing, she was still young enough and attractive enough to be eager to snatch her chance before it was too late. The Admiral was impatient – he had no intention of being balked again – and some time that spring there was another secret wedding between a Queen Dowager of England and a bold, handsome adventurer. As on the previous occasion, no record survives of where or when the ceremony took place, but the evidence points to a date in April or early May.

The next step was to find a tactful way of breaking the news. Katherine wrote again to the Admiral, probably before the marriage had actually been solemnised: 'As I gather by your letter, delivered to my brother Herbert, ye are in some fear how to frame my lord your brother to speak in your favour.' The Queen had no intention of crawling to the Protector (or to his wife, whom she disliked). 'I would not wish you to importune for his good will', she told Tom, 'if it come not freely at the first; it shall be sufficient once to require it, and then to cease. I would desire you might obtain the king's letters in your favour, and also the aid and furtherance of the most notable of the council . . . which thing obtained, shall be no small shame to your brother and loving sister, in case they do not the like.'[6] In the meantime, however, it was necessary to be discreet. 'When it shall be your pleasure to repair hither,' wrote Katherine, 'ye must take some pain to come early in the morning, that ye may be gone again by seven o'clock; and so I suppose ye may come without suspect. I pray you let me have knowledge over-night at what hour ye will come, that your porteress may wait at the gate to the fields for you.'[7]

Tom Seymour had already taken the precaution of suborning a gentleman of the Privy Chamber, one John Fowler, to further his interest with the King and act as a go-between. He also wrote to Mary, asking her to favour his suit, but got little satisfaction from this quarter. Mary was plainly shocked and disappointed, 'considering whose wife Her Grace was of late', that Katherine should even be contemplating another marriage so soon. What Elizabeth thought is, characteristically, open to question. She was probably in the secret from the beginning. Even if Katherine had not confided in her, she must have heard about those mysterious comings and goings in the Chelsea fields during the small hours. The boisterous, loud-voiced person of the Admiral was not easy to conceal at any time, and the Queen's maids would have been agog with the excitement of it all.

The unreliable Italian, Leti, in his Life of Elizabeth, records that Mary sent her sister an urgent invitation to leave their unworthy step-mother's roof and make a home with her, but that Elizabeth refused. Although expressing her grief and affliction at

seeing 'the scarcely cold body of the King, our father, so shamefully dishonoured', she considered neither she nor Mary were in
a position to risk offending so influential a couple as the Queen
and the Admiral and that their best course would be dissimulation. According to Leti, she justified this by pointing out that
Henry's memory, 'being so glorious in itself, cannot be subject
to those stains which can only defile the persons who have
wrought them'. Besides which, the Queen has shown her so great
affection and done her so many kind offices, that Elizabeth 'must
use much tact . . . for fear of appearing ungrateful'.[8]

The invitation may have been sent and, if so, would surely have
been gracefully declined – life at Chelsea, after all, promised to be
more amusing than life buried in Essex with Mary – but the whole
correspondence strikes a false note. Elizabeth was not a free agent
to live where she chose and, whatever she thought, is hardly likely
to have committed herself so far – even in a private letter to her
sister. All the same, it is true that the text, if it is genuine, has
been translated three times and may have suffered in the process.
And it is quite possible that Elizabeth was somewhat piqued by her
much-loved step-mother's precipitate remarriage. In view of subsequent events, it is reasonable to assume that she did not yet know
about Tom Seymour's earlier matrimonial intentions towards
herself. Leti again provides an elaborate apparatus of letters – an
ardent proposal and an elegantly phrased refusal, both dated in
February – but these are almost certainly inventions of his own.
Nevertheless, it was not long before Katherine Ashley had heard
the gossip about what would have happened if the Lord Admiral
'might have had his own will', and could not resist passing on
this interesting piece of information to her charge.

The Queen paid a visit to court in May and seems to have
discussed the whole question of her remarriage with the King,
explaining that no disrespect was intended to his father's memory.
Reassured on this point, Edward wrote to her on 30 May: 'since
you love my father, I cannot but much esteem you; since you love
me, I cannot but love you in return; and since you love the Word
of God, I do love and admire you with my whole heart. Wherefore,
if there be anything wherein I may do you a kindness, either in
word or deed, I will do it willingly.'[9]

News that the marriage had actually taken place had leaked out
by midsummer and the King was graciously pleased to give it his

blessing. 'I will so provide for you both', he told Katherine magnificently, 'that hereafter, if any grief befall, I shall be a sufficient succour in your godly or praisable enterprises.' But the Lord Protector, as Edward noted laconically in his Chronicle, 'was much displeased'. However, the damage was done, and the outbreak of war with Scotland later in the summer helped to distract the Protector's attention from his brother's misdeeds.

The Admiral should have commanded the Fleet in the Scottish campaign, but he preferred to remain at home to pursue certain projects of his own. He and Katherine, and Elizabeth, were now all living together – sometimes at Chelsea, sometimes further out in the country at Hanworth, another of the Queen's dower houses, and sometimes at Seymour Place, Tom's London residence. Katherine was relaxed and happy. Tom, having achieved one of his objectives, was in high good humour and the domestic atmosphere was gay and informal.

Remarkably informal, in fact, for it was at Chelsea, 'incontinent after he was married to the Queen', that the Lord Admiral began his semi-jocular pursuit of his wife's step-daughter. He

would come many mornings into the Lady Elizabeth's chamber, before she were ready, and sometimes before she did rise. And if she were up, he would bid her good morrow, and ask how she did, and strike her upon the back or on the buttocks familiarly, and so go forth through his lodgings; and sometime go through to the maidens and play with them, and so go forth.

If Elizabeth was still in bed, 'he would put open the curtains, and bid her good morrow, and make as though he would come at her. And she would go further into the bed, so that he could not come at her.' All good clean fun perhaps, and certainly quite a new experience for Elizabeth. There was one morning when the Admiral went rather too far and 'strove to have kissed her in her bed' but Mrs Ashley, who was present, 'bade him go away for shame'.[10]

When the household moved to Hanworth, Tom would 'likewise come in the morning unto her grace', but found Elizabeth up and dressed, except for two occasions when the Queen came with him 'and there they tickled my lady Elizabeth in the bed, the Queen and my lord Admiral'. Another time, in the garden at

Hanworth, 'he wrestled with her and cut her gown in an hundred pieces, being black cloth'. When Mrs Ashley scolded the princess, 'her grace answered, she could not do with all, for the Queen held her, while the Lord Admiral cut it'.[11]

Years later, Henry Clifford, writing the biography of his mistress, Jane Dormer, who had been one of Mary's favourite maids of honour, remarked of Elizabeth that 'a great lady who knew her well, being a girl of twelve or thirteen, told me that she was proud and disdainful, and related to me some particulars of her scornful behaviour, which much blemished the handsomeness and beauty of her person'.[12] Clifford can, in general, be regarded as a hostile witness, but Elizabeth always had a healthy idea of her own importance and may well have been inclined to stand on her dignity. All the same, she seems to have responded readily to teasing and for a few carefree weeks during the summer of 1547 she expanded and behaved more naturally and childishly than at any time since she was a baby. Unfortunately, however, the opportunity had come too late. At almost fourteen Elizabeth was no longer a child. Tom Seymour was a very personable man, and his thinly disguised advances naturally excited her adolescent vanity and soon began to provoke an experimentally coquettish response.

Mrs Ashley was worried. Tongues were beginning to wag. There was more romping at Chelsea, when Elizabeth, 'hearing the privy lock undo' and knowing that meant the Admiral was coming, 'ran out of her bed to her maidens, and then went behind the curtain of the bed, the maidens being there; and my lord tarried to have her come out'.[13] It was after this episode that the governess waylaid his lordship in the gallery to tell him that 'these things were complained of and that my lady was evil spoken of'. Tom was unrepentant. He meant no evil, he said, and swore, by God's precious soul, that he was being slandered and would himself complain to the Lord Protector.[14] Seeing that 'she could not make him leave it', Mrs Ashley took her troubles to the Queen, who 'made a small matter of it', but said she would come with her husband in future. 'And so', according to Mrs Ashley, 'she did ever after',[15] or for a time, at least. There were other occasions, 'at Seymour Place, when the Queen lay there' when the Admiral used 'to come up every morning in his nightgown, barelegged in his slippers'. These days, however, Elizabeth was usually up and 'at her book', so Tom had to content himself by looking in at the gallery door and bidding her good morrow before going his way. Even so, Mrs Ashley told him severely, it was an unseemly sight to come visiting a maiden's chamber so improperly dressed; 'with which he was angry, but he left it'.[16]

It is difficult to see what, if anything, the Admiral hoped to achieve by these rather questionable antics. Probably they had started simply as his idea of a joke – no doubt it gave him a pleasant sense of power to be on slap-and-tickle terms with Henry VIII's daughter – and were continued out of bravado after the joke had gone stale. For it had gone stale. Elizabeth was becoming self-conscious and Katherine, in spite of her apparent casualness, was not entirely happy about the situation. There had been a curious little incident at Hanworth, when the Queen told Mrs Ashley that 'my lord Admiral looked in at the gallery window and saw my lady Elizabeth cast her arms about a man's neck'. When Mrs Ashley taxed the princess with this, she 'denied it weeping, and bade ask all her women', but the governess knew such an accusation could not be true, 'for there came no man but Grindal, the Lady Elizabeth's schoolmaster'. She began to wonder, rather uneasily, if the Queen was growing jealous of her step-daughter and had invented the story of a strange man as a warning to Mrs Ashley to 'take more heed and be, as it were, in watch betwixt her and my Lord Admiral'.[17]

In spite of all these distractions, Elizabeth was making good progress under Grindal's tuition, and Roger Ascham did not know 'whether to admire more the wit of her who learnt, or the diligence of him who taught'.[18] Ascham was anxious to further his acquaintance with Elizabeth and took care to cultivate Mrs Ashley, writing tactful letters of congratulation on her labour and wisdom in so diligently overseeing that noble imp, her charge. He sent Elizabeth an Italian book and a book of prayers, had her pens mended, and asked to be commended to 'all that company of godly gentlewomen' who surrounded the Queen Dowager.[19]

The godly gentlewomen by this time included the ten-year-old Lady Jane Grey. She had been placed in the Queen's household by her ambitious parents, and the Admiral had persuaded her father, the Marquess of Dorset, to put her future in his hands. As the granddaughter of Henry VIII's younger sister Mary, who had married the Duke of Suffolk, Jane Grey stood close enough to the throne to be a valuable potential asset; for Henry, using the powers given him by Parliament, had bequeathed the Succession, in default of heirs from any of his own children, to the Suffolk line. Tom Seymour was not quite sure yet how he could best turn the custody of Lady Jane to his advantage, but he was full of 'fair promises' and dropped hints to the Dorsets about a possible marriage for her with the King.

Edward was, of course, the most important of the three children whom the Admiral hoped to make use of in the various undesirable ploys he had under consideration, and he lost no opportunity of ingratiating himself with the boy by flattery and gifts of pocket money.

The young King was beginning to feel a trifle overburdened with uncles. The Protector was proving a strict guardian. A 'dry, sour, opinionated man', according to Van der Delft the new Imperial ambassador, he kept Edward so strait that he could not have money at his will, and the King had conceived a perfectly dispassionate dislike for his 'uncle of Somerset'. The Admiral, on the other hand, was jovial and open-handed. Edward had no objection to the open-handedness and was in the habit of sending his uncle Tom terse demands for cash via the useful John Fowler, but he soon became irritated by the Admiral constantly urging him to assert himself, and trying to involve him in the Seymour family squabbles.

There was an acrimonious dispute in progress that autumn over some pieces of the Queen Dowager's jewellery held by the Protector. Katherine claimed they had been personal gifts from King Henry, but Somerset refused to give them up, saying they were crown property. As these items included her wedding-ring, Katherine's annoyance was understandable. Somerset had also installed a tenant, against her wishes, in one of her manors. The normally sunny-tempered Katherine was furious and threatened to 'utter her choler' to His Grace. Family relations were not improved by the attitude of the Protector's wife. The Duchess of Somerset, 'a woman for many imperfections intolerable but for pride monstrous',[20] was bitterly resentful of the fact that Katherine, as Queen Dowager, took precedence over her at state functions, and made no secret of her feelings on the subject of presumptuous wives of younger sons.

The first session of Parliament in the new reign was held in November, and the Admiral, imbued with a fresh sense of his wrongs, stamped about shouting that 'if I be thus used, they speak of a black Parliament, by God's precious soul I will make this the blackest Parliament that ever was in England'. When his cronies tried to restrain him, he exclaimed defiantly that he could better live without the Protector than the Protector without him, and that if anybody went about to speak evil of the Queen he would take his fist to their ears, from the highest to the lowest.[21]

Tom had tried to persuade Edward, now considerably in his debt financially, to sign a letter to be presented to 'the lords of the Parliament House' requesting them to favour a suit which the Admiral meant to bring before them. This suit was Tom Seymour's pet scheme to have the offices of Protector of the Realm and Governor of the King's person divided between his brother and himself. Edward, however, took the advice of his tutor, Sir John Cheke, who warned him seriously on the dangers of becoming compromised in the Admiral's intrigues, and wisely refused to sign anything he might be made to regret. The Admiral, frustrated, took to prowling the corridors of St James's Palace, remarking wistfully that he wished the King were at home with him in his house, and speculating on how easy it would be to steal the boy away under the Protector's nose.

Elizabeth paid a visit to court in December, but although she and Edward remained genuinely fond of each other their relationship had changed considerably since that day, less than a year ago, when they had cried together so bitterly over the news of their father's death. The respect exacted by a Tudor king, even one just ten years old, was formidable. An Italian visitor, Petruccio Ubaldini, thought the whole business somewhat exaggerated. Commenting on the elaborate formalities which took place when one of the King's sisters dined in the royal presence, he remarked,

> she may neither sit under a canopy nor on a chair, but must sit on
> a mere bench which is provided with a cushion, and so far distant
> from the head of the table and the King, that the canopy does not
> overhang her. The ceremonies observed before sitting down at table
> are truly laughable. I have seen, for example, the Princess Elizabeth
> drop on one knee five times before her brother, before she took her
> place.[22]

But Elizabeth had been brought up to regard the person of the sovereign with an almost superstitious reverence, and would see nothing in the least laughable about kneeling to her little brother who was also the King. At any rate she seems to have enjoyed her visit, for she asked to be allowed to stay over Christmas, and Mary was invited to join the family party.

Perhaps Elizabeth was rather glad to escape briefly from the increasingly charged atmosphere of her step-mother's household, and found reassurance in the ordered formality of the court. There was plenty of congenial male company among the group of young noblemen who surrounded the King, and she would have been able to renew her acquaintance with at least one old playmate – Robert Dudley, a dark, handsome boy just her own age whom she had known on and off since she was seven or eight. There was a long-standing connexion between the Tudors and the Dudleys, dating back to the days when Robert's grandfather had been one of Elizabeth's grandfather's hated tax-gatherers. His father had risen in the service of Elizabeth's father, and now created Earl of Warwick, was one of those members of the Privy Council standing watchfully in the shadows behind the Lord Protector.

Elizabeth returned to either Chelsea or Hanworth in January and presently suffered the loss of her tutor, William Grindal, who died of plague during that month. Elizabeth had no hesitation in her choice of a replacement. On 12 February, Roger Ascham wrote to his friend John Cheke, telling him that the princess 'is thinking of having me in the place of Grindal. . . . I was with the illustrious lady during these last days: she signified to me her pleasure and I did not try to make any bargain for my own advantage, but at once declared that I was ready to obey her orders.' It was not quite so simple as that, for Katherine and the Admiral, who were away in London, favoured appointing a man called Goldsmith, and Ascham was anxious not to appear pushing. He urged Elizabeth to follow her guardians' judgement and to think only of 'bringing to perfection that singular learning of which Grindal had sown the seeds'. However, he told Cheke, 'when the Lady Elizabeth comes to London, she will talk over this matter with the Queen and the Lord Admiral; nor do I think they will settle anything without you'.[23]

Whether as a result of her own determination, or through the growing influence of John Cheke with the Privy Council, Elizabeth got her way. Ascham obtained leave of absence from

St John's College, Cambridge, where he was a Fellow, and took up his new post in the spring of 1548.

Roger Ascham, a Yorkshireman in his early thirties, had already published *Toxophilus*, his famous treatise on archery, and was acquiring an international reputation for scholarship. He was not entirely strange to royal circles, having been called in by Cheke on several occasions to teach Edward the penmanship of which he was a notable exponent, and had played a considerable part in forming Elizabeth's exquisitely legible Italianate hand-writing; but he must have found a household dominated by the ebullient personality of Tom Seymour something of a contrast to Cambridge. Still, there were enough kindred spirits devoted to 'godly learning' in the Queen Dowager's establishment to make Roger Ascham feel at home. He was already on familiar terms with Mrs Ashley and her husband, and soon struck up a friend-ship with John Whitney, a young gentleman-in-waiting with whom he shared a bed. There was also Lady Jane Grey, already fast developing into a formidable paragon of Protestant erudition; her tutor, John Aylmer; the Queen's younger sister, Ann Parr; and, of course, Elizabeth herself who fulfilled Ascham's highest expectations as a pupil. He taught her Latin and Greek by his famous method of double translation, presenting her with passages of Demosthenes or Cicero, to be turned first into English and then back into their original languages. The mornings were usually devoted to Greek, beginning with a reading from the Greek New Testament, and followed by selected orations of Isocrates or one of Sophocles' tragedies. Ascham thought that from these sources the princess would 'gain purity of style, and her mind derive instruction that would be of value to her to meet every contingency of life'. In the afternoons they went on to Latin, and Elizabeth read almost the whole of Cicero and a 'great part' of Livy under Ascham's supervision. To these authors he added various works of St Cyprian and Melanchthon's Common-places, which he considered 'best suited, after the Holy Scrip-tures, to teach her the foundations of religion, together with elegant language and sound doctrine'.[24] It sounds an indigestible diet for a fourteen-year-old girl, but Elizabeth apparently throve on it, eagerly absorbing a carefully balanced mixture of classical ethics and Christian piety. Katherine Parr had not forgotten her zeal for 'true religion' of the reformed variety – though it was noticeable that the Lord Admiral had developed a habit of remembering urgent business elsewhere when it was time for family prayers.

Roger Ascham cannot have been more than two months in his new, intellectually stimulating surroundings when the volcano which had been simmering beneath the surface of the Queen Dowager's household for the past year suddenly erupted. Katherine was now carrying Tom's child, and a first pregnancy for a woman in her mid-thirties was no light matter in the sixteenth century. Whatever her good intentions, the Admiral's wife was no longer in any condition for chaperoning horseplay – especially in the early morning. We do not know exactly what happened to bring matters to a head, but it seems to have been something rather less innocent than hide-and-seek round the bed-curtains. According to a hearsay account given eight months after the event: 'the Queen, suspecting the often access of the Admiral to the Lady Elizabeth's grace, came suddenly upon them, when they were all alone (he having her in his arms). Wherefore the Queen fell out, both with the Lord Admiral and with her grace also. And hereupon', this same account continues, 'the Queen called Mrs Ashley to her, and told her fancy in that matter; and of this there was much displeasure.'[25]

Katherine was understandably hurt and angry, and she cannot be blamed for venting her feelings on Mrs Ashley, who does appear to have been guilty of some negligence. Quite apart from her personal distress, Katherine must also have been badly frightened. The Protector had so far shown himself remarkably forbearing towards his brother's various indiscretions, but the Queen knew that if any harm were to come to Elizabeth, a virgin of the blood royal, while in their charge, both she and her husband would find themselves in a very ugly situation. Katherine was also clearly thinking of Elizabeth herself, whose whole life could be ruined by a scandal now. At all costs that must be avoided and for everyone's sake the princess must be put out of the Admiral's reach as quickly and as quietly as possible. Arrangements were therefore made for Elizabeth and her household to leave Chelsea in the week after Whitsun 1548 for Cheshunt (or Cheston) to stay in the house of Sir Anthony and Lady Denny.

Tom Seymour's conduct towards a girl fully young enough to be his daughter living under his wife's protection was, of course, inexcusable; but Elizabeth cannot be entirely exonerated. At best she had been thoughtless, at worst stupid, and cruelly ungrateful to a woman who had loved and trusted her. That she knew she had behaved badly, and recognised the tact and generosity Katherine had shown in extricating her from an embarrassing predicament, is evident from a distinctly chastened note in the first letter she wrote to her step-mother from Cheshunt:

Although I could not be plentiful in giving thanks for the manifold kindness received at your Highness' hand at my departure, yet I am something to be borne withal, for truly I was replete with sorrow to depart from your Highness, especially leaving you undoubtful of health: and, albeit I answered little, I weighed it more deeper, when you said you would warn me of all evils that you should hear of me; for if your Grace had not a good opinion of me, you would not have offered friendship to me that way, that all men judge the contrary. But what may I more say, than thank God for providing such friends to me; desiring God to enrich me with their long life, and me grace to be in heart no less thankful to receive it than I now am glad in writing to show it; and although I have plenty of matter, here I will stay, for I know you are not quiet to read. From Cheston, this present Saturday. Your Highness' humble daughter, Elizabeth.[26]

There had obviously been an uncomfortable interview with Katherine during which Elizabeth had had to digest a number of unpalatable home-truths on the subject of light and unseemly conduct. There is, of course, no record of what passed between them on that occasion, but, according to the ever-helpful Leti, Katherine told her step-daughter: 'God has given you great qualities. Cultivate them always and labour to improve them, for I believe that you are destined by heaven to be Queen of England.' She may well have said something of the sort – perhaps offering an olive branch after certain other remarks, or in an attempt to bring a sulky girl to some realisation of what she stood to lose. It cannot have been an entirely new idea to Elizabeth. She was far too acute not to have already thought of it for herself, but perhaps it was the first time anyone had put such a thought into words, and coming from someone like Katherine it would have made a deep impression. After all, looked at dispassionately, was it so far-fetched? True, Edward seemed sturdy enough, but he was being subjected to abnormal stresses and strains for a child of his age, and had yet to pass through the adolescent years which had proved fatal to several male members of his house – his uncle Arthur, his bastard half-brother the Duke of Richmond, his first cousin the Earl of Lincoln. Then there was Mary, over thirty now, still unmarried and in poor health. Even if she were to marry at once, with her mother's history behind her the chances of her bearing children looked remote. The Tudors had not so far shown themselves either a fruitful or a long-lived stock. Henry VII had died at fifty-two, his younger daughter at thirty-eight. Even that magnificent physical specimen Henry VIII had only survived to fifty-five, and he had been an old man for some years before his death.

All the evidence points to the fact that certainly by her mid-teens the conviction that she would one day be Queen of England had taken firm root in Elizabeth's mind. It became a goal to work towards – a vision to sustain her through the difficult and frightening decade that lay ahead.

CHAPTER VII

'The Peril that Might Ensue'

THANKS to the Queen's prompt and sensible action, any immediate danger of scandal touching the princess and the Admiral had been averted. Indeed, the arrangements for Elizabeth's move were so skilfully handled that even her own household did not know the real reason for it. The Dennys may have been in the secret, but they were old friends of the family and could be trusted to be discreet. Sir Anthony Denny had been a favourite of Henry VIII, and a gentleman of his privy chamber. Lady Denny was one of those pious matrons who had been closely associated with the Queen during Henry's lifetime, and in this emergency Katherine evidently considered her the most suitable person available to take over responsibility for Elizabeth. Matters were made easier by the fact of Katherine's advancing pregnancy, for it was known that she was preparing to retire to Sudeley Castle down in Gloucestershire to await the birth of her baby.

Any unpleasantness between the Queen Dowager and her husband about what had happened was quickly smoothed over, and if Katherine felt any lingering resentment she kept it to herself. No doubt she was pinning her hopes on the coming child. If Tom had a son to think of it might steady him – make him settle down and forget all the wild whirling schemes revolving in his head.

Certainly Tom needed something to steady him. It was part of his duties as Lord Admiral to suppress the gangs of pirates which preyed on shipping in the English Channel, but instead it appeared that the Lord Admiral was well on the way to becoming a pirate himself. According to a number of justifiably irritated merchants and sea-captains, he was actually encouraging the marauders, allowing them to use his property in the Scilly Isles as a haven and taking a cut of their loot. But Tom Seymour had more important things on his mind than piracy, for he was still cherishing his ambition to wrest the guardianship of the King out of his brother's hands. If he was ever to achieve that ambition he would need powerful friends, and to buy those friends he would need money – a great deal of money. It seemed a wise move, therefore, to enlist the services of Sir William Sharington, vice-treasurer of the Bristol Mint. William Sharington had been appointed to this office in 1546, and since that time had enriched himself and his associates by such undesirable practices as the clipping and debasing of coin, and the buying-up and minting of considerable quantities of church plate. The Admiral now promised protection from the possible consequences of this form of private enterprise, if Sharington would provide him with the funds he needed. It was good always to have a mass of money ready, remarked Tom vaguely, for then 'a man might do somewhat withal'. Another time he said, 'God faith, Sharington, if we had £10,000 in ready money, that were well.' The Admiral had been reckoning how much it would cost to 'find 10,000 men a month' and boasting that 'he had more gentlemen that loved him than my Lord Protector had', but he was noticeably evasive when questioned directly about his future plans.[1]

He did not take his wife into his confidence either, but Katherine was quite intelligent enough to have guessed a good deal of what was in his mind. Although she loyally supported Tom in his personal quarrels with the Protector, she tried to lower the temperature when she could, and was understandably eager to divert his attention from any more dangerous pranks.

Katherine was particularly anxious that nothing should prevent their going down to Gloucestershire together. The baby had quickened now, and she wrote from Hanworth to her 'sweetheart and loving husband' who had been delayed in London on business: 'I have given your little knave your blessing, who like an honest man stirred apace after and before; for Mary Odell being abed with me had laid her hand upon my belly to feel it stir. It hath stirred these three days every morning and evening, so that I trust when you come, it will make you some pastime.'[2] This evoked a characteristic reply. The Admiral, 'perplexed' as usual that he could not have justice from those who should have been partial to him, was nevertheless much revived to hear that 'my little man doth shake his poll, trusting, if God should give him life to live as long as his father, he will revenge such wrongs as neither you nor I can at this present'. And the expectant father added some helpful obstetric advice: 'I do desire your Highness to keep the little knave so lean and gaunt with your good diet and walking, that he may creep out of a mouse-hole.'[3]

The Queen Dowager and her husband set out for Sudeley on Wednesday, 13 June, accompanied by a princely retinue and taking little Jane Grey with them. Jane's parents had been growing impatient, as no sign of the brilliant marriage promised for her materialised, and had tried to get her back. But the Admiral was too much for the Marquess of Dorset, being 'so earnest with him in persuasion' that Dorset could not resist him – especially perhaps as the persuasion included a substantial sum of money lent without security – and Jane stayed with Katherine, who had grown very fond of the child.

Katherine also saw to it that she and Tom maintained normal friendly relations with Elizabeth in her exile at Cheshunt. The princess had written a curiously dignified little note to the Admiral, in reply apparently to an apology of his at not being able to do her some small service:

My lord, you needed not to send an excuse to me. For I could not mistrust the not fulfilling of your promise to proceed for want of good will, but only opportunity serveth not. Wherefore I shall desire you to think that a greater matter than this could not make me impute any unkindness in you. For I am a friend not won with trifles, nor lost with the like.[4]

Elizabeth was obviously feeling out of things and missing Katherine badly. She wrote to her on 31 July:

Although your Highness' letters be most joyful to me in absence, yet considering what pain it is to you to write, your Grace being so great with child and so sickly, your commendation were enough in my lord's letter. I much rejoice . . . with my humble thanks, that your Grace wished me with you, till I were weary of that country. Your Highness were like to be cumbered if I should not depart till I were weary of being with you; although it were the worst soil in the world, your presence would make it pleasant.

She is anxious that the Admiral 'shall be diligent to give me knowledge from time to time how his busy child doth', and ended with a rather sad little attempt at a joke, 'if I were at his birth, no doubt I would see him beaten for the trouble he has put you to'.[5]

Elizabeth had not been well herself. As a little girl she had always been remarkably robust, and there is no record of her even suffering from any of the usual childish ailments. But now began that period of ill-health which was to last intermittently for the remainder of her teens. According to Mrs Ashley, 'she was first sick about mid-summer'. There is no description of the exact nature of this illness, which was to recur in the autumn and become serious enough for one of the King's physicians, Dr Bill, to be sent down to Cheshunt to attend her. In the absence of more definite information, it seems reasonable to assume that it was connected with the onset of Elizabeth's menstrual cycle, aggravated in a highly strung, sensitive girl by the effects of depression and emotional disturbance.

Katherine's baby was born on 30 August. It was a girl, christened Mary. The Admiral apparently felt no disappointment over the child's sex, and at once wrote enthusiastically to his brother with the good news. The Protector had been in the middle of a long, reproachful letter, urging Tom to mend his ways, but he added a kindly postscript: 'We are right glad to understand by your letters that the Queen, your bedfellow, hath had a happy hour; and, escaping all danger, hath made you the father of so pretty a daughter.'[6]

Tragically, however, these congratulations were premature. Katherine developed a high fever, the dreaded symptom of puerperal sepsis, and in her delirium all the carefully buried hurt of the past few months rose to the surface. 'I am not well handled,' she told her friend (and step-daughter by an earlier marriage), Elizabeth Tyrwhit, 'for those that be about me careth not for me, but standeth laughing at my grief; and the more good I will to them, the less good they will to me.' She was holding on to Tom's hand as she spoke and when he exclaimed, 'Why, sweetheart, I would do you no hurt', Katherine said, 'very sharply and earnestly', in his ear, 'No, my lord, I think so; you have given me many shrewd taunts.' Tom, distressed and somewhat embarrassed, lay down beside her on the bed in an attempt to calm her 'with gentle communication'. But Katherine was not to be pacified and rambled on that she would have given a thousand marks to have had her full talk with the physician on the day she was delivered, but 'durst not for displeasing of you'.[7] The possible implications of all this were not lost on the bystanders and inevitably a whisper began to circulate that the Queen had been poisoned.

Katherine died on 5 September 1548, and with her death was extinguished one of the most attractive personalities of the age. She was buried in the chapel at Sudeley with all the ceremonial due to a Queen Dowager of England, and ten-year-old Jane Grey officiating as chief mourner.

For a little while the Admiral seemed genuinely stricken and 'so amazed' that he had small regard to himself or his doings. For all his faults Tom was not a deliberately cruel man. The unhappiness he had caused his wife had been due more to sheer selfish thoughtlessness than any fixed desire to wound, and a servant of his, coming to Cheshunt, told Mrs Ashley that the Admiral 'was a heavy man for the Queen'.

Mrs Ashley, of course, was all agog. Knowing what she did about his lordship's earlier plans, she was already beginning to hear wedding-bells. Elizabeth was 'sick in her bed' again, and in what seems to have been a somewhat unfortunate attempt to cheer her up the governess observed archly, 'your old husband that was appointed unto you after the death of the King now is free again. You may have him if you will.' No, said Elizabeth. 'Yes,' persisted Mrs Ashley, 'yes, you will not deny it if my Lord Protector and the Council were pleased therewith.' After all, why not? The Admiral had been worthy to marry a Queen, and was 'the noblest man unmarried in this land.' But the response was disappointing, for 'her Grace would ever say, nay by her troth'.[8]

Mrs Ashley wanted the princess to write to the Admiral 'to comfort him in his sorrow', but Elizabeth remained uncooperative. She would not do so, she said shortly, 'for it needs not'. Her own feelings about Katherine's death she kept to herself. Sometime in October the household moved from Cheshunt to Hatfield – no doubt to the relief of the Dennys, for the accommodation of Elizabeth and her considerable retinue over the past five months must have put a severe strain on their resources – and John Seymour, escorting the princess on her journey, brought a message from Tom recommending him to her and enquiring 'whether her great buttocks were grown any less or no?' which certainly sounds as if he was quite his old self again.

In any case, the widower could not allow himself the luxury of mourning – there were too many urgent matters requiring his attention. In the confused period after Katherine's death, the Dorsets had insisted on removing their daughter; but Jane Grey was too valuable a property to lose without a struggle, and the Admiral was afraid (or so he said) that the Protector meant to marry her to his own son. He went to see the Dorsets and, according to the Marquess, 'was so earnestly in hand with me and my wife that in the end, because he would have no nay, we were contented she should again return to his house'.[9] Tom had re-assured the anxious parents that not only the Queen's gentle-women but also 'the maids which waited at large' should remain to attend on Jane, and that his own mother 'would be as dear unto her as though she were her own daughter'.[10] More to the point, he made Dorset another loan and renewed his promise that 'if he might once get the King at liberty' a royal marriage would be arranged. The Dorsets – chronically short of money, weak, greedy and not over-endowed with common sense – fell once again into the trap.

The Admiral was now openly canvassing support for his schemes for putting an end to the Protectorate. He asked Dorset what friends he could count on in his part of the world, and advised him to make much of the prosperous yeomen and free-holders, 'for they be men that be best able to persuade the multitude'. 'Go to their houses', urged Tom, 'carrying with you a flagon or two of wine and a pasty of venison, and use a familiarity with them, for so shall you cause them to love you and be assured to have them at your commandment.'[11] He repeated this ingenuous advice to his brother-in-law, William Parr, Marquess of Northamp-ton, and the young Earl of Rutland, telling Rutland that he would like to see the King 'have the honour and rule of his own doings'.

The Admiral did not appear to notice how lukewarm was the response, and, when Rutland had the temerity to remark that he thought his power would be much diminished by the Queen's death, brushed this aside impatiently, saying the Council never feared him so much as they did now. He continued to express his dissatisfaction with his brother's régime to anybody who would listen, and never tired of looking at 'a chart of England' which he had, and declaring how strong he was, 'how far his lands and dominions did stretch . . . and what shires and places were for him'.[12]

More sinister, though, than all this rather meaningless talk was the close proprietary interest that Tom Seymour had begun to take in the Princess Elizabeth and her affairs. Mrs Ashley, who had fallen completely under his spell, chattered away happily to Elizabeth about his intentions, how he was sure to come wooing before long, and all about the exciting possibilities which that opened up. Poor Katherine Ashley has come in for a good deal of criticism over her conduct at this time, and certainly she was not very wise. All the same, it must be remembered that she was by no means the only person to be taken in by Tom. She seems to have genuinely believed that Henry VIII would have approved the match and that it would be a good thing for her beloved princess. It was time Elizabeth had a husband. Mrs Ashley could not bear to think she might become a lonely old maid like her sister Mary. The Admiral, too, would be able to protect her – Mrs Ashley could not be expected to realise how very precarious in fact his position was.

Elizabeth did need someone to protect her. Death had removed the Queen, her only powerful and disinterested friend, and in her household of over a hundred people there was no married woman of rank to whom she could turn for advice or guidance. In the circumstances she kept her head wonderfully well, but she was not entirely proof against the relentless propaganda-campaign she was being subjected to. Mrs Ashley's husband, an observant and sensible man, warned his wife several times 'to take heed, for he did fear that the Lady Elizabeth did bear some affection to my Lord Admiral. She seemed to be well pleased therewith, and sometime she would blush when he were spoken of.'[13]

In the outside world, gossip linking the Admiral's name with the princess grew insistent, and more than one person attempted to warn Tom of the risk he was running. At the end of November, as they rode together to Parliament behind the Protector, Lord Russell, the venerable Lord Privy Seal, said seriously: 'My Lord Admiral, there are certain rumours bruited of you which I am very sorry to hear.' He was informed, he went on, that the Admiral was hoping to marry with either the Lady Mary or the Lady Elizabeth and added, 'my lord, if ye go about any such thing, ye seek the means to undo yourself and all those that shall come of you'. Tom naturally wanted to know 'the authors of that tale' and 'seemed to deny that there was any such thing attempted of his part, and that he never thought to make any enterprise therein'.

Two or three days later, however, again finding himself next to Lord Russell in the procession riding from the Protector's house to Westminster, the Admiral reopened the subject himself. 'Father Russell,' he said, 'you are very suspicious of me. I pray you tell me who showed you of the marriage that I should attempt?' Russell, very properly, refused to name his sources and renewed his warning that Tom should 'make no suit for marriage' with either of the princesses. This time the Admiral persisted. 'It is convenient for them to marry,' he said, 'and better it were that they were married within the realm than in any foreign place. . . . And why might not I, or another, made by the King their father, marry one of them?' He got an unequivocal answer. If he or any other within the realm attempted such a match, declared the Lord Privy Seal, he would 'undoubtedly procure unto himself the occasion of his utter undoing' – and Tom above all others, 'being of so near alliance to the King's Majesty'. Both Henry VII and Henry VIII, Russell pointed out, though wise and noble princes, had been well known for their suspicious natures. What was more likely than that Edward would take after his father and grandfather in this respect? If one of his uncles married one of the heirs to his crown, he would be bound to think the worst, 'and, as often as he shall see you, to think that you gape and wish for his death'. There was another thing: 'And I pray you, my lord, what shall you have with any of them?' 'Three thousand a year,' said Tom promptly and was as promptly disabused. Whoever married the princesses, Russell told him, would get no more than 'ten thousand pounds in money, plate and goods, and no land. And what', enquired the Lord Privy Seal, 'should that be to maintain his charges and estate, matching himself there?' 'They must have the three thousand pounds a year also,' said the Admiral. 'By God, they may not!' 'By God,' roared Tom, 'none of you all dare say nay to it!' But old Lord Russell was not to be intimidated. 'By God, for my part I will say nay to it; for it is clean against the King's will!'[14]

Mary and Elizabeth had each been left lands to the value of £3000 a year by their father, and the Admiral, who apparently would not be warned, now began to make detailed enquiries into

Elizabeth's finances. Her steward, or 'cofferer', Thomas Parry, came up to London shortly before Christmas and Tom Seymour took the opportunity to have several conversations with him. He wanted to know all about the state and size of the princess's household; the whereabouts and profitability of her lands; what terms she held them on; and, especially, whether or not her title to them had yet been confirmed by Letters Patent. She could get her lands exchanged for better ones, he told Parry, and wished they were situated in Wales or the West Country, significantly where most of his own strength lay. He went on to ask about her housekeeping expenses and to compare them with 'what was spent in his own house'.

It was partly a question of houses which had brought Parry to town. Elizabeth wanted to visit her brother, but Durham House, where she had been accustomed to stay when she came up to London, was now being used as a Mint. When the Admiral heard about this difficulty, he was eager to help. The princess must have his own house whenever she wanted it. He would like to see her, too. Perhaps when she moved to Ashridge – it would not be far out of his way when he went into the country. As for Durham House, Elizabeth should go to the Duchess of Somerset and 'make suit' to the Protector to grant her a suitable town-residence, and agree to the exchange of her lands before her Patent was sealed.

Parry was much impressed. When he returned to Hatfield, he told Elizabeth all about my lord's 'gentle offers' and the suggested visit. As she seemed to take this 'very gladly and to accept it very joyfully and thankfully', Parry was emboldened to ask whether, if the Council approved, she would marry the Admiral? He got small satisfaction. 'When that comes to pass,' said Elizabeth, 'I will do as God shall put into my mind.' Then she wanted to know what Parry meant by asking her such a question, 'or who bade him say so'. Nobody, the steward assured her hastily, nobody bade him say so – it was just that from the tone of the Admiral's conversation it had seemed 'he was given that way rather than otherwise'. As for his advice that she should go cap in hand to the Duchess of Somerset, Elizabeth would not believe it at first and, considering Tom's freely expressed dislike of his sister-in-law, it does seem odd to say the least. But when Parry said yes, by his faith, she was annoyed. 'Well, I will not do so,' she exclaimed crossly, 'and so tell him.' No Tudor was going to be driven to ask favours of a Seymour. 'I will not come there', said the Tudor princess, 'nor begin to flatter now.' She asked if Mrs Ashley knew of the Admiral's talk with Parry and ordered him to be sure to tell her. 'For I will know nothing but she shall know of it. In faith, I cannot be quiet until ye have told her of it.' The fifteen-year-old Elizabeth fully realised, even if nobody else did, the danger of becoming involved in anything that looked like secret negotiations.

Mrs Ashley had also been on a trip to London. She saw John Cheke's wife and Lady Tyrwhit, who told her it was being said that the Admiral was keeping the Queen's maidens together to wait on the Lady Elizabeth after they were married. Mrs Ashley then had to endure a highly unpleasant interview with the Protector's wife, during which the Duchess of Somerset 'found great faults' with her for having allowed Elizabeth to go with the Admiral in a barge on the Thames one night (this excursion must presumably have taken place the previous Christmas), and 'for other light parts'. 'She was not worthy to have the governance of a King's daughter,' said the Duchess, and threatened that 'another should have her place'.[15]

Mrs Ashley came back to Hatfield considerably subdued and began to tell Elizabeth that she might have to wait 'till the King's majesty came to his own rule', for it looked as if 'my Lord Protector's grace nor the Council would not suffer a subject to have her'; and not to set her mind on the marriage 'seeing the unlikelihood of it'.[16] Mrs Ashley, in fact, was becoming a little frightened. She had not altogether liked the sound of the Admiral's behaviour recently; if he was planning to do anything without the Council's consent, it would be disastrous for all concerned, and especially for herself.

But in spite of her newly acquired circumspection, Mrs Ashley presently enjoyed a cosy gossip with Thomas Parry on the subject uppermost in both their minds. This conversation took place on the day before Twelfth Night 1549 and, judging by its general tone, was accompanied by something guaranteed to keep out the cold and loosen the tongue.

Parry remarked on the goodwill which he had noticed 'between the Lord Admiral and her Grace'. Oh, said Mrs Ashley, it was true. 'I would wish her his wife of all men living,' sighed the governess. 'Yes, he might bring it to pass at the Council's hands well enough.' But, she told Parry, she had had such a 'charge' from the Duchess of Somerset that she dared not speak of it; 'and so fell again in praising the Admiral'.

Parry observed that for all that he had heard much evil report of the Admiral, 'that he was not only a very covetous man and an oppressor, but also an evil jealous man; and how cruelly, how dishonourably and how jealously he had used the Queen'. Non-sense, said Mrs Ashley, 'I know him better than ye do, or those that so report him.' No, he would make but too much of Elizabeth, and she knew it. As for the stories about the Admiral's jealousy, 'I will tell you,' went on Mrs Ashley with one of those rare flashes which illuminate a landscape: ' As he came upon a time up a stairs to see the Queen, he met with a groom of the chamber upon the stairs with a coal basket coming out of the chamber; and because the door was shut, and my lord without, he was angry and pretended that he was jealous.'

The Admiral loved Elizabeth 'but too well, and had so done a good while' confided Mrs Ashley, and forgetting all discretion she proceeded to tell Parry about the Queen's jealousy, how Elizabeth had been discovered in the Admiral's arms and had had to be sent away to Cheshunt.

Something in the steward's reaction, perhaps the eagerness of his 'Why, hath there been such familiarity indeed between them?' brought Mrs Ashley up short, for she 'seemed to repent that she had gone so far' and begged him several times never to repeat what she had said, 'for her Grace should be dishonoured for ever and she likewise undone'. Of course not, said Parry, of course not, he would 'rather be pulled with horses'.[17]

A couple of days later Parry was in London again and saw the Admiral briefly in his room at the court. It was an unsatisfactory interview, for it seemed to the cofferer that his lordship was either 'in some heat, or very busy, or had some mistrust of me'.[18] Tom Seymour had, in fact, come very nearly to the end of the road. The Protector had heard about his proposed visit to Elizabeth, and said with unwonted sternness that he would clap his brother in the Tower if he went anywhere near the princess. More serious was the fact that William Sharington's malpractices were at last coming to light. Sharington's house had been searched on 6 January and evidence discovered of his dealings with the Admiral. Tom was summoned to give an account of himself to the Protector in private, but with astonishing pigheadedness he refused to go until it should be more convenient for him.[19]

After this there was nothing for it but to lay the whole matter before the Council. The Council had put up with a good deal from the Admiral, but reports of his 'disloyal practices' were growing too numerous and too circumstantial to be ignored any longer. Finally, after 'divers conferences had at sundry times' it was unanimously decided at a meeting held on 17 January 1549 'to commit the said Admiral to prison in the Tower of London, there to remain till such further order be taken with him as the case . . . shall require'.[20]

At the last moment Tom seems to have come to some realisation of his danger. He told the Marquess of Northampton on the day before his arrest that the Council had been having great secret conferences, and, although he knew the matter touched him, he could learn nothing of it.[21] Walking in the gallery of his house with Lord Dorset after dinner on 17 January, he said that the Earl of Rutland had accused him, and he showed himself 'to be much afraid to go to the Council'. He would not go, he declared, without some pledge that he might return home again. Dorset's brother, Thomas, who was also present, observed with irritating good sense: 'Knowing yourself a true man, why should you doubt to go to your brother, knowing him to be a man of much mercy? Wherefore, if you will follow my advice, you shall go to him; and if he list to have you, it is not this house that can keep you, though you have ten times so many men as you have.'[22]

In spite of having boasted that, by God's precious soul, he would thrust his dagger into whosoever laid hands on him, when the Council's agents came for him that night the Admiral went quietly, protesting his innocence and swearing that no poor knave was ever truer to his prince.

Within the next couple of days John Harington, the Admiral's confidential servant, William Sharington and the serviceable John Fowler of the Privy Chamber had followed him to the Tower, and a party headed by Lord St John, Great Master of the Household, Anthony Denny and Sir Robert Tyrwhit was despatched to Hatfield. Mrs Ashley and Thomas Parry were taken away for questioning, and Robert Tyrwhit was left behind to obtain a statement from the Princess Elizabeth concerning her own guilty knowledge of the Admiral's subversive activities.

When Elizabeth was told that her governess and her steward
had been arrested, 'she was marvellous abashed and did weep
very tenderly a long time' demanding to know whether they had
confessed anything or not. This sounded promising, and Robert
Tyrwhit was not anticipating any great difficulty in his assign-
ment. But when the princess summoned him, saying she had forgotten to tell Lord St John and Denny of certain matters which
she would now open to him, it turned out to be no more than a
letter she had written to the Admiral requesting some favour for
her chaplain and asking him to credit her trusty servant, Parry, her
cofferer, in all other things. This, said Elizabeth, had only meant
that she wanted the Admiral's help in getting Durham House
back. Oh, and there was one other thing. Mrs Ashley had written
to the Admiral telling him he had better not visit the princess 'for
fear of suspicion', and when Elizabeth heard about this she had
been much offended and advised Mrs Ashley not to write so,
'because she would not have her to take upon her the knowledge
of any such thing'.

Tyrwhit was disappointed. Elizabeth must clearly be made to
realise that she was in no position to play games. 'After all this,'
he wrote to the Protector, 'I did require her to consider her
honour and the peril that might ensue, for she was but a subject.'
Having allowed Anne Boleyn's daughter to digest this ominous
piece of advice, he continued,

> I further declared what a woman Mistress Ashley was . . . saying that
> if she would open all things herself, all the evil and shame should
> be ascribed to them and her youth considered both with the King's
> Majesty, your Grace and the whole Council. But in no way she will
> not confess any practice by Mistress Ashley or the cofferer concern-
> ing my Lord Admiral; and yet I do see it in her face that she is
> guilty, and do perceive as yet she will abide more storms ere she
> accuse Mistress Ashley.

Tyrwhit felt he had every reason to believe that Elizabeth was
being deliberately obstructive, for when Thomas Parry had heard
the 'sudden news that my Lord Great Master and Master Denny
was arrived at the gate' he had rushed to his chamber and said to
his wife: ' "I would I had never been born, for I am undone",
and wrung his hands and cast away his chain from his neck and

his rings from his fingers'.[23] If that did not sound like guilt, reasoned Robert Tyrwhit, what did?

On the following day, 23 January, he wrote again to the Protector. He had had another interview with Elizabeth, but was obliged to admit: 'All I have gotten yet is by gentle persuasion, whereby I do begin to grow with her in credit.' The princess had told him how the Admiral had kindly offered to lend her his house in London 'for her time being there to see the King's Majesty', and had repeated most of the conversation she had subsequently had with Parry. It was not much, but, wrote Tyrwhit hopefully, 'this is a good beginning, I trust more will follow.' All the same, he ended, 'I do assure your Grace, she hath a very good wit, and nothing is gotten of her but by great policy'.[24]

Elizabeth needed all the wit and self-control she could muster. She was in a tight corner and knew it. She was now not merely alone, she was surrounded by enemies and spies. She was being called upon to answer the kind of charge, based chiefly on backstairs gossip, which is always most difficult to refute. She faced continual interrogation, designed to trap her into admissions which would have ruined her good name for ever and probably cost her any chance of succeeding to the throne. Her liberty might well be at stake, and, for all she knew of the political situation in London, perhaps even her life. And she was still only fifteen years old.

Robert Tyrwhit now resorted to that time-honoured device of showing Elizabeth a letter from the Protector, pretending 'with a great protestation' that he would not for a thousand pounds have it known that he had done so. Elizabeth thanked him for his kindness, but was not deceived. A false friend, Lady Browne, was introduced into the household in the hopes that the princess might be persuaded to confide in her sympathetic ear. But on 28 January, after more than a week of concentrated effort, Tyrwhit had nothing further to report. 'I do verily believe', he wrote to Somerset, 'that there hath been some secret promise between my Lady, Mistress Ashley and the cofferer, never to confess till death; and if it be so, it will never be gotten of her, but either by the King's Majesty, or else by your Grace.'[25]

The Protector had now taken a hand in the game and written to Elizabeth himself. Tyrwhit was slightly cheered to note that she 'hath been more pleasant since the receipt thereof than she hath been at any time since my being here'. Not surprisingly, for Elizabeth had seen her chance, and in her reply to Somerset she took it with both hands. His lordship had counselled her 'as an earnest friend' to declare all she knew of the matter and Elizabeth was perfectly willing to oblige. Out it all came again – the matter of her chaplain, the Admiral's offer of his house, Parry's report of his conversations with the Admiral, Mrs Ashley's letter to the Admiral, some (though not all) of Mrs Ashley's badinage. There had been no secret understanding of any sort. 'As concerning Mrs Ashley, she never advised me unto it, but said always (when any talked of my marriage) that she would never have me marry, neither in England nor out of England, without the consent of the King's Majesty, your Grace's, and the Council's.' Elizabeth herself, of course, would never have agreed to such a thing without the Council's consent. 'And as for Katherine Ashley or the cofferer, they never told me they would practice it. These be the things which I both declared to Master Tyrwhit', she continued, 'and also whereof my conscience beareth me witness, which I would not for all earthly things offend in any thing; for I know I have a soul to save, as well as other folks have.' But if she should remember anything else, she would either write it herself, 'or cause Master Tyrwhit to write it'. Elizabeth ended with an indication of the sort of tactics which were being employed against her.

> Master Tyrwhit and others have told me that there goeth rumours abroad which be greatly against my honour and honesty (which above all other things I esteem), which be these; that I am in the Tower; and with child by my Lord Admiral. My lord, these are shameful slanders, for the which, besides the great desire I have to see the King's Majesty, I shall most heartily desire your lordship that I may come to Court after your first determination, that I may show myself there as I am.[26]

This famous letter, polite but businesslike, written in a beautifully neat schoolgirl hand, is by any standards a masterpiece of its kind. Elizabeth had wasted no paper on protestations of innocence or outraged modesty. She had defended herself and her servants against unwarrantable accusations with courage and dignity, and more than hinted that she would expect an apology.

Unfortunately, however, not everyone possessed the qualities of Elizabeth Tudor. Parry and Mrs Ashley both made detailed confessions with which, on 5 February, Tyrwhit was able to confront the princess. 'She was much abashed and half breathless,' he reported, 'and perused all their names particularly', although, as Sir Robert added scornfully, she knew both Mrs Ashley's hand and the cofferer's 'with half a sight'. Parry had been the first to break, he told her. Mrs Ashley would say nothing until she and Parry were brought face to face, when the steward stood fast to all he had written and 'she seeing that, she called him false wretch and said that he had promised he would never confess it to death'. Then, commented Elizabeth simply, 'it was a great matter for him to promise such a promise, and to break it'. Tyrwhit went on, 'I will tomorrow travail all I can, to frame her for her own surety and to utter the truth.'[27]

But by the next day Elizabeth had had time to recover from her embarrassment and to think. It had been acutely humiliating to see the details of those merry romps at Chelsea and Hanworth set out in writing for all to read. They made her look more like a giggling servant girl than a princess. That was bad enough, but it was not remotely treasonable. Parry and Mrs Ashley did not show up in a particularly good light either, but that was all. There was nothing in their statements to implicate any of them in actual treason; no evidence that either they, or Elizabeth, had ever been involved in a secret matrimonial plot. When Robert Tyrwhit returned to the attack, the princess allowed him to take down her formal 'confession' but, apart from a few additional details, it contained absolutely nothing new. 'They all sing the same song,' wrote the exasperated Tyrwhit, 'and so I think they would not do, unless they had set the note before.'[28]

In spite of Elizabeth's spirited defence of Mrs Ashley, the Council had come to the conclusion that the governess had 'shown herself far unmeet' to occupy her position and appointed Elizabeth Tyrwhit, Sir Robert's wife, instead, hoping that the princess would 'accept her service willingly'. The princess did nothing of the kind. She was furious and showed it. 'Mrs Ashley was her mistress,' she said, 'and she had not so demeaned herself that the Council should now need to put any more mistresses unto her.' Lady Tyrwhit replied tartly that 'seeing she did allow Mrs Ashley to be her mistress, she need not be ashamed to have any honest woman to be in that place'. But Elizabeth 'took the matter so heavily, that she wept all that night and lowered all the next day'. Sir Robert felt sure he knew the reason for these tantrums. 'All is no more,' he wrote in yet another of his reports to the Protector, 'she fully hopes to recover her old mistress again. The love she beareth her is to be wondered at. I told her if she would consider her honour and the sequel thereof, she would, considering her years, make suit to your Grace to have one, rather than to make delay to be without one one hour.' However, the princess could not 'digest such advice in no way' and Tyrwhit, who had plainly had just about enough, added that in his opinion she needed not one governess but two.[29]

The Protector had now replied to Elizabeth's letter, and Tyrwhit had offered more advice on drafting a suitable reply which Elizabeth again 'would in no wise follow, but writ her own fantasy. She beginneth now a little to droop', he went on, 'by reason she heareth that my Lord Admiral's house be dispersed. And my wife telleth me now that she cannot bear to hear him discommended but she is ready to make answer therein; and so she hath not been accustomed to do, unless Mistress Ashley were touched, whereunto she was very ready to make answer vehemently.'[30]

On 21 February Elizabeth wrote 'her own fantasy' to the Duke of Somerset. She understood that he had taken her previous letter 'in evil part' and thought she was altogether too sure of herself. The princess was sorry, but the Protector had asked her to be plain with him and she had only told the truth. Regarding her complaint about the rumours being spread of her 'lewd demeanour', Elizabeth did not see that 'your Grace has made any direct answer at this time'. 'Howbeit,' she continued, 'you did write "that if I would bring forth any that had reported it, you and the Council would see it redressed". Which thing, though I can easily do it, I would be loath to do, because it is mine own cause.' It was not for Elizabeth herself, she indicated, to be forced to bring counter-charges to clear her name. That would only get her the evil will of the people which thing she would be loath to have. However,

if it might seem good to your lordship and the rest of the Council to send forth a proclamation into the countries that they refrain their tongues, declaring how the tales be but lies, it should make both the people think that you and the Council have great regard that no such rumours should be spread of any of the King's Majesty's sisters, (as I am, though unworthy) and also that I should think myself to receive such friendship at your hands as you have promised me. . . . Howbeit, I am ashamed to ask it any more, because I see you are not so well minded thereunto.[31]

This letter was another masterly piece of tactics, in which Elizabeth had neatly out-manœuvred the Protector and regained the initiative by putting him subtly in the wrong. In fact, she knew by this time that, although the war was by no means over, her own immediate battle had been won. The cost had been great, how great she could not yet know, but the challenge had been met and met with fortitude. During the past month she had grown from a girl into a woman and, for better or worse, she would never be the same again.

CHAPTER VIII

Sweet Sister Temperance

IF the Government had expected that Elizabeth would prove a star witness in the case against Tom Seymour, they had certainly been disappointed; but, as it turned out, there was no shortage of other people only too eager to turn King's evidence.

William Sharington had thrown himself on the Protector's mercy and made a full and abject confession. John Fowler, too, sought safety in offering a circumstantial account of the part he had played in assisting Tom's efforts to win his nephew's affection. Those surreptitious gifts of pocket-money, so gratefully accepted at the time, were now produced as evidence of treasonable intent. The Lords Dorset, Rutland and Northampton all came forward with statements about their dealings with the Admiral. Even the King obligingly remembered certain conversations he had had with his uncle over the past two years. The only person, in fact, who made any attempt to speak up for Tom was his friend, John Harington.

The Council met on 22 February to consider the result of their enquiries and came to the conclusion that 'the Lord Admiral was sore charged of divers and sundry Articles of High Treason, great falsehoods and marvellous heinous misdemeanours against the King's Majesty's person and his Royal Crown'.[1] It looked an open and shut case, but Tom himself had so far made no confession. It was therefore decided that the Lord Chancellor and the rest of the Council should 'repair unto the Tower, and there propound and declare unto the said Lord Admiral the said heinous Articles which were objected unto him . . . to the intent that he should, if he could, clear himself of them, or show some excuse or pretence, if he had any, whereby he could think to purge himself of them'.[2]

Thirty-three Articles, or charges, had been drawn up in a form of indictment and, on the following day, this was solemnly read aloud to the Admiral in the Tower. Tom remained uncooperative, refusing to make any answer 'except he had his accusers brought before him, and except he were brought in upon trial of arraignment, where he might say before all the world what he could say for his declaration'.[3] He would not budge from this position, and the Council were finally obliged to depart empty-handed, leaving him 'in his old custody'.

On 24 February the lords reported their failure to the Protector and it was agreed that the law should now be allowed to take its course, and 'specially for so much as these things have chanced to be revealed in the time of His Majesty's High Court of Parliament, that the Parliament should have the determination and order thereof'.[4] In other words, that the proceedings should take the form of an Act of Attainder. First, however, the matter must be laid before the King and his consent obtained. Later that same day, 'after the King's Majesty had dined', the Council assembled in his presence, the Lord Chancellor declared 'the heinous facts and treasons of the Admiral', and made a formal request for permission to proceed against him 'according to the order of justice and the custom of the realm in like cases'. One by one the members of the Council cast their votes in favour. Last of all came the Lord Protector who, 'declaring how sorrowful a case this was unto him, said that he did yet rather regard his bounden duty to the King's Majesty and the Crown of England than his own son or brother, and did weigh more his allegiance than his blood, and therefore he could not resist nor would not be against the Lords' request, but as his Majesty would, he would most obediently be content'.[5] Now it was the King's turn. 'We do perceive', announced the eleven-year-old Edward, 'that there is great things which be objected and laid to my Lord Admiral, mine uncle, and they tend to treason, and we perceive that you require but justice to be done. We think it reasonable, and we will well that you proceed according to your request.'[6] At these words, 'coming so suddenly from his Grace's mouth of his own motion', the Council, much relieved by the King's commendably unsentimental attitude, 'were marvellously rejoiced, and gave his Highness most hearty praise and thanks'.[7]

The gravamen of the long and repetitive list of charges against the Admiral was that he had intended to overthrow the legally constituted government of the country, and had taken deliberate steps to put his plans into action. There can be little doubt on the evidence that, technically, he was guilty of treason, but whether such a recklessly inefficient conspirator had ever represented any serious danger to the state is at least questionable.

When he realised that he was not going to have an open trial and that he could expect no rescue operation from his brother or his nephew, Tom Seymour finally agreed to make some sort of answer. He had already vehemently denied meaning any hurt to the Protector, or planning to take the King from him by force. Now he admitted that he had given Fowler and others secret presents of money for the King, and that he had 'sought out certain precedents' for dividing the offices of Protector and Governor of the King's person but, he said, he had become 'ashamed of his doings and left off that suit and labour'. He also admitted that he had tried to persuade Edward to sign a memorandum to be presented to Parliament, favouring a change in his guardianship. Having gone thus far, Tom suddenly bade his interrogators to be content, saying plainly that 'he would answer no more before them'.[8] He could not be prevailed upon to break his silence again. The whole of that ebullient, energetically self-confident façade seems to have collapsed into apathy and introspection.

The Bill declaring the Admiral to be 'adjudged and attainted of high treason' had passed both Houses of Parliament by 5 March. It now lay with the Protector to take the final decision on his brother's fate. There was silence for nearly a week while, presumably, the unfortunate Somerset wrestled with his conscience. Then the Earl of Warwick, who was quietly waiting for the Seymour brothers to destroy each other, applied some discreet pressure on his colleagues, and on 10 March the Council waited on the King and asked permission to proceed 'without further troubling or molesting in this heavy case either his Highness or the Lord Protector'. Edward, with Somerset at his side, thanked the lords for the great care they had taken for his surety, and gave the necessary permission. On 15 March the Admiral was warned to prepare for his execution. On the twentieth he was led out on to Tower Hill, there to suffer the same fate which had befallen another Queen Dowager's widower, in the market square at Hereford eighty-eight years previously. Unlike Owen Tudor, though, Tom Seymour left no legacy for posterity. His infant daughter, stripped of her inheritance and abandoned to the reluctant care of the dowager Duchess of Suffolk, disappeared into obscurity and is generally believed to have died in childhood.

It is said that Tom spent his last night on earth writing to the princesses, urging them to beware of the Protector's influence with the King, and 'enforcing many matters against him to make these royal ladies jealous of him'. The Admiral entrusted these missives, laboriously inscribed with a pen improvised from 'the aglet of a point that he plucked from his hose', to a servant who had sewn them into the sole of a velvet shoe; but as he mounted the scaffold his muttered reminder to the man to 'speed the thing that he wot of' was overheard, and the letters were discovered and destroyed.[9]

Tom met his end calmly, but not, it seems, in the articulately repentant frame of mind considered proper on such occasions. This led Bishop Latimer to remark, in a sermon not noticeably pervaded with the spirit of Christian charity, that 'he died very dangerously, irksomely, horribly' and to conclude that God had clean forsaken him. 'Whether he be saved or no,' continued the Bishop, 'I leave it to God, but surely he was a wicked man, and the realm is well rid of him.'[10]

When Elizabeth was told the news down at Hatfield, she is reputed to have said: 'This day died a man with much wit, and very little judgement.' The authority is Leti who could never leave an occasion unimproved, but it cannot have come as any surprise to Elizabeth by this time to hear that Tom was dead and she may well have prepared some suitably dispassionate public reaction. What had she really felt about him? The detailed testimony of eye-witnesses makes it plain that she had never been indifferent. He had undoubtedly roused and stimulated her nascent sexual aware-ness, and she had some affection for him as a friend; although, had she seen more of him, she must soon have become bored by his essential shallowness and irritated by his stupidity. The reality of Tom's attentions seems to have half-excited, half-repelled her. In the abstract, of course, they acquired the glamour of forbidden fruit, inspiring private fantasies and public blushes and side-long looks. However, from the evidence available, it seems per-fectly safe to say that Elizabeth had never for a moment entertained the idea of a runaway marriage. She may sometimes have yearned for the Admiral's embraces, but if anything had been needed to drive home the lesson that physical love brought danger, terror and violent death the consequences of her first tentative experiment in this field, coming just at the age of puberty, had certainly provided it. Elizabeth knew now, at the deepest level of consciousness, that sexual fulfilment was forbidden to her. She could play with physical desire, circle round it, approach it as close as she dared with a sort of delicious defiance but there was a point beyond which she might never, could never go. It was always to be the same type of man who roused this desire – handsome, showy, athletic. She once remarked brutally of a would-be suitor that, like her father, she loved a man who was a man and not one who would sit at home all day among the cinders. She loved, in fact, the kind of man who reminded her of Tom Seymour – the kind of man who reminded her of her father.

Elizabeth had learnt a more immediately useful lesson during the month of February 1549. Her own innate intelligence and political sense had kept her out of really serious trouble, but now the necessity of cultivating habits of caution and dissimulation, of concealing her true feelings at all costs, had been forcibly instilled. It became part of her nature to face the world from behind a mask, by no means always the same mask, but always one which exactly suited the purpose of the moment. At this particular moment, in the spring of her sixteenth year, Elizabeth's purpose was to repair her damaged reputation. She had got the promise of a proclamation from the Protector, but she knew the smear left by her connexion with the Admiral would not easily be removed. There were plenty of people who still vividly remembered the fall of Anne Boleyn and who would be only too glad of an opportunity to rake up old scandals. There were plenty of people to say that of course blood will out, like mother like daughter, and no smoke without a fire. Gossip sizzled pleasurably. One especially hoary chestnut going the rounds concerned the midwife summoned mysteriously at dead of night and taken blindfold to a strange house, where she delivered a child which was then 'miserably destroyed'. The approved conduct for midwives who found themselves in such a situation was to snip a piece from the bed-curtains when no one was looking. In the current version of the legend, however, the midwife seems to have omitted to take this sensible precaution and could only swear afterwards that her patient had been 'a very fair young lady'.[11] But everybody who had a friend who knew someone whose aunt or cousin had heard the midwife's tale from her own lips could make an informed guess as to the fair young lady's identity.

Elizabeth was well aware that she had a long campaign ahead of her, and her first step was to get Katherine Ashley out of prison. She had three reasons for requesting her governess's release she told the Protector in a letter dated 7 March

> First, because that she hath been with me a long time, and many years, and hath taken great labour and pain in bringing me up in learning and honesty; and, therefore, I ought of very duty to speak for her. . . . The second is, because I think that whatsoever she hath done in my Lord Admiral's matter, as concerning the marrying of me, she did it because knowing him to be one of the Council, she thought he would not go about any such thing without he had the Council's consent thereunto; for I have heard her many times say 'that she would never have me marry in any place without your Grace's and the Council's consent'. The third cause is, because that it shall, and doth make men think, that I am not clear of the deed myself; but that it is pardoned to me because of my youth, because she that I loved so well is in such a place.[12]

Elizabeth ended with a plea for Mr Ashley, 'which, because he is my kinsman, I would be glad he should do well'.

Elizabeth seems to have become more or less reconciled to Lady Tyrwhit, who remained in the household for a while, but Mrs Ashley was released, and was back with her princess probably by the autumn. So, too, was Thomas Parry and this despite the fact that Sir Robert Tyrwhit, who had been going through the cofferer's accounts, had discovered that Parry's sins were not confined to meddling in affairs of state, for his books were 'so undiscreetly made that it doth well appear he had little understanding to execute his office'. Elizabeth, it seemed, had been overspending and would have 'to abate her charges'. She had immediately requested that Parry's place should not be filled. One of his clerks could easily take over, she said, and that would save her £100 a year.[13] Clearly, though, her motive was not economy but a determination to keep the post vacant. It is also clear that Elizabeth harboured no resentment against Mrs Ashley or Parry for their betrayal of her. She knew something of the pressures they had been subjected to and did not blame them for succumbing. Once Elizabeth gave her love or trust it was not lightly withdrawn, but above all she was a realist. Katherine Ashley and Parry were her friends and whatever their imperfections she needed them and wanted them with her, and would protect them so far as she was able.

After his return Parry sometimes served the princess in the capacity of secretary. In September she received a courtesy visit from the Venetian ambassador, who spent a day at Hatfield, hunting and talking with her Grace, 'at sundry times'. Parry, at Elizabeth's request, at once wrote to inform the Protector; 'not for that the talk did import weight, but that her Grace will neither know nor do in matters that either may sound or seem to be of importance without doing of my Lord's Grace to understand thereof '.[14] Parry's letter was addressed to his distant kinsman, the Protector's secretary, young Mr William Cecil. This is not the first recorded instance of Elizabeth's connexion with the man who was to be so closely associated with her that it is virtually impossible to think of them separately. A letter written by Mrs Ashley, dated August 1548 and with a postscript in Elizabeth's own hand, shows that friendly relations existed between them even then.

About a fortnight after the Venetian ambassador's visit to Hatfield, Cecil's master suffered political eclipse. The year 1549 had been marked by a general and increasing popular discontent. This was partly economic in origin, caused by rising prices and widespread unemployment; and partly due to the reaction of a largely conservative population against sweeping religious innovations now being introduced by the government. This discontent erupted into two quite serious revolts, one in the West Country and one in Norfolk. The ruling classes were alarmed by the Protector's mild attitude to these demonstrations which, although it earned him the title of the Good Duke among the common people, did not endear him to the nobility and gentry. His increasing arrogance and refusal to take advice was also alienating many of his colleagues on the Council. His friend, William Paget, who had played such a large part in engineering his elevation, warned him bluntly 'that unless your Grace do more quietly show your pleasure in things wherein you will debate with other men, and hear them again graciously say their opinions, when you do require it, that will ensue whereof I would be right sorry, and

your Grace shall have first cause to repent. . . . Howsoever it
cometh to pass I cannot tell', Paget went on,

> but of late your Grace is grown in great choleric fashions whensoever
> you are contraried in that which you have conceived in your head. A
> king which shall give men occasion of discourage to say their
> opinions frankly, receiveth thereby great hurt and peril to his realm.
> But a subject in great authority, as your Grace is, using such fashion
> is like to fall into great danger and peril of his own person.[15]

But the Protector, it seems, was no longer willing to face the
realities of the political scene, or to accept the position of *primus
inter pares* which had originally been envisaged for him. His
image, too, had been fatally damaged by the Admiral's death – just
as the Earl of Warwick had known it would be. Somerset's coldly
correct attitude towards his brother's attainder and execution had
disgusted many people, who now stigmatised him as 'a blood-
sucker and a ravenous wolf'.

In mid-September Warwick returned to London, after successfully and ferociously suppressing the rebellion in Norfolk, and
judged the time was now ripe for a move to dislodge the
Protector.

> Suddenly, upon what occasion many marvelled, but few knew, every
> Lord and Councillor went through the City weaponed, and had their
> servants likewise weaponed, attending upon them in new liveries, to
> the great wondering of many; and, at the last, a great assembly of the
> said Councillors was made at the Earl of Warwick's lodging, which
> was then at Ely Place in Holborn, whither all the confederates in this
> matter came privily armed, and finally concluded to possess the
> Tower of London.[16]

Somerset was at Hampton Court with the King, attempting
ineffectually to raise support, when he learnt that the 'London
Lords', as the opposition had become known, intended to pay
him an unfriendly visit. On 6 October, between nine and ten in
the evening, he routed Edward out of bed and bundled him off to
seek sanctuary at Windsor Castle – an unnerving experience for
which the King never really forgave his uncle. But the London
Lords, under the skilful and determined leadership of the Earl of

Warwick, were too strong for him. A few days later the Protector had surrendered and been conveyed under arrest to the Tower. It was not, as might have been expected, the final disaster. The Duke still had a considerable popular following, both in London and the country at large, and Warwick was far too astute to risk over-reaching himself at this stage. Somerset was presently released, even temporarily regaining a seat on the Council, but his reign was over and his end merely postponed.

The Lords had addressed a somewhat specious letter of explanation and justification of their proceedings to the heiress-presumptive, Princess Mary, and thought it worth while to send a duplicate to her younger sister. Elizabeth probably welcomed the news, guessing that this shift at the seat of power was likely to be to her advantage. She needed something to distract her thoughts for, although her emotional involvement with Tom Seymour may not have gone very deep, reaction after the strain she had undergone was inevitable. She was not at all well, suffering from catarrh and what sounds like severe attacks of migraine. References to 'my evil head', 'the pain in my head' and even to 'a disease of the head and eyes' recur in her letters over the next few years.

In spite of her headaches and other troubles, Elizabeth did not abandon her studies. After the parting from Katherine Parr she had, in fact, clung to Roger Ascham with something like desperation. So much so that Ascham began to find her demands on his time a trifle irksome. He wrote to a former pupil at St John's in July 1548 that he would willingly have paid a visit to his friends at Cambridge on the occasion of the last meeting of the Senate, had not his illustrious mistress prevented him. This may have been due to the fact that there had recently been a case of plague at his old college and Elizabeth was not risking the loss of another tutor or simply, as Ascham rather plaintively put it, 'because she never lets me go away anywhere'. He was hoping, he said, to return to the University for good at Michaelmas, 'if I can get my lady's permission which I can hardly hope, for she favours me wonderfully'. This plan came to nothing – either permission was not forthcoming, or Ascham had had second thoughts. 'Many men', he observed, 'who have become courtiers, praise their former life of retirement, but have not courage to leave the splendour of a court: I cannot promise anything about myself, but I think somewhat about it.'[17] He did, however, spend Christmas at Cambridge, returning to Hatfield just as the storm over the Admiral was about to break. He was not personally involved and remained with Elizabeth throughout the crisis, but, in the misfortunes of his friends the Ashleys, he had plenty of opportunity to observe at first hand the sort of pitfalls which lay in wait for courtiers.

In January 1550 he himself suffered 'shipwreck', as he described it, 'overcome by court violence and wrongs'. In a letter to John Cheke he complained fluently of the injuries done him, as a result of which, through no fault of his own, he had either been forced to resign or had been dismissed from the princess's service. The details of this episode remain obscure, but there had evidently been intrigue against him in the household – the chief trouble-maker being Thomas Parry, who was probably jealous of Ascham. Elizabeth, too, seems to have developed a coolness towards her tutor, and in her nervy irritable state had allowed herself to be influenced by malicious tale-bearing.

Whatever the cause of the temporary rift between them, Roger Ascham did not blame his 'illustrious Lady', for the following April he addressed his famous letter in praise of the princess to Johann Sturm, Rector of the Protestant University of Strasbourg. 'She has just passed her sixteenth birthday', he wrote,

and shows such dignity and gentleness as are wonderful at her age and in her rank. Her study of true religion and learning is most energetic. Her mind has no womanly weakness, her perseverance is equal to that of a man, and her memory long keeps what it quickly picks up. She talks French and Italian as well as English; she has often talked to me readily and well in Latin, and moderately so in Greek. When she writes Greek and Latin, nothing is more beautiful than her hand-writing. She is as much delighted with music as she is skilful in the art. In adornment she is elegant rather than showy, and by her contempt of gold and head-dresses, she reminds one of Hippolyte rather than of Phaedra. . . . Whatever she reads she at once perceives any word that has a doubtful or curious meaning. She cannot endure those foolish imitators of Erasmus, who have tied up the Latin tongue in those wretched fetters of proverbs. She likes a style that grows out of the subject; chaste because it is suitable, and beautiful because it is clear. . . .

'I am not inventing anything, my dear Sturm,' he concluded, 'it is all true: but I only seek to give you an outline of her excellence, and whilst doing so, I have been pleased to recall to my mind the dear memory of my most illustrious lady.'[18]

This is a remarkable encomium, coming from a scholar of Ascham's reputation. In writing to Sturm he had no particular reason to flatter Elizabeth, except in so far as the achievements of his former pupil must of necessity reflect some glory on himself, and his admiration seems genuine. 'I teach her words,' he had told his friend John Aylmer, 'and she me things. I teach her tongues to speak, and her modest and maidenly looks teach me works to do. For I think she is the best disposed of any in all Europe.'[19]

Elizabeth continued for the most part to live very quietly in the country, dividing her time between Hatfield and Ashridge. Her retired existence is traditionally ascribed to the fact of her still being in disgrace following the Seymour scandal. This tradition does not, however, stand up to close examination, for it was perfectly well known in government circles that no sort of case had ever been established against her. Her own indifferent health and the dangerously unsettled state of the political scene are much more likely causes for her avoidance of the limelight – not, in fact, that her rustication was as complete or as prolonged as is sometimes stated. It is true that she did not come to London again until after the Protector's fall, but it is hardly surprising that Somerset, beset on every side, should have discouraged visits from a potentially powerful young woman who had no reason to feel well disposed towards him. On 19 December 1549, however, Van der Delft, the Imperial Ambassador, informed his master that: 'The Lady Elizabeth, sister to the King, arrived at Court the other day, was received with great pomp and triumph, and is continually with the King.'[20]

After her return to Hatfield, Elizabeth maintained a dutiful correspondence with her brother. Edward asked to have a portrait of her, and complying with this request she wrote somewhat sententiously:

For the face, I grant, I might well blush to offer; but the mind I shall never be ashamed to present. For though from the grace of the picture the colours may fade by time, may give by weather, may be spotted by chance; yet the other nor time with her swift wings shall overtake, nor the misty clouds with their lowerings may darken, nor chance with her slippery foot may overthrow. Of this, although yet the proof could not be great, because the occasions hath been but small; notwithstanding, as a dog hath a day, so may I perchance have a time to declare it in deeds, where now I do write them but in words. And further I shall most humbly beseech your Majesty, that when you shall look on my picture you will witsafe to think, that as you have but the outward show of the body afore you, so my inward mind wisheth, that the body itself were oftener in your presence.[21]

In spite of her bodily absence, Elizabeth kept a close watch on her interests. During the first half of 1550, possibly as a result of her Christmas visit, her financial position was put on a firmer footing when the King, in fulfilment of Henry VIII's Will, formally granted his sister lands to the value of £3000 a year. But when Elizabeth discovered that Hatfield was to be given to the Earl of Warwick she protested vigorously. The old palace, once the property of the Bishops of Ely, pleasantly situated on a wooded hill with the River Lea winding through its grounds, is traditionally associated with Elizabeth's girlhood, and, although until now she does not appear to have spent more time there than at the other royal manors in the Home Counties, she seems to have had a special affection for it. At any rate, she was not prepared to give it up without a struggle. On 22 June it was recorded in the minutes of the Privy Council that: 'Where the Lady Elizabeth's Grace desired to have the house, parks and lands of Hatfield of the Earl of Warwick she to have the same in exchange for as much lands of hers in value again to the said Earl.'[22] The princess relinquished a manor in Lincolnshire and everyone, presumably, was satisfied.

Elizabeth was naturally careful to keep on friendly terms with Warwick and that autumn Jehan Scheyfve, who had now replaced Van der Delft as the Emperor's ambassador in London, picked up an odd little rumour which he thought worth passing on. 'I have heard from a safe source', he wrote, 'that my lord Warwick is about to cast off his wife and marry my Lady Elizabeth, daughter of the late King, with whom he is said to have had several secret and intimate personal communications; and by these means he will aspire to the Crown.'[23] There is no reason to suppose that there was a word of truth in this particular item of gossip, but it throws an interesting glimmer of light on the kind of thin ice Elizabeth was learning to tread. She was seventeen now, an age when it was unusual for a sixteenth-century princess to be still unmarried, or at least unbetrothed. There were, as there always had been, foreign suitors under consideration. Those whose names occur in the early fifties were a French duke and the eldest son of the King of Denmark, but nothing came, or seemed at all likely to come, of their pretensions. The future was altogether too uncertain.

Early in 1551 Elizabeth made another of her carefully spaced public appearances. On 21 January, Jehan Scheyfve reported her arrival in London a few days previously, accompanied by a great suite of gentlemen and ladies and escorted by one hundred of the King's horse. 'She was most honourably received by the Council', wrote Scheyfve, 'who acted thus in order to show the people how much glory belongs to her who has embraced the new religion and is become a very great lady.'[24]

If anyone was now officially out of favour it was the King's elder sister and the Emperor's cousin, which accounts for the acid note in Scheyfve's despatches. The religious question was again becoming acute, and the wretched Mary was once more being hounded for her beliefs – this time by her brother's ministers. Two years earlier the Act of Uniformity had established the new English Prayer Book – the result of Cranmer's programme of liturgical reform begun in the last reign – as the only service book of the Church of England. It came into official use on Whitsunday, 1549, and it meant the end of the ancient Latin Mass. When Mary saw the very foundation and cornerstone of her faith being threatened, she appealed frantically to the Emperor for help, and Charles had responded more energetically than usual. He instructed his ambassador to obtain a guarantee from the Protector that Mary should be allowed to hear Mass undisturbed in her own household for as long as she chose. After some argument, Van der Delft had extracted a verbal promise from Somerset that the princess could do as she thought best until the King came of age. There the matter might have rested. Mary was an old friend of the Somersets, the Duchess had once been one of her mother's maids and the Duke was a man of his word. Unfortunately, however, the Earl of Warwick was not a man to be bound by anyone's word. He found it convenient to form an alliance with the extreme Protestants – men far to the left of Cranmer – and by the summer of 1550 Mary's position had become so intolerable to her that, for the second time in her life, she wanted only to escape from England and seek sanctuary with the Emperor. The battle of the Princess Mary's Mass continued to rage intermittently for the rest of Edward's life, poisoning the relationship between brother and sister, and finally reducing Mary to practising her religion in fear, behind locked doors.

Elizabeth at least had no problems of this nature to contend with and her own relationship with her brother remained unclouded to the end. Indeed, it was later said that 'there was between these two princes a concurrency and sympathy in their natures and affections, together with the celestial conformity in religion which made them one, and friends; for the King ever called her his sweetest and dearest sister, and was scarce his own man, she being absent, which was not so between him and the Lady Mary'.[25] It suited Protestant hagiographers, writing in the seventeenth and eighteenth centuries, to present an idealised picture of two such notable stalwarts of the Protestant faith as Edward and Elizabeth, and in doing so they both exaggerated and over-simplified the situation. Edward was genuinely fond of his elder sister, and genuinely troubled over the difficulties caused by her religious fervour which presented a mirror image of his own; but he naturally felt more at ease with Elizabeth, so much nearer to him in age and sharing so much more of his background and upbringing.

Elizabeth had by now virtually succeeded in obliterating any unfortunate impression created by the Seymour affair – at any rate among those predisposed in her favour. She adopted a severely plain style of dressing, which no doubt suited her admirably, and John Aylmer remarked approvingly on her maidenly apparel – so dramatically contrasted to the noblemen's wives and daughters who went 'dressed and painted like peacocks'. Even after the visit to court in 1551 of Mary of Guise, Queen Dowager and Regent of Scotland, on her way back from France, had awakened a new interest in French fashions, Elizabeth would alter nothing 'but kept her old maiden shamefacedness'.[26] She was setting the fashion herself for high-born Protestant maidens; and Jane Grey, receiving a mouth-watering present from Mary of a dress of 'tinsel cloth of gold and velvet, laid on with parchment lace of gold', is

Elizabeth I in her coronation robes

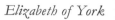
Elizabeth of York

ELIZABETHA · VXOR
HENRICI · VII ·

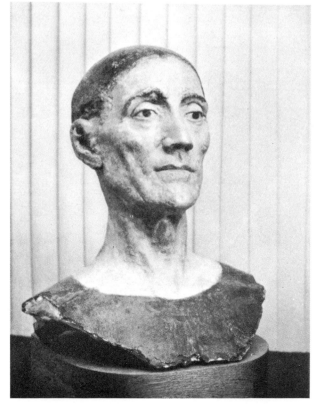

Funeral effigy of Henry VII in Westminster Abbey

Anne Boleyn

Henry VIII

*Effigy of Sir Thomas Boleyn
in Hever Church, Kent*

Edward VI

Mary I

Philip II of Spain

Thomas, Lord Seymour of Sudeley

Thomas Parry

Katherine Astley

The Old Manor at Chelsea

The Old Palace at Woodstock

The Old Palace of Hatfield

said to have complained: 'What shall I do with it?' 'Marry, wear it,' answered one of her ladies in surprise. 'Nay,' said Jane, never noted for her tact, 'that were a shame to follow my Lady Mary against God's word, and leave my Lady Elizabeth, which followeth God's word.'[27]

It was inevitable that the Protestant faction should look hopefully towards Elizabeth, although she never made a parade of her beliefs – merely conforming without unnecessary comment. She always had a strong sense of public decorum, and, as much as many Catholics, may have disliked the current excesses of the anti-ritualists, the spoliation of the parish churches and the coarse derision being hurled at the old worship; but, if so, she kept her opinions to herself. As well as her carefully unadorned appearance, her quiet, modest demeanour was winning her the reputation of having 'a marvellous meek stomach', and Edward is said to have called her 'his sweet sister Temperance'.

After her New Year visit of 1551, sweet sister Temperance left London again for Hertfordshire, resolutely avoiding any involvement in the controversy over Mary and her Mass, or indeed any involvement in anything even remotely controversial. She maintained her connexion with William Cecil, and had appointed him Surveyor of her landed property at a salary of £20 a year. Cecil, shortly to become Sir William, now held the influential post of Principal Secretary to the Earl of Warwick, and Elizabeth obviously relied on him to hold a watching brief on her interests at court. Thomas Parry, forwarding a letter from Elizabeth to Warwick, which was to be delivered by Cecil, observes in his covering note: 'Her Grace commanded me to write this: "Write my commendations in your letter to Mr Cecil, that I am well assured, though I send not daily to him, that he doth not, for all that, daily forget me; say, indeed, I assure myself thereof."' Elizabeth was still having to use Parry as a secretary, and he goes on: 'I had forgotten to say to you that her Grace commanded me to say to you, for the excuse of her hand, that it is not now as good as she trusts it shall be; her Grace's unhealth hath made it weaker, and so unsteady, and that is the cause.'[28]

Elizabeth's household books for the period October 1551 to September 1552 show how simply she was living. On 13 February 1552, she received a visit from the King's drummer and fife and John Heywood's troupe of child actors which cost her altogether

£7 9s 0d. In April she paid Beaumont, the King's servant, ten shillings 'for his boys which played before her grace'. There are some other scattered entries in August:

For Farmor that played on the lute	30s
More the harper	30s
My lord Russell's minstrels	20s

But apart from these musical interludes the household seems to have spent nothing on entertainment. Elizabeth paid £26 0s 0d for velvet coats and £78 18s 0d for liveries for her yeomen, but her own expenditure on clothes was moderate. A pair of silk-lined upper-bodies cost her 2s 8d in October 1551. On the thirty-first of the month Anthony Brisquet's account for 'a piece of wrought velvet containing twenty yards and a half and a half quarter', and another ten yards or so of black velvet for a pair of sleeves, two French hoods and partlets came to £43 7s 2d. Rafe Hope was paid nine shillings and eightpence on 8 November 'for lining of her grace's kirtles'. Elizabeth Slannying received £8 15s 3d on 1 April for 'certain damask and crimson satin' and, later in the month, £79 0s 0d for velvet, silk and other necessaries to her grace's use. Cauls and linen cloth cost only 22s 4d, and Warren, the tailor, charged £21 10s 0d for 'making diverse robes for her grace'. Other miscellaneous items in the Chamber and Robe Accounts give a fascinating insight into the trivialities of daily life. Mrs Ashley spent twelve shillings on six ells of holland for towels, and one and fourpence on thread. Forty-four and ninepence was paid 'to him that made her grace a table of walnut tree', and five shillings 'to a poor woman which brought six chickens and two capons'. Brooms for the chamber cost three shillings, and Elizabeth paid seventeen shillings for lute strings. She was not particularly open-handed, for her total expenditure on alms given 'at sundry times to poor men and women' over this period amounted to no more than £7 15s 8d, and she only spent £32 3s 10d on gilt plate for New Year's gifts in 1552. Thomas Parry was getting no opportunity to feather his nest these days, for every page of his accounts was meticulously signed and countersigned by Elizabeth and her chamberlain, Walter Buckler.[29]

But, in spite of her economies at home, she knew when it paid to put on a good show. In March 1552 she came up to town for what was to prove her last state visit to Edward, having demanded and got the loan of St James's Palace for herself and her suite. Henry Machyn, the undertaker, recorded in his diary that:

The 17th day of March rode through London unto St James in the field, the King's place, the King's sister, my Lady Elizabeth, with a great company of lords and knights and gentlemen, and after her a great number of ladies and gentlewomen to the number of two hundred on horseback, and yeomen. The 19th day of March [she] came from St James through the park to the Court, and from Park gate unto the Court was strewn with sand fine, and afore her came dukes, lords and knights, and after ladies and gentlewomen a great company, and so she was received into the Court goodly.[30]

There had been some significant political developments since Elizabeth's last appearance at court. John Dudley, Earl of Warwick, was now Duke of Northumberland, and the last act of the Seymour tragedy had been played out. Dudley had found it impracticable to spare his defeated rival indefinitely, and on 22 January, three years almost to the day after Tom's execution, Somerset had suffered a similar fate on Tower Hill. In January 1551 Jehan Scheyfve had told the Emperor that Warwick was 'the man who governs absolutely' and now the new Duke, although he never officially adopted the title of Protector, wielded as much, if not more, influence over the King as ever Somerset had done. Northumberland favoured a more athletic and open-air régime for his charge, and Edward had grasped the opportunity to prove his manhood with pathetic eagerness. Elizabeth may not have liked or trusted John Dudley – few people did – but the King seemed well and happy in his care. When she said good-bye to Edward, after what appears to have been quite a short visit, Elizabeth, percipient as she was, can hardly have guessed that she would never see her brother again.

CHAPTER IX

The Queen's Sister

At the beginning of April 1552, Edward developed a rash and a high temperature. He himself recorded in his Chronicle 'I fell sike of the mesels and the smallpokkes.' This would surely have been a lethal combination and the trouble was probably a sharp attack of measles. He recovered quickly and was able to reassure Elizabeth, for she wrote on the twenty-first to congratulate him on his 'good escape out of the perilous diseases'. 'And that I am fully satisfied and well assured of the same by your Grace's own hand,' she went on, 'I must needs give you my most humble thanks, assuring your Majesty, that a precious jewel at another time could not so well have contented, as your letter in this case hath comforted me.'[1]

The King was able to take part in the St George's Day celebrations at Westminster Abbey on 23 April, wearing his Garter robes. On the thirtieth the court moved to Greenwich, where Edward ran at the ring and attended a 'goodly muster of his men at arms' on Blackheath. On 27 June, still in good spirits, he left London to make a progress through the south and west, but people noticed that he was looking pale and thin. That unlucky bout of measles, coming just at the most dangerous age for Tudor boys, followed by a strenuous summer had fatally weakened him. When he returned to Hampton Court, a few days before his fifteenth birthday, tuberculosis was already established. By Christmas it had become obvious that the King was far from well, and a more than usually elaborate programme of festivities was arranged to distract attention from this uncomfortable fact. Mary came to court at the end of January, but found Edward in bed with a fever and unable to see her for three days.

Elizabeth had sent word that she, too, was 'determined about Candlemas to come to see the King's Majesty'. She was still trying to get Durham House back, although she had apparently been offered the great mansion which the Duke of Somerset had built for himself in the Strand as a town residence. She could not have her things ready there in time, she declared, and again applied for the loan of St James's Palace. Northumberland, remarking appreciatively that he was sure her Grace would have done no less though she had kept Durham House still, stalled her. He did not want Elizabeth at court just then and her visit was postponed. John Dudley was worried about the future. If the King were to die, the edifice of his own power, so carefully built up over the past four years, would collapse overnight, for at best he could expect total political extinction from Mary and her friends. He was doing all he could to conceal the gravity of Edward's illness but, despite reassuring bulletins issued from the court, it was impossible to stop the rumours spreading. Jehan Scheyfve reported at the end of April: 'I hear from a trustworthy source that the King is undoubtedly becoming weaker as time passes, and wasting away. The matter he ejects from his mouth is sometimes coloured a greenish yellow and black, sometimes pink like the colour of blood.'[2]

Elizabeth must have heard some of these disquieting stories and was far too intelligent not to realise that she was being deliberately prevented from seeing her brother. Some time in the spring of 1553 she made a determined effort to reach him and actually set out on the journey to London. Half-way there she was intercepted by a messenger, supposedly from the King, who 'advised' her to turn back. After that there was nothing she could do but return to Hatfield and wait upon events. She continued to write to Edward, but it is unlikely that any of her letters reached him. Once he knew the King was dying, Northumberland had gone to considerable pains to separate him from his sisters. It was essential that no external influences should be brought to bear on the boy, and also that neither of the princesses should learn of certain interesting plans being made for their future.

The secret seems to have been well kept, although, as time passed and Edward grew steadily worse, the court and City seethed with speculation, for no one expected the Duke would give up his dictatorship without a fight. Scheyfve at first believed that he meant to use Elizabeth as his instrument; either by marrying her to his eldest son, after first causing him to divorce his wife, or else – again – 'that he might find it expedient to get rid of his own wife and marry Elizabeth himself'. In fact, Northumberland

had devised a simpler and more radical scheme. Edward was
to be persuaded to make a Will passing over both his sisters and
bequeathing the Crown directly to his cousin Jane Grey. Mary
and Elizabeth were to be declared unfit to succeed because both
were (*a*) illegitimate, (*b*) related to the King by half-blood only,
and (*c*) liable to marry foreign princes who would gain control of
the government and thus 'tend to the utter subversion of the
commonwealth'. The question of whether or not either or both
of Henry VIII's daughters could properly be regarded as having
been born in wedlock was just the kind of nice point guaranteed
to keep lawyers and theologians happily occupied for a lifetime.
The other two grounds cited for their exclusion from the succession were constitutionally merely frivolous. As for Jane Grey's
claim, it was true that Henry had settled the Crown, in default of
heirs from his own children, on the descendants of his younger
sister; but, if Mary and Elizabeth were to be disabled, the next
heir was Jane's mother, Frances. Apart from all this, no Will made
by Edward could have any validity while the 1544 Act of Succession, 35 Henry VIII, remained on the Statute Book. But, from
Northumberland's point of view, the legality of the plan mattered
less than the speed and efficiency with which it was carried out.
Once Mary and Elizabeth were safely in his hands and Jane
established on the throne, he had little doubt of being able to
persuade Parliament to repair any constitutional deficiencies.

On Whitsunday, 21 May 1553, fifteen-year-old Jane Grey was
married, much against her own will but with the eager connivance
of her deplorable parents, now Duke and Duchess of Suffolk, to
one of Northumberland's numerous sons, Guildford Dudley. It
only remained to draft the Will, and bully or cajole the rest
of the Council into acquiescence. Edward had at first been reluctant to upset his father's arrangements and to disinherit his
sisters. Mary's religion told against her, of course, but the same
objection could not be raised in Elizabeth's case. The Duke, however, pointed out that Elizabeth might easily be forced by
circumstances into marrying a Catholic, which would make her
succession as fatal to the Protestant cause as Mary's. It was the
duty of a prince to set aside all considerations of blood, he told
the King, where God's glory and the subjects' weal might be en-
dangered. If Edward were to forget that duty, he could expect
revenge 'at God's dreadful tribunal'.[3] Edward, now suffering as

much from the remedies being inflicted upon him as from his disease and very near his end, was not proof against arguments of that nature. His 'Device for the Succession' was drawn up during the first half of June and the Privy Council, more or less reluctantly, had appended their signatures before the end of the month.

Northumberland had worked fast but he was only just in time. The last of the Tudor kings died on 6 July 1553, and that night a fearsome thunderstorm broke over London, as if presaging other storms to come. For the first time in nearly three-quarters of a century England was faced with a disputed succession and all the unpleasant consequences which that inevitably entailed. Also, the very contingency which Henry VIII had laboured so murderously to avoid was now at hand; for the first time since the days of Matilda of unhappy memory, England was to be ruled by a woman.

Northumberland, choosing his moment carefully, had already despatched letters to Mary and Elizabeth summoning them to Edward's deathbed. These letters must have reached their destinations about the fourth or fifth of July; and Mary, then at Hunsdon, obediently set out on the journey. She had got as far as Hoddesdon on the London road when, on the evening of 6 July, she received an anonymous warning that the summons was a trap. This warning may have come, as he later claimed, from Nicholas Throckmorton. It is just as likely that its author was William Cecil. Elizabeth, warier or better informed than her sister, never set out at all. There is no record that she, too, received a specific warning, but it would surely be odd if certain unobtrusive travellers had not been riding the road to Hatfield during the past few weeks carrying letters or, more probably, verbal messages from Master Secretary Cecil to the Lady Elizabeth. William Cecil had already been fortunate enough to survive one change of régime, but he was a careful man, and no doubt took steps to provide himself with as much insurance as possible.

As soon as she realised that the *coup d'état* was under way, Elizabeth, according to most accounts, gave out that she was too ill to go to London and prudently retired to bed. All the same, the next fortnight must have been an extremely anxious time for her If Northumberland won, and on the face of it the odds seemed heavily in his favour, she knew that the most she could expect at

his hands would be marriage to some obscure Protestant prince-
ling – a marriage which would take her out of England and give
her a husband with no power to insist on her rights. According
to Camden, the Duke sent emissaries to the princess offering large
financial rewards if she would surrender her claim to the throne.
It seems unlikely that Northumberland would have wasted time
on such an obviously pointless errand, but, if the story is true,
Elizabeth made the only answer possible – 'that they must first
make their agreement with her elder sister, during whose lifetime
she had no claim or title to resign'.

Mary, meanwhile, had fled, first to Kenninghall in Norfolk, and
subsequently to Framlingham Castle, accompanied only by six
loyal members of her household, and narrowly evading capture
by a party of horse under the command of Robert Dudley, sent
out in pursuit of her. The King's death was kept secret for three
days, but when it became apparent that Mary had, temporarily at
least, slipped through his fingers Northumberland was obliged to
proceed without her. On 9 July Nicholas Ridley, Bishop of
London, in a sermon at Paul's Cross, referred to both princesses
as bastards, and Bishop Latimer, never one to mince words,
declared it would be better that God should take away the ladies
Mary and Elizabeth, rather than by marrying foreign princes they
should endanger the existence of the Reformed Church. On
10 July Jane Grey was summoned to Syon House and officially
informed of the contents of Edward's Will. Her protests were
ignored, and later that day she was brought in state to the Tower,
her formidable mother bearing her train and Guildford Dudley,
resplendent in white and silver, preening himself at her side. At
seven o'clock in the evening 'was made a proclamation at the
Cross in Chepe by three heralds and one trumpet with the King's
sheriff of London, Master Garrard, with divers of the guard for
Jane the Duke of Suffolk's daughter to be Queen of England,
but', added the chronicler ominously, 'few or none said God
save her'.[4]

The Duke of Northumberland was not a man to take public
opinion into account, but this was to prove a fatal omission. The
English people had always had a soft spot for Mary and, even
more to the point, they loathed the whole tribe of Dudley as
greedy, tyrannical upstarts. Richard Troughton, the bailiff at
South Walshen in Lincolnshire, hearing of Mary's flight from his

friend James Pratt, as they stood together by the cattle drinking-
place called hedgedyke, was moved to exclaim: 'Then it is the
Duke's doing and woe worth him that ever he was born, for he
will go about to destroy the noble blood of England. I wish this
dagger at the villain's heart with my hand at it, as hard as I can
thrust, face to face and body to body, whatsoever may become of
me. May God's plague light upon him and may God save the
Queen's majesty and deliver her grace from him.'⁵ John Dudley
might control the capital, the fortress of the Tower with its
armoury and its Mint, he might have the Council in his pocket;
but Richard Troughton spoke for England, and England had had
more than enough of John Dudley and was not prepared to stand
by while King Harry's daughter was cheated out of her natural
inheritance.

On 9 July Mary had written defiantly to the Council from
Kenninghall. It seemed strange, she said, that they had failed to
inform her of 'so weighty a matter' as her brother's death and
added that she was not ignorant of their consultations to undo the
provisions made for her preferment, although she was still prepared to believe in their loyalty. Her letter ended with a command
that her right and title was to be proclaimed in her City of
London.

The news that Mary meant to show fight came as an unwelcome
surprise to her enemies, but not even the most optimistic of her
well-wishers believed she had any chance of winning. At the
Imperial embassy, where Jehan Scheyfve had recently been
reinforced by three envoys extraordinary, there was only gloom.
The ambassadors scarcely thought it worth their while to pass on
to the Emperor Mary's desperate pleas for help, and could think
of nothing better to do than beg the Council to be good to her.
But the Duke knew on what a fragile foundation his power really
rested, and every day that Mary remained at large undermined it
further. Already disquieting news was coming in of the support
rallying to her. The Earls of Bath and Sussex had joined her,
together with quite a few substantial gentlemen and their
tenantry, not to mention 'innumerable companies of the common
people'. On 12 July a muster was proclaimed in Tothill Fields to
collect an army 'to fetch in the Lady Mary' and that night, says
Henry Machyn, 'was carried to the Tower three carts full of all
manner of ordnance, as great guns and small, bows, bills, spears,

morris-pikes, harness, arrows, gunpowder and victuals'.[6] On Friday, 14 July, 'the Duke of Northumberland with other lords and knights with a great power of horsemen with artillery and munitions of war departed from London towards Norfolk to suppress the rebels, as he took them which had taken the Lady Mary's part'.[7] But as the impressive cavalcade passed through Shoreditch, the Duke was heard to say 'to one that rid by him, "The people press to see us, but not one sayeth God speed us" '.[8]

Northumberland had been manœuvred into taking the field himself by his fellow councillors, but although he had the reputation of being 'the best man of war in the realm' on this occasion his genius seems to have deserted him. He allowed his followers to waste precious time burning and looting and falling out over the spoils, and his soldiers began to remember pressing engagements elsewhere. In the Tower, his associates, relieved of his hypnotic presence, began to suffer from cold feet. When they heard that the crews of the royal ships, sent to lie off Yarmouth to cut off Mary's escape route to the Continent, had gone over to her in a body, it became a question of not whether but when the Council would do the same. On 18 July the decision was taken and on the nineteenth, between five and six o'clock in the afternoon, they proclaimed Queen Mary 'Queen of England, France, and Ireland, and all dominions, as the sister of the late King Edward VI and daughter unto the noble King Henry VIII'. This time, reported an anonymous correspondent in the City, 'the number of caps that were thrown up at the proclamation were not to be told. The Earl of Pembroke threw away his cap full of angels. I saw myself money was thrown out at windows for joy. The bonfires were without number, and what with shouting and crying of the people, and ringing of the bells, there could no one hear almost what another said, besides banquetings and singing in the streets for joy.'[9]

That night, while the citizens were still drinking the health of Queen Mary and destruction to the Dudleys in the wine and beer flowing in every street, the Earl of Arundel and William Paget slipped away, riding post into Norfolk to explain to the new Queen that the Privy Council had always remained her true subjects in their hearts, but until now had seen no possibility of declaring their loyalty 'without great destruction and bloodshed'. There seems to be no record of how or when the news reached

Hatfield, but it was not long before Elizabeth heard of her sister's triumph and wrote to congratulate her. On 29 July she came riding through Fleet Street to Somerset House accompanied, according to Henry Machyn, by two thousand horsemen all in green garded with white velvet or satin taffeta.

Mary was now making her way slowly down to the capital and on the following day Elizabeth set out to meet her. She passed through the City 'at twelve of the clock in the forenoon, being Sunday, and rode out at Aldgate towards the Queen's Highness, accompanied with a thousand horses of gentlemen, knights, ladies and their servants'.[10] It was some time since the sisters had last met, possibly not since the Christmas of 1547, but they had continued to correspond and, on the surface at any rate, remained good friends. Mary greeted Elizabeth affectionately, kissed all the ladies in her sister's train, and the two processions formed up for the Queen's entry into London.

The royal party reached Whitechapel at seven o'clock in the evening of 3 August, and Mary paused only to change her dress before resuming her triumphal progress. At Aldgate, which was 'goodly hanged with cloths', she was received by the Lord Mayor and his aldermen and then passed on into the City, with the Earl of Arundel, who had successfully made his peace, riding ahead bearing the sword and Elizabeth following immediately behind the Queen. They must have made a poignant contrast, those two daughters of Henry VIII, as they rode together through the gaily decorated streets, with the citizens cheering themselves hoarse on every side, the trumpets sounding before them and the church bells ringing in their ears. Mary, dressed in purple velvet and satin heavy with goldsmith's work, a baldrick of gold, pearl and stones round her neck and a rich billament of stones and great pearl on her hood, was thirty-seven years old. As a girl she had been pretty, small and finely made, with the delicate pink and white complexion which often goes with red hair. Now she was painfully thin and, although dispassionate foreign observers still described her as 'fresh-coloured', the long years of unhappiness, ill-health and unkindness had left their indelible mark upon her. Elizabeth would be twenty in a month's time. She was never, even in the full bloom of youth, strictly beautiful, but the Venetian ambassador considered her face and figure 'very handsome' and her bearing regally dignified. There can be no doubt that to very many people in those welcoming crowds of Londoners she represented all the hope for England's future.

When the Queen's procession reached the Tower, she was met at the Gate by four kneeling figures – the old Duke of Norfolk, who had lain there under sentence of death ever since King Henry died; Stephen Gardiner, Bishop of Winchester, who had spent most of Edward's reign in prison; Somerset's termagant Duchess and young Edward Courtenay, now virtually the only surviving member of the ancient royal line of Plantagenet. Mary raised them all and kissed them, saying 'these are my prisoners'. There were certain other inmates of the Tower currently enjoying Her Majesty's hospitality who were not in evidence on that auspicious occasion – the Duke of Northumberland and his brood of sons, and Jane Grey, whose palace had now become her prison.

The Queen remained at the Tower for about a fortnight and then the court moved to Richmond. These first few weeks of the new reign were a difficult period of adjustment for Elizabeth. Accustomed, ever since she had begun to grow up, to thinking of her sister as 'poor Mary' – bullied, downtrodden and neglected, dismissed by Northumberland and his like as a weepy, neurotic old maid – she must now get used to the idea of Mary as Queen. Elizabeth never seems to have found the least difficulty in according her younger brother the exaggerated respect due to royalty. All the evidence points to the fact that she never really found it easy to do the same for her elder sister.

While her brief, incredulous flush of happiness lasted, Mary showed Elizabeth a flattering degree of attention, holding her by the hand whenever they appeared in public together and always giving her the place of honour at her side, but this satisfactory state of affairs was inevitably short-lived. Mary had inherited all her mother's pride, courage and stubbornness – none of her father's subtlety and political acumen. A 'good' woman, narrow in outlook, limited in intelligence, fanatical in the religious beliefs which for so long had been her only solace, and still carrying that terrible burden of guilt, she was to prove a dangerous person to deal with – and especially dangerous for Elizabeth. Mary had never borne malice to the child who had been the innocent cause of so much of her sufferings, but she soon made it clear that she could neither like nor trust the young woman – the past and their mothers' ghosts lay too heavily between them. Added to this, there was now a poisoning element of sexual jealousy in their relationship. Mary's friends had naturally been in the forefront of those ready to believe the worst of Anne Boleyn's daughter four years ago, and it would be strange indeed if Mary had not heard and been influenced by the stories circulating at that time. No least breath of scandal had ever touched Mary's name, no man had ever come near her, her virtue was unassailable; but, as one of her biographers has remarked, even a good woman can regret things which she ought not.[11] The Queen, looking at her young half-sister's demurely inscrutable countenance, must on occasion have been assailed by some highly regrettable pangs of envy and curiosity. None of this could be acknowledged, of course, but there was one issue between them which would soon have to be brought into the open, and that was the prickly question of Elizabeth's religious faith.

Mary had not the least doubt that her unexpected victory had been due entirely to the personal intervention of the Almighty, nor that it was now her duty to lead her people back into the fold of the true Church. On this point, she told the Emperor's ambassador, she felt so deeply that she was hardly to be moved. Unfortunately, however, she had misjudged the mood of the country almost as disastrously as Northumberland had done. Living in rural retreat, surrounded by her Catholic household, she had, not surprisingly, failed to realise how strongly a nationalistic form of Protestantism had taken hold – especially among the artisan classes in London and the south-east – during the past few years; and had completely misinterpreted the rapturous welcome she had received. The people were thankful to be rid of Northumberland and delighted to see the true line of succession re-established. They had no intention of returning meekly to the dominance of Rome. Within a month of the Queen's accession there had been unmistakable and violent demonstrations of this feeling in the streets of London.

For a time Mary clung to her hopes for a peaceful reconciliation. Her 'determination and pleasure' uttered to the Council on 12 August was that she did not mean to 'compel or constrain other men's consciences', but trusted that God would put into their hearts a persuasion of the truth.[12] Shortly afterwards a proclamation was issued in which the Queen expressed the hope that the religion which she herself had professed from infancy would now be quietly and charitably embraced by all her subjects.

Mary had never made any secret of her beliefs and, although it was still officially illegal, Mass was now being openly celebrated at court – not once, as the Emperor was informed at the end of August, but six or seven times a day with the Councillors assisting. There was, however, one notable absentee, for the Queen's sister and heiress had not so far put in an appearance. The religious problem was a particularly delicate one for Elizabeth. The Protestant party was already turning to her as their figurehead and white hope for the future, and, so far as it is possible to tell, her own private inclinations lay with the Protestant right wing. Elizabeth was not the stuff of which martyrs are made and had no intention of becoming one if she could help it, but it would not do to alienate her friends. Added to this, if she apostatised too ardently, she would be tacitly admitting her own illegitimate birth. On the other hand, she dared not offend the Catholics too deeply, and Mary's attitude was beginning to show that she would soon have to make some gesture to placate them. Early in September the gesture was made, an event which, as Simon Renard of the Imperial embassy reported sardonically to his master, 'did not take place without a certain amount of stir'.

Alarmed by her sister's sudden coldness, Elizabeth had asked for a private audience, which was held in one of the galleries at Richmond Palace with a door or half-door separating the participants. Elizabeth fell on her knees and shed tears. She saw only too clearly, she said, that the Queen was not well disposed towards her and could think of no other cause except religion. She might, however, be excused on this point as she had been brought up in the way she held and had never been taught the doctrine of the ancient faith. She begged Mary to send her books 'contrary to those she had always read and known hitherto' so that she might see if her conscience would allow her to be persuaded; 'or that a learned man might be sent to her, to instruct her in the truth'. These requests were granted and Elizabeth apparently found her conscience easily persuadable, for on 8 September, the day after her twentieth birthday, she accompanied the Queen to Mass. The effect of this from the Catholic point of view was somewhat marred by the fact that 'she tried to excuse herself, saying she was ill and complained loudly all the way to Church that her stomach ached, wearing a suffering air'.[13]

Simon Renard had no illusions about the true worth of Elizabeth's conversion and Antoine de Noailles, the French ambassador, told the King of France on 22 September, 'everyone believes that she is acting rather from fear of danger and peril from those around her than from real devotion'.[14]

The religious difficulty was only part of the quagmire surrounding Elizabeth and waiting hungrily for her least false step. Mary, accustomed all her adult life to relying on her mother's relations for support and advice, now turned as naturally and trustfully to Simon Renard as once she had turned to Eustace Chapuys; and Renard, the shrewd and skilful diplomat who had taken over as the Emperor's resident ambassador, was dedicated to cementing the important English alliance with Spain and the Empire. The Queen listened eagerly to the sage counsel passed on by her cousin's ambassador. She was to move cautiously at first in matters of religion and refrain from taking too harsh a revenge on her enemies. But Mary had no desire for revenge and only three of the Northumberland conspirators, the Duke himself and two of his closest confederates, were executed. In Renard's opinion the same fate should properly have overtaken Jane Grey, but here Mary proved unexpectedly intractable. 'As to Jane of Suffolk, whom they had tried to make Queen,' he reported, 'she could not be induced to consent that she should die.' Jane had written to Mary, admitting she had done wrong in accepting the Crown but vehemently denying that she had either consented or been a party to Northumberland's intrigues. Mary believed her and told Renard that her conscience would not permit her to have Jane put to death. The ambassador pointed out that 'power and tyranny had sometimes more force, especially in affairs of state, than right or justice' but the Queen was immovable. Nevertheless, she promised to be careful and to take all the necessary precautions before setting the usurper free! Renard could only shrug up his shoulders and hope, without much conviction, that Mary would not regret her astonishing clemency.[15] But, however much he might deplore Jane's preservation, he regarded Elizabeth as potentially even more dangerous. The Queen's heretical heir would be an obvious focal point for all discontent, both religious and political, and her name recurs in his despatches with relentless iteration. He told the Emperor, in a curiously felicitous phrase, that she had a spirit full of enchantment (*qu'est ung esprit plain d'incantation*) and was greatly to be feared.[16] He told the Queen at every opportunity not to trust her sister 'who might, out of ambition, or being persuaded thereto, conceive some dangerous design and put it to execution, by means which it would be difficult to prevent, as she was clever and sly'.[17]

The overt enmity of Simon Renard was formidable enough by itself, but Elizabeth knew she had as much or more to fear from his rival, Antoine de Noailles, who professed to be her friend. The French ambassador's chief business was to prevent, if possible, too close an alliance between England and Spain. Such an alliance could only be hostile to France, and as rumours began to spread that the Queen of England was contemplating marriage with the Emperor's son, Philip, French alarm increased. There was another compelling reason for the King of France's close interest in English affairs – a reason represented in the person of the young Queen of Scots, now nearing her twelfth birthday, who was being brought up at the French court as the intended bride of the Dauphin. Mary Stuart was the granddaughter of Margaret Tudor, Henry VIII's elder sister, who had married James IV of Scotland. In spite of Henry's Will, which arbitrarily excluded the Scottish line, by all the laws of primogeniture Mary Stuart had an excellent claim to the English crown. No slur had ever been cast on her birth, and many people felt she had every right at least to be regarded as the heiress presumptive. The King of France was naturally attracted by the prospect of seeing his future daughter-in-law become queen of both the island kingdoms and, if some sufficiently lethal form of dissension could be stirred up between the Tudor sisters he was not unhopeful of the outcome. De Noailles was an accomplished intriguer and could be relied upon to do his best in this direction.

Mary was already beginning to entertain grave doubts as to the purity of Elizabeth's motives in attending Mass, and 'asked her if she firmly believed what the Catholics now believed and had always believed concerning the holy sacrament'. She begged her 'to speak freely and declare what was in her mind'.[18] Oddly enough Elizabeth might have been wiser, at this stage, to have done just that. Mary's own sincerity was patent and she could respect genuine scruples of conscience in others. Unfortunately, however, the gulf between the sisters was now so wide that no trust or confidence was possible. Elizabeth told the Queen that she was considering making a public declaration 'that she went to Mass and did as she did because her conscience prompted and moved her to it; that she went of her own free will and without fear, hypocrisy or dissimulation'.[19] Mary could not believe her and the suspicion that Elizabeth was deliberately using the religious faith which the Queen held sacred as a political weapon did nothing to improve her opinion of the girl.

All the same, by using these somewhat dubious methods, Elizabeth succeeded in maintaining a foothold at court and in securing her proper place at Mary's coronation, which took place on 1 October. She was paired with that old friend Anne of Cleves, still living in England in comfortable and respected retirement. They rode together 'in a chariot covered with cloth of silver' in the procession through the City from the Tower, and later both dined at the Queen's table at the banquet in Westminster Hall.[20] But even at the coronation festivities Renard was watching Elizabeth closely and reported that she appeared to be conspiring with the French ambassador. Apparently the Princess had complained to de Noailles about the weight of her coronet and he answered brightly that she must have patience, for soon this crown would bring her a better one.[21]

Mary's first Parliament met on 5 October and proceeded to repeal the divorce of Henry VIII and Catherine of Aragon, pronouncing their marriage to have been lawful and valid. Mary can hardly be blamed for wanting to vindicate her mother's memory and doing what she could to right that old wrong, but it was embarrassing for Elizabeth to have her bastard state thus emphasised. In fact, and contrary to Renard's expectations, the re-establishment of Mary's legitimacy did not affect her own position vis-à-vis the succession. Under the peculiar powers granted to Henry VIII by Parliament, as long as the 1544 Act of Succession remained in force, Elizabeth was still next in line to the throne if Mary died childless. So far, the present Parliament, although willing to oblige the Queen up to a point, had shown no disposition to interfere with this arrangement, but Elizabeth could have no illusions about what her sister might do if the opportunity presented itself. In one hysterical outburst that autumn, Mary had cried out that it would be a scandal and a disgrace to the kingdom to allow Elizabeth to succeed, for she was a heretic, a hypocrite and a bastard.[22] On another occasion the Queen went so far as to say that she could not even be sure that Elizabeth was King Henry's bastard. Her mother had been an infamous woman and she herself 'had the face and countenance' of Mark Smeaton, the lute-player.[23] No doubt all this was faithfully repeated to the Princess, and on 25 October de Noailles reported that 'Madame Elizabeth is very discontented, and has asked permission to withdraw from this Court'.[24]

Permission was refused, and Simon Renard, who saw heretical plots behind every bush and the hands of Elizabeth and de Noailles in all of them, urged the Queen to send her sister to the Tower without more ado. Mary would not go as far as that, but in November she was foolish enough to insult Elizabeth publicly, by giving precedence to the Countess of Lennox and the Duchess of Suffolk at state functions. To be made to follow Margaret Douglas, daughter of Margaret Tudor's second marriage to the Earl of Angus, or the Duchess of Suffolk, mother of the convicted traitor Jane Grey, was too much for Elizabeth's temper. There was something perilously close to an open quarrel, and Elizabeth showed her feelings by sulking in her own apartments. Mary's friends cut her, but the younger element at court – especially the younger male element – openly sided with the Princess.

Renard heard rumours that she was entertaining de Noailles in secret, and although Elizabeth had no difficulty in clearing herself from this accusation the atmosphere had become so strained that she renewed her demands to be allowed to retire into the country. As things turned out, she might have done better to have stayed where she was, but her desire to escape from the intolerable situation at court is very understandable.

This time leave was granted, and at the beginning of December the sisters met to say good-bye. Mary had been given a good talking-to by Renard, who told her she would have to make up her mind what to do about Elizabeth. If she would not put her in the Tower, then, for reasons of policy, she must treat her with at least outward civility. His words had some effect for, although he wrote 'I had much difficulty in persuading the Queen to dissemble', Mary made a heroic effort and gave Elizabeth an expensive parting-present of a sable hood. Her dislike of her younger sister had by now grown into a near obsession. Renard observed that 'she still resents the injuries inflicted on Queen

Catherine, her lady mother, by the machinations of Anne Boleyn, mother of Elizabeth', and it is tempting to speculate whether there was something about Elizabeth at this time which reminded Mary with especial vividness of the hated Anne – something which made all that long pent-up bitterness come welling uncontrollably to the surface. All the courtesies, however, were observed at their leave-taking and de Noailles heard that there had been a complete reconciliation. According to Renard, Elizabeth 'addressed a petition to the Queen, asking her not to believe anyone who spread evil reports of her without doing her the honour to let her know and give her a chance of proving the false and malicious nature of such slanders'.[25]

Before she was allowed to leave London, the Princess received a visit from the Earl of Arundel and William Paget, who 'spoke to her frankly and said what they thought salutary for her to hear, namely that if she left the straight road and intrigued with the heretics and French, she might have reason to regret it'.[26] If Elizabeth found anything ironic in this homily from two gentlemen, neither of whom was exactly noted for following the straight road himself, she gave no sign of it and merely repeated her assurance 'that as for religion she was not acting hypocritically but according to the dictates of her conscience'. She would show her good intentions by her way of living, she told them. She would take priests into her household, dismiss any of her servants who might be suspect and 'do all in her power to please the Queen'. On the day of her departure Renard himself, anxious to leave no stone unturned, went to see her and 'spoke seasonable words calculated to counteract the effects of French intrigues'. 'Nevertheless,' he assured the Emperor, 'care was being taken to have her every action observed.'[27]

Elizabeth was bound for Ashridge, which lay close to the Great North Road, and Renard was highly suspicious of a request previously made by de Noailles 'to have posting-houses on the road to Scotland'. De Noailles had told the Council that this was for the convenience of his colleague, the Sieur d'Oysel, when he passed through England on his way north to take up the post of French ambassador in Scotland; but Simon Renard felt convinced that it was all part of some dark scheme being hatched with Elizabeth's connivance.

As Elizabeth rode out of the capital, her purest emotion was probably relief at getting away. She knew it could only be a temporary respite, the storm signals were too unmistakable, and she was well aware that she was still surrounded by spies; but she could relax her vigilance just a little, while she prayed to be delivered from her friends.

CHAPTER X

'We Are All Englishmen'

THE bulk of the work of Mary's first Parliament had consisted of repealing various treason Acts passed during the two preceding reigns, and sweeping away the whole of the Edwardian religious settlement. With this, for the time being, the Queen had to be content, although her ultimate objective, as revealed to Parliament by Stephen Gardiner, Bishop of Winchester and now Lord Chancellor, was to return unconditionally to the authority of Rome. The solid conservative core of the nation as represented in the House of Commons was willing enough to return to the *status quo* which had existed at King Henry's death – in other words, to a form of Anglo-Catholicism. Further than that they were not so far prepared to go, and Mary found she was still saddled with the unwanted title of Head of the Church. The spirit of national pride and independence fostered by Henry's defiance of the Pope was a powerful driving-force and, even more to the point, a large number of family fortunes had been founded on the spoils of the Reformation. Certainly no holder of Church lands was now going to part with a foot of his plunder without a bitter struggle.

If the Queen was dissatisfied, so too was the Protestant left wing, a noisy and well-organised minority which manifested its opposition to her policy by acts of hooliganism in the churches, physical assaults on priests and the dissemination of a shower of highly inflammatory anti-Catholic propaganda. It was not, however, the religious dispute *per se* which brought about the first and most narrowly contested trial of strength between Mary and her people. By the beginning of November 1553, it had become generally known that the Queen seriously intended marriage with Philip of Spain, who was not merely a foreigner and a Catholic but the representative of the most formidable Catholic power bloc in Europe. It looked as if all Northumberland's direst predictions were going to be fulfilled, and public reaction was sharp and immediate. The Protestant pressure groups redoubled their efforts; both Houses of Parliament sent a joint deputation to the Queen begging her to marry an Englishman and there were grave misgivings within the Privy Council itself.

No one, of course, questioned that the Queen must marry and the sooner the better. The idea of a single woman attempting to rule such a turbulent nation as England was not to be thought of, especially as Mary had already shown that she possessed neither the taste nor the aptitude for government. Obviously she must have a husband to support her and undertake, as Simon Renard delicately put it, 'those duties which were not the province of ladies'. In the opinion of many people and in particular of the Lord Chancellor, the Queen's wisest choice of consort would have been Edward Courtenay, 'the last sprig of the White Rose'. Courtenay, a good-looking, charming but rather weak-witted young man now in his mid-twenties, was a grandson of one of Edward IV's daughters and had spent nearly half his life in prison for that very reason. Mary was prepared to be kind to him – she created him Earl of Devon and arranged that he should be given special opportunities to make up for the time he had wasted in prison – but she made it perfectly clear that she had no intention of marrying him, or indeed any other Englishman. Her desire for Philip, although politically and, as it turned out, personally disastrous, was natural enough in the circumstances. The fact that the Prince of Spain happened to be the most brilliant match available weighed less with Mary than the fact that he was a Spaniard and one of her mother's kin. Having been skilfully and patiently piloted by Renard through the shoals of her maidenly shrinking, self-doubt and indecision, Mary was now more than half in love – a heady emotion for one of her naturally affectionate temperament who had so far always schooled herself to an almost nun-like renunciation of the flesh.

One of the reasons which had been officially advanced in favour of the Queen's marriage was to secure an heir to safeguard the succession but, although nobody was tactless enough to say so, few people seriously believed that Mary would ever bear a child. Mary herself was not so sure. After all, God had already worked one miracle for her. Why should He not work another and give her a son to guarantee the continued success of her mission? For, with Philip at her side, surely nothing could prevent her from bringing England safely back to Rome. She did not reach her decision lightly, but when on 29 October, after many weeks of heart-searching, tears and prayer, Mary finally gave her word to Renard she had convinced herself that it was God's will for her to marry Philip and after that, of course, she was immovable.

The Lord Chancellor was the only person with sufficient prestige and authority to try to make the Queen understand the sort of trouble she was storing up for herself and for the country, but unfortunately there was always a fatal element of awkwardness and reserve in their relationship. Mary could not forget that Stephen Gardiner had once been one of her father's most trusted and able instruments in the struggle for the divorce, and Gardiner was especially hampered on this occasion by his known personal fondness for Courtenay. As Mary snappishly remarked, was it suitable that she should be forced to marry someone simply because a bishop had made friends with him in prison? Gardiner could only reiterate that the people would never stomach a foreigner who would make promises that he would not keep. The Queen retorted that if her Chancellor preferred the will of the people to her wishes, then he was not keeping *his* promises. The Chancellor, with his past experience of Tudor obstinacy, gave in, saying it was too dangerous to meddle in the marriages of princes. With the parliamentary delegation, Mary took an even higher tone. It was none of their business, she told them, to dictate to her on such a matter. She could be trusted to remember the oath she had taken at her coronation and always to put her country first. Anyway, she added in a burst of petulance, if they forced her to marry against her will, she would not live three months and they would only be defeating their own ends.[1] In fact, as the Queen indicated defiantly to all and sundry, she meant to have Philip or nobody.

Across the Channel, the French, seeing themselves threatened with encirclement, were full of despondency. Mary's ambassador, Nicholas Wotton, had been instructed to tell the King of France that, no matter whom she married, she intended to continue to live in peace and amity with him, but that cynical monarch was not convinced. 'It is to be considered', he remarked to Wotton, 'that a husband may do much with his wife; and it shall be very hard for any wife to refuse her husband any thing that he shall earnestly require of her.' Wotton had been abroad in the world, continued the King, and knew how subtle and crafty the Spaniards were, so that whatever good intentions Mary might profess now it was very doubtful whether she would be able to keep to them in the future.[2] Indeed, the fear that England would be dragged into war with France was one of the most serious objections to the Spanish marriage, and, as it turned out, a fear which was to prove only too well founded.

Meanwhile, in London, de Noailles had not given up hope that even now the marriage might be prevented. Although the Emperor, throughout the delicate process of negotiation, was doing his utmost to avoid treading on English corns – an alliance which would give him command of the sea route between Spain and the Netherlands was worth any amount of diplomacy – the English people in their present mood of suspicion and xenophobia preferred to believe the various horrific rumours being carefully spread by interested parties; that a horde of Spaniards all armed to the teeth would shortly land on their coast; that England was to be reduced to the status of a province of the Empire and the Pope's authority forcibly reimposed. The country was clearly ripe for mischief and de Noailles thought he knew best how to put the finishing touches to it. Mary might have refused to have young Courtenay, but there was still Elizabeth. 'From what I hear,' he told the King of France in December, 'it only requires that my Lord Courtenay should marry her, and that they should go together to the counties of Devonshire and Cornwall. Here it can easily be believed that they would find many adherents, and they could then make a strong claim to the crown, and the Emperor and Prince of Spain would find it difficult to suppress this rising.' Elizabeth and Courtenay should certainly have made a virtually irresistible combination, but de Noailles was too clear-headed not to see at least one of the snags. 'This misfortune', he continued, 'is that the said Courtenay is of such a fearful and timid disposition that he dare not make the venture. . . . There are many, of whom I know, who would be ready to give him encouragement and all help in carrying out some plan to his advantage, and I do not see what should hinder him, except his weakness, faint-heartedness and timidity.'[3] The ambassador seems to have taken Elizabeth's co-operation for granted but if she ever had any idea of raising rebellion against her sister, of which there is no proof whatever, the timorous Courtenay was the last person with whom she would have been likely to throw in her lot.

Nevertheless, ambitious plans for armed resistance against the proud Spaniard and 'the coming in of him or his favourers' were now being laid. They were still maturing when, on 2 January 1554, the Emperor's envoys, led by Count Egmont, arrived 'for the knitting up of the marriage' between the Queen and the Prince of Spain. Egmont and his coadjutors landed at Tower Wharf to the salute of 'a great peal of guns' from the Tower batteries, and on Tower Hill a reception committee headed by Courtenay was waiting to conduct them ceremoniously through the City. They got no welcome from the watching crowds, for 'the people, nothing rejoicing, held down their heads sorrowfully'. On the previous day the embassy servants had been pelted with snowballs, but at least nothing was actually thrown at the distinguished visitors.[4]

On 12 January the marriage treaty was finally signed and its terms, as outlined by the Lord Chancellor two days later in an eloquent oration to the lords, nobility and gentlemen in the presence chamber at Westminster, should have been generous enough to satisfy the most exacting Englishman. But unfortunately the rising tide of panic and prejudice could no longer be stemmed by reasoned argument. The mindless rallying-cry 'We will have no foreigner for our King' had temporarily driven out common sense, and Gardiner's announcement, according to one chronicler, was 'heavily taken of sundry men, yea and thereat almost each man was abashed, looking daily for worse matters to grow shortly after'.[5] Within a week word reached London that Sir Peter Carew was up in Devonshire 'resisting of the King of Spain's coming'. Almost simultaneously the Council heard that Sir Thomas Wyatt, son of the poet, and a number of others were up in Kent 'for the said quarrel in resisting the said King of Spain . . . and partly for moving certain councillors from about the Queen'. About this time, according to the same account, 'Sir James Crofts departed to Wales, as it is thought to raise his power there', and news also came in that the Duke of Suffolk had mysteriously disappeared from his house at Sheen.[6]

The rising had originally been timed for March, to coincide with Philip's actual arrival, but someone had let the secret out. It was generally believed that Courtenay, always the weak link in the chain, had taken fright and confessed to Gardiner or else that the Chancellor, becoming suspicious and alarmed for his protégé, had somehow extracted the story from him. The other conspirators, not knowing to what extent their plans had been betrayed and too deeply committed to draw back, were forced to move prematurely. The movement in the West Country was virtually still-born. It had always depended very largely on Courtenay's presence and the prestige of his name; without him, its morale rapidly collapsed and Peter Carew fled to France. In Kent, however, things looked serious. Thomas Wyatt had taken Rochester Bridge, and the crews of the royal ships lying in the Medway had gone over to him with their guns and ammunition.

While these stirring events were taking place, Elizabeth remained lying close at Ashridge. Earlier in the month Mary had written to her asking for news and received a letter in reply saying that Elizabeth was not at all well. She had been troubled, she said, with such a cold and headache as she had never felt before, and for the past three weeks had had no respite from the pain in her head and arms. Then came the outbreak of armed rebellion, and rumours began to circulate that Ashridge was being provisioned for a siege. Gardiner's agents picked up a report that the Princess intended moving to Donnington Castle, a semi-fortified house near Newbury in Berkshire, and on 26 January, the day after Wyatt entered Rochester, Mary wrote again to her sister:

> We tendering the surety of your person, which might chance to be in some peril, if any sudden tumult should arise, either where you now be, or about Donnington, whither (as we understand) you are bound shortly to remove, do therefore think it expedient you should put yourself in readiness with all convenient speed to make your repair hither to us, which, we pray you, fail not to do, assuring you, that as you may more surely remain here, so shall you be most heartily welcome to us. And of your mind herein we pray you return answer by this messenger.[7]

Velvet gloves were still being worn, but the hint of steel in the invitation was unmistakable. Elizabeth returned a verbal answer. She was too ill to travel, she said. The officers of her household felt it prudent to follow this up with a letter addressed to the

Lord Chancellor. 'Albeit we attend here on my Lady Elizabeth's Grace, our mistress,' they wrote,

> in hope every day of her amendment, to repair towards the Queen's Highness, (whereof we have, as yet, none apparent likelihood of health,) yet, considering this dangerous world, the perilous attempts and the naughty endeavours of the rebels . . . we do not forget our most bounden duty, nor yet our readiness in words and deeds to serve Her Highness by all the ways and means that may stand in us, both from her Grace, our mistress, and of our own parts also.[8]

There, for the moment, the matter rested; during the next fortnight the Queen and Council were too busy coping with a major crisis on their doorstep to have any leisure to spare for Elizabeth.

A hastily collected force, consisting of men of the Queen's guard and the City train bands, had been sent down to Kent; but the Londoners and a fair proportion of the guard promptly defected to the rebels with rousing cries of 'We are all Englishmen!' In the words of one Alexander Brett, they preferred to spend their blood 'in the quarrel of this worthy captain, Master Wyatt' and prevent at all costs the approach of 'the proud Spaniards' who, as every right-thinking Englishman knew, would treat them like slaves, despoil them of their goods and lands, ravish their wives before their faces and deflower their daughters in their presence.[9]

Thus reinforced, Wyatt resumed his advance on the capital. From Blackheath on 30 January he announced his terms: the custody of the Tower with the Queen in it, the removal of several councillors and their replacements to be chosen by him. London was in a turmoil and everything depended on the loyalty of the citizens, which appeared doubtful to say the least. It was Mary herself who saved a very ugly situation. Like all her family, she showed to the best advantage in a crisis which demanded a display of physical and moral courage. Disregarding advice that she should seek her own safety, she rode into the City on 1 February and made a fighting speech in the crowded Guildhall that not even Elizabeth could have bettered. Her audience rose to her, and when Wyatt reached Southwark two days later he found the bridge heavily defended against him. A period of uneasy stalemate followed, during which the Lord Mayor and the sheriffs got into armour and commanded the householders to be ready 'in harness to stand every one at his door, what chance soever might happen'. It was a long time since London had been besieged and 'much noise and tumult was everywhere' as shops were shuttered, market stalls hastily dismantled and weapons and armour unearthed from store and prepared for use. The Queen had refused to allow the Tower guns to be turned on the rebels in case any of the innocent inhabitants of Southwark should suffer, and finally, on Shrove Tuesday, 6 February, Wyatt withdrew his men from 'the bridge foot' and marched down-river to Kingston, where they crossed to the northern bank before turning eastwards again. But the steam had gone out of them by now. They were tired and hungry, and too much time had been wasted. Still they came on through the western suburbs. There was some skirmishing with the royalist forces under the command of the Earl of Pembroke around St James's and Charing Cross, and some panic at White-hall when, in the general confusion, a cry of treason was raised within the precincts of the palace as a rumour spread that Pembroke had gone over to the enemy. 'There', remarked one observer, 'should ye have seen running and crying of ladies and gentlewomen, shutting of doors, and such a screeching and noise as it was wonderful to hear.' But still the Queen stood fast and 'many thought she would have been in the field in person'.[10] Wyatt and a handful of followers got through Temple Bar and on down Fleet Street, but found Ludgate barred and defended against them. As they turned back they realised that they had become separated from the main body of their army and Pembroke was coming up to cut off their retreat. A few minutes later it was all over and Wyatt had yielded to Sir Maurice Berkeley at Temple Bar.

Once the immediate danger had passed and the rank and file of the insurgents were being rounded up and crammed into make-shift prisons, the government was able to turn its attention to unravelling the threads of the conspiracy. Before the end of January, Gardiner, believing with some justification that de Noailles was involved up to his neck, had resorted to highway robbery on one of the ambassador's couriers. As a result indisputable evidence emerged that de Noailles had known all about the plot and the names of the plotters for at least two months. Even more interesting, the Lord Chancellor's men discovered a copy of Elizabeth's last letter to the Queen on its way to the

French King by diplomatic bag. From this it seemed reasonable to assume that the Queen's heir was in correspondence with the emissaries of a foreign power. Whether she had been actively involved in the recent disturbance remained to be proved, but although Wyatt had never openly invoked her name there could be no doubt that she, if anyone, had stood to gain from his success. At all events, it was time she came to London to give an account of herself. Mary was already suspicious of the convenient illness Elizabeth was still using as an excuse for skulking in the country, and two of the royal physicians, Drs Owen and Wendy, were despatched to examine the patient and report on her condition. On 10 February, the medical team was reinforced by a commission consisting of Lord William Howard, the Lord Admiral and Elizabeth's maternal great-uncle, Sir Edward Hastings and Sir Thomas Cornwallis.

According to a highly coloured and quite unsubstantiated account by that enthusiastic martyrologist John Foxe, their orders were to bring the Princess back with them 'either quick or dead'. Holinshed says they arrived late at night and insisted on forcing their way unbidden into her bedroom. The commissioners themselves reported more soberly to the Queen on the following day that 'immediately upon our arrival at Ashridge, we required to have access unto my Lady Elizabeth's Grace; which obtained, we delivered unto her your Highness' letter; and I, the Lord Admiral, declared the effect of your Highness' pleasure'. The doctors had given it as their opinion that Elizabeth could be moved 'without danger of her person' and the commission therefore felt that 'we might well proceed to require her in your Majesty's name (all excuses set apart) to repair to your Highness with all convenient speed and diligence'. They found the invalid 'very willing and conformable' but still fighting a determined rearguard action, for 'she much feared her weakness to be so great that she should not be able to travel and to endure the journey without peril of life'. Elizabeth knew that the peril lay not in the journey but its destination and begged a further respite, 'until she had better recovered her strength'. It was, however, politely but firmly made clear that the time for such delaying tactics had passed, and she gave in with becoming meekness, agreeing to set out on the following day.[11]

Although, for obvious reasons, she was making the most of it, there is no doubt that her illness was genuine. When her escort

'had her forth' at nine o'clock in the morning of Monday,
12 February, 'she was very faint and feeble and in such case that
she was ready to swound three or four times' before they could
get her into the Queen's litter which had been brought to carry
her. From the description of her symptoms – her face and limbs
were so distended that she was said to be 'a sad sight to see' –
Elizabeth appears to have been suffering from acute nephritis, or
inflammation of the kidneys, and it has been suggested that she
may have had an attack of scarlet fever of which this form of
Bright's Disease is often a complication.[12] But her physical discomfort can scarcely have compared with her mental anxiety. The
situation she had been dreading ever since Mary's accession was
now at hand and there could be no disguising the fact that she
stood in deadly danger. The litter jolting its way slowly but
inexorably through the frost-rutted Hertfordshire lanes might
well be taking her towards a traitor's death.

In deference to his charge's fragile condition, Howard had
planned the thirty-mile journey to Westminster in very easy
stages, expecting it to last five days; but he had reckoned without
Elizabeth's talent for procrastination and it was 22 February
before the cortège was able to leave Mr Cholmeley's house at
Highgate and descend into the City. Simon Renard reported that
Elizabeth, who was wearing unrelieved white for the occasion,
'had her litter opened to show herself to the people' and the
people themselves, clearly expecting the worst, came flocking
gloomily to gaze on the swollen, pallid countenance of their
Princess. According to Renard, she appeared 'proud and
haughty', an expression which in his opinion was assumed to
mask the vexation she felt.[13]

Elizabeth's feelings on that dismal Thursday afternoon can only
be guessed at, but the sights which greeted her as she was carried
through Smithfield and on down Fleet Street can have done
nothing to raise her spirits. The government had had a bad fright
and the work of exemplary justice was proceeding briskly.
Gallows had been erected throughout the City, in Bermondsey, at
Charing Cross and Hyde Park Corner, and all the gates into
London were decorated with heads and dismembered corpses.[14]
The great were suffering with the simple. Courtenay was back in
the Tower. The Duke of Suffolk, who owed his life and liberty
after Northumberland's *coup* entirely to the Queen's generosity,

had tried to raise the Midlands against her and was now awaiting execution. Mary had also reluctantly been brought to agree that Jane Grey would have to die. Innocent she might be of any complicity in Wyatt's rebellion but the very fact of her existence had come to represent an unacceptable danger. Her father's disastrous behaviour had proved that beyond doubt. Diminutive, freckle-faced Jane, who was not yet seventeen, had followed her young husband to the block on the day Elizabeth left Ashridge – a piece of news which more than any other must surely have brought home her own nearness to the abyss. If Mary could be persuaded to kill Jane of whom, despite her heresy, she had always been rather fond, there seemed even less chance that she would be in any mood to spare the sister she so overtly distrusted.

When Elizabeth reached Whitehall the portents were bad. She had already been separated from most of her household. The Queen refused to see her and she was lodged in a part of the Palace from which, said Renard, neither she nor her remaining servants could go out without passing through the guard. There she stayed for nearly a month, a prisoner in fact if not in name, while determined efforts were made to build up the case against her. Renard could not understand the delay in sending her to the Tower, since, he wrote, 'she has been accused by Wyatt, mentioned by name in the French ambassador's letters, suspected by her own councillors, and it is certain that the enterprise was undertaken for her sake. Indeed, Sire,' he told the Emperor in some exasperation, 'if she does not seize this opportunity of punishing her and Courtenay, the Queen will never be secure.'[15]

It is impossible, at this distance in time, to say just how deeply Elizabeth had in fact been implicated in the rebellion. There was some circumstantial evidence – enough, it must be admitted, to justify an enquiry. But it soon turned out to amount to very little in real terms. Wyatt, who was being rigorously interrogated, admitted having sent Elizabeth two letters; one advising her to retreat to Donnington, where she could have defended herself until the insurrection had succeeded; the other informing her of his arrival at Southwark. Francis Russell, the Earl of Bedford's son, confessed to acting as postman but the replies, if any, had been verbal and non-committal. Sir James Crofts, one of the conspirators now in custody, had been to see Elizabeth at Ashridge, and according to a report from Mr Secretary Bourne dated 25 February had incriminated William Saintlow, a member of her household. But William Saintlow, examined by the Council, 'stoutly denied' knowing anything of Wyatt's plans, 'protesting that he was a true man, both to God and his prince'.[16] 'Crofts is plain and will tell all,' wrote Bourne hopefully, and Renard, in a despatch dated 1 March, declared that Crofts had 'confessed the truth, written his deposition, and admitted in plain terms the intrigues of the French ambassador with the heretics and rebels'.[17] Possibly the wish was father to the thought – in actual fact Sir James, although 'marvellously tossed', does not appear to have revealed anything of importance. Even the discovery of that letter in de Noailles's postbag was not in itself evidence against Elizabeth. There was nothing to prove that she herself had given it to de Noailles or had permitted anyone else to do so.

While it is difficult to believe that she had been entirely ignorant of the conspiracy, it is equally hard to credit that she had either approved or been actively involved. On the other hand, she could scarcely have betrayed the men who, however wrong-headed, believed themselves to be her friends, and had they been successful, she would have found it impossible to stand aside. There can be little doubt that one of the first consequences of such a success would have been the removal of Mary and an attempt to replace her by putting Elizabeth and Courtenay jointly on the throne. Since everything we know about Elizabeth leads to the conclusion that this was the last way she would ever have chosen to come into her inheritance, her most likely course is the one which, in the light of the available evidence, she may be said to have pursued – to try to know as little as possible and hope to keep out of it.

On 15 March Wyatt was brought to trial and convicted. The next day, which was the Friday before Palm Sunday, Elizabeth received a visit from Stephen Gardiner and nineteen other members of the Council, who 'burdened her with Wyatt's conspiracy' as well as with the 'business made by Sir Peter Carew and the rest of the gentlemen of the West Country'. It was the Queen's pleasure, they told her, that she should go to the Tower 'while the matter were further tried and examined'. Elizabeth was aghast. She denied all the charges made against her, 'affirming that she was altogether guiltless therein', and said desperately that she trusted the Queen's Majesty would be a more gracious lady

unto her than to send her to 'so notorious and doleful a place'.
Stony-faced, the deputation indicated that there was no alternative, the Queen was fully determined, and they trooped out 'with
their caps hanging over their eyes'. Barely an hour later four of
them were back again. Her own servants were removed and six
of the Queen's people appointed to wait on her, so that 'none
should have access to her grace'. A hundred soldiers from the
north in white coats watched and warded in the Palace gardens
that night, and a great fire was lit in the Hall, where 'two certain
lords' kept guard with their company.[18]

It is not difficult to imagine the twenty-year-old Elizabeth lying
awake in the darkness, listening to the tramp of feet beneath her
window and knowing that the net was closing round her. Within
a few hours, short of some miracle, she would be in 'that very
narrow place' the Tower, from which few prisoners of the blood
royal had ever emerged alive. But, on the following morning,
when the Earl of Sussex and another lord whom Foxe tactfully
omits to name (he was probably the Marquess of Winchester, the
same who as Lord St John had once ridden down to Hatfield with
Robert Tyrwhit), came to tell her that the barge was waiting and
the tide now ready 'which tarrieth for nobody', Elizabeth made it
clear she had by no means given up the fight. It was a time for
clutching at straws. She asked to wait for the next tide and was
refused. Then, if she might not see the Queen, she begged at least
to be allowed to write to her. Winchester said he dared not permit
such a thing, adding that in his opinion it would do Elizabeth
more harm than good. But Sussex, suddenly kneeling to the
prisoner, exclaimed that she should have liberty to write, and, as
he was a true man, he would deliver her letter to the Queen and
bring an answer 'whatsoever came thereof'.[19]

Writing-materials were hastily produced, and with her escort
hovering in the background Elizabeth sat down to begin what
might well prove to be the most important letter of her life. Her
pen flowed easily over the first page, in sentences which she must
have been polishing during the watches of the night. 'If any ever
did try this old saying', she wrote,

> that a King's word was more than another man's oath, I most
> humbly beseech your Majesty to verify it in me, and to remember
> your last promise and my last demand, that I be not condemned

without answer and due proof, which it seems that now I am; for that without cause proved I am by your Council from you commanded to go into the Tower, a place more wonted for a false traitor than a true subject. . . . I protest afore God, who shall judge my truth, whatsoever malice shall devise, that I never practised, counselled nor consented to anything that might be prejudicial to your person any way, or dangerous to the state by any means. And I therefore humbly beseech your Majesty to let me answer afore yourself, and not suffer me to trust to your councillors; yea, and afore that I go to the Tower, if it is possible; if not, afore I be further condemned. . . . Let conscience move your Highness to take some better way with me, than to make me condemned in all men's sight afore my desert [be] known.

It might be dangerous to remind Mary of Tom Seymour and yet she had to risk it. 'I have heard in my time', she went on,

of many cast away for want of coming to the presence of their Prince; and in late days I heard my Lord Somerset say that if his brother had been suffered to speak with him, he had never suffered; but the persuasions were made to him too great, that he was brought in belief that he could not live safely if the Admiral lived, and that made him give his consent to his death. Though these persons are not to be compared to your Majesty, yet I pray God as evil persuasions persuade not one sister against the other. . . .

So far so good – she had reached the end of the page – but the strain was telling and as she turned over mistakes and corrections began to come thick and fast. Perhaps Sussex was at her elbow by this time, urging her to make an end. 'I humbly crave to speak with your Highness,' scribbled Elizabeth,

which I would not be so bold to desire if I knew not myself most clear as I know myself most true. And as for the traitor Wyatt, he might peradventure write me a letter, but on my faith I never received any from him. And for the copy of my letter sent to the French king, I pray God confound me eternally if ever I sent him word, message, token or letter by any means. And to this my truth I will stand to my death.

She had said all she could say, but more than half her second sheet was left blank – an open invitation to some forger to add a last-minute confession or damaging admission – so Elizabeth scored the page with diagonal lines, before adding her final appeal at the very bottom. 'I humbly crave but only one word of answer from yourself. Your Highness's most faithful subject that hath been from the beginning and will be to my end, Elizabeth.'[20]

She might have saved herself the trouble. Mary flew into a royal rage when the letter was brought to her. She roared at the Council that they would never have dared to do such a thing in her father's time and wished, in a triumph of illogicality, that he were alive again if only for a month.[21] All the same, Elizabeth had won twenty-four hours respite for she had contrived to miss the tide. The great boat-shaped starlings which supported the piers of old London Bridge restricted the flow of the river and turned the water beneath it into a mill-race. 'Shooting the bridge' was a hazardous business at the best of times, but when the tide was flooding it became impossible – there could be a difference of as much as five feet in the level of the water on either side. The government had no intention of courting a riot by taking the Princess through the streets, but the bridge would not be navigable again until midnight and the danger that a rescue attempt might be mounted under cover of darkness seemed too great to risk. It was therefore reluctantly decided to wait for daylight.

At nine o'clock on the morning of Palm Sunday Sussex and Winchester came for her again. This time there was no question of any reprieve. 'If there be no remedy', said Elizabeth dully, 'I must needs be contented.' As she was hurried through the damp gardens to the riverside, she looked up at the windows of the Palace, perhaps in a faint hope of seeing Mary, but there was no sign. Even now she seems to have been half-expecting a miracle, for she cried out that she marvelled much at the nobility of the realm who would suffer her to be led into captivity 'the Lord knew whither, for she did not'.[22] No miracle was forthcoming and she embarked at the Privy Stairs with the two peers, three of the Queen's ladies and three of her own, her gentleman usher and two grooms. The barge was cast off and rowed away downstream. The nightmare – the horror which had been lying in wait for Elizabeth in the dark places of her mind all her conscious life – was a nightmare no longer. It was actually happening in the

bleak daylight of a wet Sunday morning. Not quite eighteen years
ago her mother had travelled on this same river to the same
destination. It would surely be a crowning irony if Thomas
Wyatt, whose father had loved Anne Boleyn, was now to drag
Anne's daughter down with him.

In their haste to be rid of their uncomfortable charge, Sussex
and Winchester had misjudged the tide and there was a tense
moment under the bridge when the barge 'struck upon the
ground, the fall was so big and the water so shallow'. Then they
were through and the grey, ghost-ridden bulk of the Tower
loomed ahead. It was the end of Elizabeth's journey. Here her
mother had died with the five young men accused of being her
lovers. Her mother's cousin – poor, silly, wanton Katherine
Howard – had come this way by water from Syon House. There
were so many others – Tom Seymour and Tom's brother;
Northumberland, 'that great devil'; Suffolk, the weak fool; her
own cousin, Jane Grey, with whom Elizabeth had once shared
lessons and gone to Christmas parties and who had met the
executioner with such perfect courage – this had been the end of
the journey for them all.

Now the boatmen were shipping their oars and tying up at the
Water Gate – Traitor's Gate. And still Elizabeth was struggling.
At first she refused to land, she was no traitor, besides she would
be over her shoes in water. The two lords had gone on ahead, but
when they were told the prisoner would not come Winchester
turned back and told her brutally that she could not choose. He
offered her his cloak, which she rejected 'with a good dash' and
then, with one foot on the stairs, exclaimed: 'Here landeth as true
a subject, being a prisoner, as ever landed at these stairs; and
before Thee, O God, I speak it, having none other friends but
Thee alone!' If that were so, said Winchester, unimpressed, it was
the better for her. A company of soldiers and Tower warders were
drawn up on the landing-stage and Elizabeth took the opportunity of making another little speech for their benefit. 'O Lord,'
she said, 'I never thought to have come in here as prisoner; and
I pray you all, good friends and fellows, bear me witness that I
come in no traitor, but as true a woman to the Queen's majesty
as any is now living; and thereon will I take my death.' She was
rewarded by a voice from the ranks crying 'God preserve your
Grace!' and, turning to the Lord Chamberlain, Sir John Gage,

she asked if all these harnessed men were for her. 'No, madam' was the reply, and another voice added helpfully that it was the use so to be, when any prisoner came thither. But Elizabeth was not going to have her effect spoilt. 'Yes,' she insisted mournfully, 'I know it is so. It needed not for me, being, alas! but a weak woman.' A few steps further on she suddenly stopped and sank down 'upon a cold stone'. 'Madam, you were best to come out of the rain,' said the Lieutenant of the Tower, 'for you sit unwholesomely.' 'It is better sitting here than in a worse place,' answered Elizabeth, 'for God knoweth, I know not, whither you will bring me.' This was too much for her gentleman usher, who burst into tears and was promptly rounded on by his mistress demanding to know what he meant 'so uncomfortably to use her, seeing she took him to be her comforter, and not to dismay her'. Especially, she added sharply, since she knew her truth to be such that no man had cause to weep for her. Then, her courage restored, or perhaps having played out the scene to her satisfaction, she got up from her wet stone and swept on into the Tower.

She was lodged in the Bell Tower, and Winchester and Sir John Gage began at once to 'lock the doors very straitly' and to discuss further security arrangements. But the Earl of Sussex, who had throughout shown himself more compassionate – or more long-sighted – intervened. They would be wise, he pointed out, not to be over-zealous and to remember that Elizabeth was 'the King our master's daughter' as well as being the Queen's sister. 'Therefore,' said Sussex, 'let us use such dealing that we may answer it hereafter, if it shall so happen; for just dealing is always answerable.' This significant reminder that their prisoner might yet become their Queen seems to have gone home, and the escort departed a trifle thoughtfully.[23]

Elizabeth might have been cheered if she had known just how deeply the government was divided on the subject of her future, and that it was only after heated discussion and because no one would accept the responsibility of her safe-keeping that the decision to send her to the Tower had been taken. Sussex told her that several members of the Privy Council 'were sorry for her trouble' and, he himself was sorry he had lived to see this day; but now, abandoned in the prison which seemed only too likely soon to become her grave, there was little comfort to be gained from mere sympathy and her spirits sank to a very low ebb. Years later she was to tell a foreign ambassador how, having no hope of escape, she had planned to beg the Queen, as a last favour, to have a French swordsman brought over for her execution as had been done for Anne Boleyn – anything rather than suffer the clumsy butchery of the axe.

CHAPTER XI

Elizabeth, Prisoner

I N spite of all the passions it had aroused; in spite of the fact that it had already led to one of the most serious rebellions against the authority of the crown in living memory, and that popular opposition still rumbled ominously, preparations for the royal wedding continued to go forward. Count Egmont, who had slipped unobtrusively away while the trouble was at its height, returned to England early in March, bringing with him the ratification of the marriage treaty, and on the sixth Philip and Mary had been formally betrothed in the binding form of *verba de praesenti*, with Egmont standing proxy. In fact, all that was lacking now was the presence of the bridegroom, but Simon Renard, only too conscious of his heavy responsibilities, had begun to have serious misgivings about the wisdom of allowing the Prince to hazard his precious person in a country so ungrateful for the honour bestowed on it – at least as long as Elizabeth and Courtenay were alive to provide figure-heads for future insurrections. In Renard's opinion a more than suspicious negligence was being shown over bringing these two 'great persons' to trial, and could only conclude that 'delays were being created in the hope that something may crop up to save them'.[1]

Renard saw the Queen on Easter Saturday and took advantage of the occasion to express some of his doubts on the subject of Philip's future safety. He indicated, in the most tactful manner, that until 'every necessary step' had been taken he would not feel able to recommend the Prince's coming to her country. The blackmail was implicit and Mary replied, with tears in her eyes, that 'she would rather never have been born than that any harm should be done to his Highness'.[2] She promised to see to it that Elizabeth's and Courtenay's trials were over before his arrival.

However, it was continuing to prove unexpectedly difficult to collect enough evidence against either of the suspects even to begin proceedings. As far as Courtenay was concerned, the circumstances were certainly suspicious and there had certainly been a good deal of loose talk; but he had not apparently actually *done* anything. He had not gone down to Devonshire. He had not at any time taken up arms against the Queen. He had not attempted to escape. The plan to marry him to Elizabeth had been openly suggested by William Paget, a member of the Privy Council, the previous autumn; but Courtenay had rejected it, on the grounds that it would be beneath the dignity of one of his unblemished lineage, and there was no evidence that he had ever had any secret correspondence with her. Renard suspected that Stephen Gardiner was deliberately shielding his young friend, but had there been any direct proof against Courtenay it is unlikely that the Chancellor's influence could have saved him. As for Elizabeth herself, nothing fresh had so far come to light. Wyatt was being kept alive in the hope that he might yet be induced to incriminate her further, but although he is said to have signed a statement to this effect no such document has ever come to light.

About a week after her committal to the Tower, the Princess was visited by Gardiner and some other members of the Council, who 'examined her of the talk that was at Ashridge, betwixt her and Sir James Crofts, concerning her removing from thence to Donnington Castle, requiring her to declare what she meant thereby'. In spite of her vehement protestations of innocence, Elizabeth seems to have been a little touchy on the subject of Donnington. She began by saying that she did not even remember owning a house of that name but then, perhaps seeing that this would not do, she pulled herself together and admitted that she did have such a place, but had never been there in her life and could not remember anyone suggesting that she should. She was then confronted with James Crofts and asked by Gardiner what she had to say to him? Elizabeth replied calmly that she had little to say to him, or 'to the rest that were then prisoners in the Tower'. 'But my lords', she went on, 'you do examine every mean prisoner of me, wherein, methinks, you do me great injury. If they have done evil, and offended the Queen's majesty, let them answer it accordingly. I beseech you, join not me in this sort with any of these offenders.' Having regained command of the situation, she proceeded to dispose of the subject of Donnington. She remembered now, she said, that there had been some talk between

James Crofts and certain officers of her household about the possibility of her moving there, but what was that to the purpose? Surely she had a perfect right to go to one of her own houses at any time?

It was at this point that the Earl of Arundel, who was a member of the examining body, unexpectedly fell on his knees exclaiming, 'Your Grace saith true, and certainly we are very sorry that we have so troubled you about so vain matters.' Elizabeth took her cue at once. 'My lords, you do sift me very narrowly,' she said, with a sad, reproachful dignity, 'but well I am assured you shall not do more to me than God hath appointed; and so God forgive you all.'³ Since Arundel was one of the leaders of the pro-Spanish faction on the Council and therefore counted as one of her enemies, his outburst must have encouraged Elizabeth considerably. Exactly what lay behind his sudden change of heart remains obscure but he may have begun to feel, like Sussex, that it would be wise to think of the future. In fact, he later became one of the most determined of her English suitors, so perhaps Elizabeth was already fishing for men's souls 'with so sweet a bait that no one could escape her network', and perhaps Arundel was among the first of those poor fish 'who little knew what snare was laid for them'.⁴

The Lord Chancellor, on the other hand, after a period of hesitation, had apparently made up his mind that the Princess would have to be sacrificed. He told Renard at the beginning of April that 'as long as Elizabeth lived he had no hope of seeing the kingdom in peace'. Renard himself continued to impress on the Queen how essential it was to have Elizabeth and Courtenay tried and executed to make England safe for Philip; but he was irritated to discover that, as matters stood, the laws of England did not provide penalties applicable – at any rate to Elizabeth. The Queen assured him that fresh proof against the Princess was coming in every day 'and there were several witnesses to assert that she had gathered together stores and weapons in order to rise with the rest and fortify a house in the country, whither she had been sending her provisions'.⁵ The house in the country was, presumably, Donnington, but this apparently promising line of enquiry had already turned into a blind alley, and Elizabeth swore that any defensive preparations made at Ashridge were simply as a protection against the Duke of Suffolk, who had been in the neighbourhood at the time. Unpalatable though it might be to some, the fact remained that the government were no nearer to making out a case against her than they had been two months earlier.

Meanwhile, even in the Tower, life settled down into a daily routine. To begin with there had been some housekeeping problems. Elizabeth had to provide (and pay for) her own and her attendants' food, and the officers of her household responsible for making such provision found they had to deliver their mistress's diet into the hands of 'common rascal soldiers' at the outer gate of the fortress. This seemed to Elizabeth's people both dangerous and unsuitable and they accordingly waited on the Lord Chamberlain to protest, 'beseeching his honour to consider her Grace and to give such order that her viands might at all times be brought in by them which were appointed thereunto'. They got short shrift from Sir John Gage, who declared that the Princess was a prisoner to be served with the Lieutenant's men like any other, and he saw no reason why she should be given preferential treatment. The deputation took offence at these 'ungrateful words', whereupon Sir John lost his temper and 'sware by God (striking himself upon the breast), that if they did either frown or shrug at him, he would set them where they should see neither sun nor moon'. However, representations were made at a higher level, with the result that Elizabeth's servants were given permission to bring her food in and cook and serve it themselves. The Lord Chamberlain, who was also acting Constable of the Tower, did not at first take kindly to having his authority set aside but when, after some skirmishing in the kitchen, he contrived to secure the services of the Princess's cook for himself as well, matters went more smoothly. 'And good cause why,' observed John Foxe sardonically, 'for he had good cheer and fared of the best, and her Grace paid well for it.'[6]

After about a month's close confinement and 'being very evil at ease therewithal', Elizabeth began to agitate for some fresh air and exercise. At first she was only allowed to walk in the Queen's lodgings, 'the windows being shut and she not suffered to look out at any of them', but presently this licence was extended to include a small garden, 'the doors and gates being shut up'.[7] There were other slight diversions in the shape of the five-year-old son of the Keeper of the Wardrobe, who brought the Princess

posies of spring flowers, and two little girls – Susanna, who was
'not above three or four years old', and another who came to give
the captive a tiny bunch of keys, so that she might unlock the
gates and go abroad.[8] These touching visits were, however,
brought to an abrupt end by the Lord Chamberlain, in case the
children might be used to convey other, less innocent, messages.

The Tower was crowded with political prisoners at this time,
and stringent measures were in force to prevent any unauthorised
person from speaking to, or even seeing, the Princess. As well as
several officers of her own household, there were a number of old
friends among her fellow inmates. John Harington, who had once
been Tom Seymour's man, was now undergoing one of those
periodic spells in jail which were an occupational hazard for anyone connected with the great, and Elizabeth's childhood playmate
Robert Dudley and his surviving brothers were still suffering the
consequences of their father's ill-judged activities of the previous
summer. A long-standing tradition maintains that, despite all
official precautions, Elizabeth and Robert Dudley managed to
meet in prison and lay the foundations of their peculiar, life-long
relationship. If this is true, it must at least have helped to alleviate
the gloom and boredom of their incarceration.

Thomas Wyatt was finally executed on 11 April. On the scaffold
he explicitly exonerated both Elizabeth and Courtenay from having had any guilty knowledge of the rebellion, and although the
government attempted to suppress or deny it the news spread
rapidly and joyfully through the City. It was now clear that there
was no chance whatever of getting a legal conviction against
the Princess. Barely a week after Wyatt's execution Nicholas
Throckmorton was acquitted of a charge of treason by a London
jury, and there were renewed demonstrations against both the
Queen's religion and her marriage. A dead cat, dressed as a priest,
was found hanging on the gallows in Cheapside. Pamphlets were
scattered in the streets – one adjuring all Englishmen to stand
firm and keep out the Prince of Spain – another, so Renard reported angrily, 'as seditious as possible and in favour of the Lady
Elizabeth'. There had also been the scandalous but ingenious
affair of 'The Voice in the Wall' which, when addressed with the
words 'God Save Queen Mary' remained silent, but responded
to 'God Save the Lady Elizabeth' with an emphatic 'So be it'.
This remarkable phenomenon attracted admiring crowds until the

Voice was unmasked as a servant girl, cunningly concealed in an empty house.

Quite apart from the inflamed state of public opinion, the Council itself was split from top to bottom. On 22 April Renard sent the Emperor a vivid word-picture of the situation. 'Since I last wrote', his despatch began, 'quarrels, jealousy and ill-will have increased among the Councillors, becoming so public that several of them, out of spite, no longer attend the meetings. What one does, another undoes; what one advises, another opposes; one strives to save Courtenay, another Elizabeth; and such is the confusion that one can only expect the upshot to be arms and tumult.' Renard believed that the Queen would be persuaded to pardon Courtenay altogether, and, as for Elizabeth, 'the lawyers can find no sufficient evidence to condemn her'. 'Even if there were evidence,' he went on, 'they would not dare to proceed against her because her relative, the Admiral, has espoused her cause, and controls all the forces of England.'[9] There had already been some high words between Lord William Howard and John Gage on the subject of Elizabeth, and the influential Lord Admiral certainly opposed any undue show of severity towards his great-niece.

Elizabeth owed her apparently miraculous preservation to a number of factors – her own unfathomable discretion, the surprising strength of her popularity, government weakness and lack of direction – but most of all she owed it to her sister. Early in March the Queen had told Renard bitterly that 'Elizabeth's character was just what she had always believed it to be' but, in spite of her personal dislike of the girl and in spite of the pressure being exerted on her most vulnerable flank, Mary remained true to her principles. Her conscience had insisted on a painstaking examination of all the evidence, and although she herself remained highly sceptical, as long as the case remained 'not proven', Elizabeth would continue to be given the benefit of any doubt.

The fear of judicial execution might have receded, but Elizabeth knew she was by no means out of the wood. Renard had not abandoned his efforts to get her removed before Philip's arrival, and if she could not be put to death there were other – though admittedly less efficient – ways of disposing of her. In the present mood of the country any attempt to persuade Parliament to disinherit her would obviously be pointless, but there was still marriage; not, of course, marriage to an Englishman, but one of the Emperor's vassals who could be trusted to keep her safely under control. Emmanuel Philibert, Duke of Savoy and Prince of Piedmont, seemed the most suitable candidate and his name was to become wearisomely familiar to Elizabeth as time went by.

Other less obvious but equally nerve-wracking fears kept her awake at night and dogged her through the long, monotonous days. Mary's always precarious health had not been improved by the strain of the past few months and there were those among her friends with little to hope for from her successor. Thoughts of some desperate act which could not be undone must have passed through several minds. Elizabeth took what precautions she could against poison and a rumour went round that a warrant for her immediate execution, 'subscribed with certain hands of the Council', had been delivered to the Lieutenant of the Tower, but honest John Brydges, fortunately noticing that the Queen's signature was missing, refused to act upon it.

Then, on 5 May, Sir John Gage was relieved of his office as Constable and 'one Sir Henry Bedingfield placed in his room'. Bedingfield marched in to take over command of the Tower bringing with him a hundred men in blue liveries, and Elizabeth's reaction to this 'sudden mutation', at least as described by John Foxe, clearly illustrates her state of mind. The arrival of Sir Henry, being 'a man unknown to her Grace and therefore the more feared', seems to have induced a fit of panic. She demanded to be told 'whether the Lady Jane's scaffold were taken away or no?' Reassured on this point, but still not entirely satisfied, she went on to ask who Sir Henry Bedingfield was and whether, 'if her murdering were secretly committed to his charge, he would see the execution thereof?'[10]

In the circumstances, Elizabeth's alarm was understandable but it proved groundless. Henry Bedingfield was no ogre. A stolid country squire in his mid-forties from Oxborough in Norfolk, he was a staunch Catholic and one of those gentlemen who, with their tenantry, had gone to Mary's aid when she was standing embattled at Framlingham the year before. He was also, ironically enough, son of Edmund Bedingfield who had been Catherine of Aragon's custodian during her last sad years at Kimbolton Castle. As Elizabeth's jailer, Sir Henry has naturally come in for a lot of hard words from such vigorous Protestant partisans as John Foxe, but in actual fact he seems to have performed an unenviable task, if not with much tact or imagination, at least with resolute and incorruptible integrity.

The question of the Princess's future had become something of an embarrassment to the government. She could not be left in the Tower indefinitely but she was still under too much of a cloud to be set free. Neither would it be 'honourable, safe nor reasonable' to expect the Queen to receive her at court. Some face-saving formula would have to be found and Mary fell back on the time-honoured expedient of sending her sister to live under restraint in a remote country house. After a period of some indecision, the manor of Woodstock – once a hunting-lodge favoured by the Plantagenets – had been chosen, although Renard would have preferred a castle in the North, where the people were Catholics.

Having been officially consigned to Bedingfield's charge, Elizabeth left the Tower on Saturday, 19 May, at one o'clock in the afternoon and was taken by river to Richmond. Antoine de Noailles, although in disgrace with the Queen for dabbling in Wyatt's treason, was still taking a close interest in the Princess and had picked up a rumour that two envoys from the Emperor were to meet her at Richmond on the following day and would 'lay before her the proposals for her marriage with the Duke of Savoy'. In order to try to find out more about what was going on, de Noailles sent one of his agents to follow Elizabeth 'under the pretext of carrying her a present of apples', but he had been misinformed. There were no envoys at Richmond, and Bedingfield got an early opportunity to prove his zeal by seizing the messenger and stripping him to his shirt.[11] Fortunately there was nothing on him but the apples, though it was possibly as a result of this incident that the Princess was again separated from her own people 'which were lodged in out-chambers'. Whether she still harboured suspicions of Bedingfield's intentions or was just sick of the whole dreary business, Elizabeth – at any rate according to Foxe – seems to have thought herself in some special danger, for she called to her gentleman usher as he left her 'and desired him with the rest of his company to pray for her: "For this night", quoth she, "I think to die" '.[12]

However, the night, though 'doleful', passed quietly and next morning the cavalcade set off for Woodstock. Elizabeth, who was riding in a warped and broken litter, did not hesitate to say that she was being led 'like a sheep to the slaughter'; but in fact the journey soon turned into something suspiciously like a triumphal progress. Bedingfield, conscientiously reporting from Sir William Dormer's house at West Wycombe at the end of the second day, told the Council that: 'Her grace passed the town of Windsor with much gazing of people unto Eton College, where was used the like, as well by the scholars as other; the like in villages and fields unto Wycombe where most gazing was used, and the wives had prepared cake and wafers which, at her passing by them, they delivered into the litter. She received it with thanks until by the quantity she was accombered . . . and desired the people to cease.'[13] The next day, at Aston, the church bells were rung for her and that night was spent at Lord Williams's house at Ricote, where 'her grace was marvellously well entertained'. In fact Bedingfield considered that Lord Williams had rather overdone his hospitality to one who was, after all, 'the Queen's majesty's prisoner and no otherwise' and warned that there might be 'after-claps' of royal displeasure; but his lordship replied sharply that 'he was well advised of his doings', adding 'that her grace might and should in his house be merry'.[14]

All the rest of the way, through the Oxfordshire villages of Wheatley and Stanton St John, Islip and Gosford, the country people crowded the roadside to cheer the Princess as she passed with cries of 'God save your Grace', and Bedingfield must have breathed a sigh of relief when he finally got his charge to Woodstock. The house itself turned out to be in a state of considerable dilapidation. Elizabeth was accommodated in the gatehouse, where four rooms had been prepared for her, but Sir Henry was disquieted to find that only three doors in the whole building could be locked and barred. To do him justice, he was as nervous of possible assassins getting in, as of his prisoner getting out.

Elizabeth was to spend nearly ten months in detention at Woodstock under conditions which, though irksome, were hardly intolerable. Bedingfield was responsible for seeing 'that neither she be suffered to have conference with any suspected person out of his hearing, nor that she do by any means either receive or send any message, letter or token to or from any manner of person'. However, the Queen's instructions were that her sister was to be treated 'in such good and honourable sort as may be agreeable to

our honour and her estate and degree'.[15] Elizabeth had a respect-
able number of servants to wait on her. She was able to walk in
the 'over and nether gardens' and the orchard, and was also to be
allowed any books, within reason, to help pass the time. All the
same, it was not a very stimulating existence and, once the
Princess had recovered from her initial distrust of Bedingfield, she
could not resist teasing him with demands for all sorts of small
indulgences. Sir Henry, never quite sure whether she was in
earnest or not and 'marvellously perplexed whether to grant her
desires or to say her nay', took refuge in clinging tenaciously to the
letter of his instructions and insisting on referring every detail to
London. He was not above getting in an occasional sly dig on his
own account. Elizabeth had been asking for that suspiciously heretical object, an English Bible, and Bedingfield offered her instead
some Latin books which he had by him, 'wherein, as I thought,'
he reported blandly, 'she should have more delight, seeing she
understandeth the same so well'. Elizabeth retaliated by accusing
him of failing to pass on any of her requests to the Council and
then refused to speak to him.[16] However, there does not seem to
have been any real malice on either side and the relationship between prisoner and custodian came to be based on a grudging but
mutual respect.

Although she may have derived a certain amount of amusement
from baiting Sir Henry, Elizabeth had a more serious underlying
purpose. The events of the past few months had plainly demonstrated the importance of public opinion as a weapon in her
armoury; but memories were short and she was evidently afraid
that, buried in the country, she might be forgotten and that
Renard would seize the opportunity to have her shipped abroad.
In spite of Bedingfield's care, she may have got wind of a scheme,
currently being propounded by the Emperor, to send her to
Brussels to the court of his sister, the Dowager Queen of Hungary.
At any rate, Elizabeth had no intention of allowing the authorities
to forget her, and on 12 June Bedingfield apologised to the
Council for the fact that he was being 'enforced, by the im-
portunate desires of this great lady, to trouble your lordships with
more letters than be contentful to mine own opinion'.

Elizabeth was now nagging for permission to write to the
Queen herself and eventually got it, although it does not appear
to have done her much good. Mary's only response was to send

Bedingfield a terse note, telling him that she did not wish to receive any more of her sister's 'disguised and colourable letters'. This having been faithfully reported to Elizabeth, she demanded that Bedingfield should write to the Council on her behalf. When he refused, she told him that she was being worse treated than any prisoner in the Tower and, on second thoughts, worse than the worst prisoner in Newgate.

She was ill again towards the end of June with a recurrence of her nephritis, being 'daily vexed with swelling in the face and other parts of her body'. She wanted the Queen's physicians to be sent down to Woodstock, but for various reasons they were not available. Dr Owen wrote to Bedingfield explaining that her grace's body was 'replenished with many cold and waterish humours, which will not be taken away but by purgations meet and convenient for that purpose'. However, apparently it was not the right time of year for such ministrations and Elizabeth would have 'to take some patience'. In the meantime, Owen sent a diet-sheet for her to follow which 'would preserve her grace from the increase of such humours', and recommended the services of Dr Barnes and Dr Walbeck, 'two honest and learned men remaining at Oxford'. But, although she continued to be 'very evil at ease', the Princess indignantly refused to make any strangers privy to the estate of her body and preferred, she said, to commit it to God.[17]

So the battle went on. In July the Queen agreed to allow Elizabeth 'to write her mind' to the Council via Bedingfield. The letter granting this concession was dated the seventh, but it was three weeks before the prisoner condescended to take advantage of it. 'My Lady Elizabeth,' wrote Bedingfield at last,

> this present 30th of July, required me to make report of her grace's mind as her suit to your honours, to be means to the Queen's majesty on her behalf to this effect. To beseech your lordships all to consider her woeful case, that being but once licensed to write as an humble suitress unto the Queen's highness, and received thereby no such comfort as she hoped to have done, but to her further discomfort in a message by me opened, that it was the Queen's highness's pleasure not to be any more molested with her grace's letters. That it may please the same, and that upon very pity, considering her long imprisonment and restraint of liberty, either to charge her with

special matter to be answered unto and tried, or to grant her liberty
to come unto her highness's presence, which she sayeth she would
not desire were it not that she knoweth herself to be clear even before
God, for her allegiance.

Elizabeth ended her appeal by requiring Bedingfield 'to move
chiefly' those members of the Council who had been executors
'of the Will of the King's majesty her father' and requesting that
the Queen would at least allow some of them to visit her and hear
her state her case in person. 'Whereby she may take release not
to think herself utterly desolate of all refuge in this world.'[18]
Deferentially phrased though it was, the mention of King Henry's
Will was a shrewd reminder that, outcast and disgraced though
she might be, Elizabeth still remained the heiress-presumptive.

Meanwhile, having delayed for as long as he decently could,
Philip of Spain had finally arrived in England. He disembarked
at Southampton on 20 July and five days later he and Mary were
married in Winchester Cathedral amid scenes of great splendour.
Philip, a good-looking young man of twenty-seven, privately
considered himself a sacrifice on the altar – literally – of political
expediency, but in public he and his train were studiously polite.
On 18 August the Queen brought her bridegroom in triumph to
London. The gallows had been removed and decorations more
suitable to the occasion substituted. The citizens, well primed with
free drink, were in a benevolent mood and, although there was
plenty of jealousy and backbiting behind the scenes at court, and
the Spaniards complained they were being charged twenty-five
times the proper price for everything in the shops, on the surface
things went reasonably well.

Elizabeth may have hoped that Mary would soften towards her,
now that she had achieved her heart's desire, but Mary, apparently
absorbed in gaiety, made no sign and Elizabeth had to possess
herself in patience as best she could. According to the story preserved by Foxe and Holinshed, it was at Woodstock that she
scratched 'with her diamond in a glass window very legibly' the
famous couplet:

> Much suspected of me,
> Nothing proved can be:
> > Quoth Elizabeth, prisoner.

It seems uncharacteristic of Elizabeth that she would have gone so far as even to admit anything *could* have been proved. More credible is the old tale that she envied the freedom of 'a certain milkmaid singing pleasantly' in the Park, saying that 'her case was better and life more merrier'.[19] Once, in a fit of pious resignation, she wrote on the flyleaf of her edition of the Epistles of St Paul: 'I walk many times into the pleasant fields of the Holy Scriptures, where I pluck up the goodlisome herbes of sentences by pruning, eat them by reading, chew them by musing, and lay them up at length in the high seat of memorie, by gathering them together, that so having tasted their sweetness I may less perceive the bitterness of this miserable life.'[20]

She was by no means always so resigned, however, and Bedingfield continued to be harassed by the various whims and importunities of 'this great lady', as he persistently referred to her. Elizabeth complained bitterly about the Council's failure to respond to her appeal and pestered Bedingfield to let her write again herself. When he refused to take the responsibility without first going through the usual channels, she told him that their lordships would smile in their sleeves at his 'scrupulosity'. But, after the necessary permission had been laboriously obtained and Bedingfield had doled out pen, ink and paper, the Princess changed her mind and made him write at her dictation, declaring haughtily that she was not accustomed to communicate with the Council except through a secretary and overriding his rather feeble protests.

Elizabeth's general tiresomeness was, in some ways, the least of Sir Henry's worries. He lived in daily dread of leaks appearing in his security system, and the activities of Thomas Parry in particular were a constant source of anxiety. As the Princess's cofferer, Parry was responsible for feeding and paying her household, and had set up his headquarters at the sign of The Bull in Woodstock village. The Bull, in Bedingfield's opinion, was 'a marvellous colourable place to practise in'. Elizabeth's servants were always finding excuses for slipping off there and it was becoming, Sir Henry was gloomily convinced, a haunt and resort for all her undesirable friends. As time went by, with no release in sight for anyone, other pressing problems began to arise. The house would have to be put into a better state of repair before the winter if they were not all to freeze to death. Already, in early

October, the nights were becoming too long and cold for the
Queen's soldiers to continue their watch 'standing upon the hill'
and they would have to be brought within the gates. The men's
pay, too, was a month in arrears, and the inhabitants of Woodstock
were making it clear that unless some ready money was forthcoming soon they would cut off supplies. But, in spite of the
heart-rending pictures drawn by Bedingfield of the plight of the
soldiers and the poor folk of Woodstock, the government was
very slow to respond and eventually he was forced to advance
money to the local people out of his own pocket, to avoid, as he
put it, 'their daily exclaiming'.[21]

On 28 October Dr Owen and Dr Wendy came down to see
Elizabeth and took some blood from her arm and foot. 'Since
which time,' reported Bedingfield, 'thanks be to God, as far as
I see or hear, she doeth reasonably well.'[22] Probably the enforced
period of rest and quiet had done her as much good as anything.
At any rate, no more is heard about headaches or kidney trouble.
The Council, however, remained deaf to her repeated appeals for
her case to be reopened. The Queen was apparently determined to
wring some admission of guilt and contrition from her sister before she would consider restoring her to liberty. The winter closed
in and the household at Woodstock settled down grimly to wait
out the contest of Tudor stubbornness.

In London, events were taking place which had temporarily
pushed the problem of Elizabeth's future into the background.
Mary believed she was pregnant, and on 12 November she and
Philip together opened the Parliament which, if all went well,
would see the re-establishment of Rome's authority over the
Church in England. On 24 November, Cardinal Pole, the first
papal Legate to set foot on English soil since the days of Wolsey
and Campeggio, came up-river from Gravesend. He brought with
him the Pope's absolution for her excommunicated country, and
as Mary greeted him she felt certain 'that the babe had quickened
and leapt in her womb'.[23] Reginald Pole, who had been living in
exile for nearly thirty years, was another offshoot of the
Plantagenet tree, the son of Mary's old friend and governess the
butchered Countess of Salisbury, and he was a reminder of happy
childhood days as well as being the symbol of her future hopes.

A few days later the reconciliation with Rome had been effected.
Parliament, in an orgy of emotional remorse, voted a 'supplica-

tion' and, as both Houses knelt 'in the Great Chamber of the Court at Westminster' to receive absolution from the Bishop of Winchester, England was taken back into the bosom of the Catholic Church. The negotiations leading up to this remarkable moment had been going on throughout the autumn, while water-tight arrangements were devised to safeguard the property rights of all holders of Church lands. Once that was done, the Commons, who had been carefully chosen from 'the wise, grave and Catholic sort', were ready to undo the Reformation and restore the old laws and penalties against heresy.

As the time of Mary's delivery approached, the question of Elizabeth came once more into prominence. Stephen Gardiner was frankly of the opinion that any attempts to eradicate Protestantism in England would amount to no more than strip-ping the leaves and lopping the branches as long as the root of the evil – Elizabeth herself – remained untouched. Now was the time, he urged, to frame a Bill to disinherit her once and for all, but there was no enthusiasm for this project and it was quietly dropped. Philip's approach to the problem was a good deal more pragmatic. A measure had been passed which would give him the Regency if Mary died in child-birth and her child survived. But what if neither mother nor child survived? In the resulting chaos, he and his Spaniards would find themselves isolated among a hostile population and Elizabeth might then be a useful hostage. Anyway, he wanted the whole matter of the succession put on a regular basis. Elizabeth could not be left in limbo for ever and, according to Bedingfield, she was conducting herself like a good Catholic these days. Far better, reasoned Philip, to make a friend of this unknown young woman at a time when she was likely to be suitably grateful for his support. She could then be married to a Prince subservient to Spain, and the future of the English alliance would be secured.

On or about 20 April 1555, Bedingfield at last received a sum-mons to convey his charge to Hampton Court, where the Queen had gone to prepare for her lying-in. The journey from Woodstock was made in typical blustery spring weather, and on the first day out the party encountered violent gusts of wind which got under the ladies' skirts and more than once blew the Princess's hood from her head. She wanted to take shelter in a near-by gentleman's house to repair the ravages but Bedingfield, with his usual inflexibility, refused to allow even this slight deviation from his itinerary, and Elizabeth was obliged to do up her hair under a hedge as best she could.[24]

After three over-night stops – the last being at The George at Colnbrook, where about sixty of her gentlemen and yeomen had come to catch a glimpse of her – she entered Hampton Court 'on the back side'. She was still a closely guarded prisoner, but according to a French report Philip paid her a private visit three days after her arrival and the Queen sent a message telling her to be sure and wear her best clothes for the occasion.[25] Nearly another fortnight went by, and then she was waited on by the Lord Chancellor, the Earls of Arundel and Shrewsbury and the Secretary Petre. Elizabeth greeted them with the words: 'My lords, I am glad to see you; for methinks I have been kept a great while from you, desolately alone.' Gardiner went on his knees to her and begged her to submit herself to the Queen. If she did so, 'he had no doubt that her majesty would be good to her'. Elizabeth answered sharply that she would rather lie in prison all the days of her life. She wanted no mercy from the Queen, 'but rather desired the law, if ever she did offend her majesty in thought, word or deed'. Besides, she went on, 'in yielding, I should speak against myself and confess myself to be an offender, which I never was, towards her majesty, by occasion whereof the King and the Queen might ever hereafter conceive of me an evil opinion. And therefore I say, my lords, it were better for me to lie in prison for the truth, than to be abroad and suspected of my prince.'

Next day, Gardiner returned to the attack. The Queen marvelled, he told her, 'that she would so stoutly use herself, not confessing that she had offended'. It made it look as if she thought she had been wrongfully imprisoned. No, replied Elizabeth, the Queen must deal with her as she felt it right. 'Well,' said Gardiner, 'her majesty willeth me to tell you that you must tell another tale ere that you be set at liberty.' Elizabeth would only repeat that she would rather stay in prison 'with honesty and truth' than go free under a cloud. 'And this that I have said I will stand unto,' she declared, 'for I will never belie myself.' Gardiner tried another tack. Dropping on his knees again, he said: 'Then your grace hath the vantage of me, and other the lords, for your wrong and long imprisonment.' 'What vantage I have', answered the Princess, 'you know; taking God to record I seek no vantage at your hands for your so dealing with me. But God forgive you and me also.'[26]

It looked like stalemate. There was silence for a week. Then, without any warning, at ten 'clock one night, came a summons for Elizabeth to go at once to the Queen. She had been angling for a personal interview for over a year, but now the moment had arrived she was understandably shaken. It was probably to cover her nervousness, in case it might be misconstrued, that she asked her attendants to pray for her, saying 'she could not tell whether ever she should see them again or no'.

Susan Clarencieux, Mary's close friend and Mistress of the Robes, had come to fetch her, and escorted by Bedingfield, with her ladies following and her gentleman usher and grooms of the chamber going before to light the way, Elizabeth walked the short distance across the garden in the summer night till she reached the foot of the staircase which led to the Queen's lodging. There the procession halted. Bedingfield and the others waited outside while Elizabeth, accompanied only by Susan Clarencieux and one of her own ladies, went up the stairs to her sister's bedroom. Without waiting for Mary to speak, she knelt and once again proclaimed her innocence. She was a true subject and begged the Queen so to judge of her. She would not be found the contrary, whatsoever reports had gone of her. 'You will not confess your offence', said Mary out of the shadows, 'but stand stoutly to your truth. I pray God it may so fall out.' 'If it doth not,' answered Elizabeth, 'I request neither favour nor pardon at your majesty's hands.' 'Well,' came the somewhat ungracious rejoinder, 'you stiffly still persevere in your truth. Belike you will not confess but that you have been wrongfully punished.' 'I must not say so, if it please your majesty, to you.' 'Why then,' persisted the Queen, 'belike you will to others.' 'No, if it please your majesty, I have borne the burden and must bear it. I humbly beseech your majesty to have a good opinion of me, and to think me to be your true subject, not only from the beginning, but for ever, as long as life lasteth.'

Looking at the supple figure kneeling before her in the candlelight, Mary knew she had lost the battle of wills. She must accept, however reluctantly, Elizabeth's movingly worded assurances of loyalty and make her peace with Anne Boleyn's daughter. There is a tradition that Philip was present at their meeting, hidden behind a curtain – a tradition based perhaps on the report that Mary made some remark in her husband's language. The interview ended with a few 'comfortable' words from the Queen, but, added John Foxe darkly, 'what she said in Spanish, God knoweth'.[27]

CHAPTER XII

'A Second Person'

ABOUT a week after that nocturnal interview with Mary, Elizabeth said good-bye to Henry Bedingfield – it would probably be difficult to say whether prisoner or jailer was the more relieved – and his departure marked the end of a period of close restraint which had lasted just over fifteen months. The Princess remained at Hampton Court still under a limited form of surveillance, not appearing in public outside her own rooms. She was, however, able to set up her own household again, and some of the courtiers were given permission to visit her, although, commented the Venetian ambassador, 'they all avail themselves of it with great reserve'.[1]

In the circumstances, such caution was hardly surprising. At no time since the days of the Wars of the Roses had England been in such a nervous and unsettled state. The government was weak, divided and unpopular. The uncertain outcome of the Queen's impending childbed, bringing with it the dread of another minority, dominated this time by a Spanish regency, hung like a fog blotting out the future. To make matters gloomier still, the religious persecution which has left such an indelible stain on the memory of Mary's reign had now begun. The first heretics went to the stake in February 1555, and the burnings were to continue intermittently for the next three years. In all some three hundred people, including sixty women, suffered this peculiarly horrific form of death. It was not, however, by contemporary standards, an especially vicious campaign (by contemporary Continental standards it was mild), and it has to be remembered that in the eyes of the government Protestantism had, with justification, become synonymous with sedition, treason and open rebellion. It nevertheless remains an unpleasant episode – one of its least attractive features being the fact that the vast majority of the victims were humble people. The better-to-do Protestants either conformed just sufficiently to satisfy the authorities' not very exacting standards, or else went abroad more or less unhindered. From the point of view of what it hoped to achieve, the Marian persecution was a total and monumental failure in tactics. By giving the Reformers their martyrology, it also gave them respectability in the eyes of many to whom they had formerly appeared as little more than a gang of violent, loud-mouthed trouble-makers. The deaths of the Bishops Hooper, Latimer and Ridley who, with Thomas Cranmer, were virtually the only sufferers of note, did indeed light such a candle in England as, with God's grace, never was put out. Apart from a certain native distaste for religious persecution *per se*, Catholicism, in the current political climate, began to become ineradicably associated with foreign oppression in the minds of Englishmen, and now were sown the seeds of an implacable fear and hatred of Rome and all its works. These seeds, carefully watered by the outpourings of such men as John Foxe (the Protestants always did have the edge in the propaganda war), blossomed and burgeoned over the remainder of the century and, indeed, over three centuries to come.

As Head of State, Mary must, of course, bear ultimate responsibility for the acts committed in her name, but how far she personally initiated the persecution which earned her her unenviable nickname remains in some doubt. In many ways she was the most merciful of her family. Certainly towards her political enemies her leniency bordered on recklessness. Even the retribution visited on the Wyatt rebels was soon being tempered by the Queen's clemency, a clemency which extended beyond the rank and file. Edward Courtenay, after a period of incarceration at Fotheringay Castle, had been released shortly before Elizabeth was brought up from Woodstock, and sent to travel abroad. However doubtful his guilt, he would not have been so fortunate under Henry VIII. There had been a general spring-cleaning, too, at the Tower and the remaining prisoners left over from both the Northumberland and Wyatt affairs were pardoned and dispersed to their homes. Henry VIII would never have taken such a risk; neither would his younger daughter. Treason against herself Mary was ready to forgive, but heresy smacked of treason against God and that was another matter. The heretics were also imperilling their immortal souls and infecting others by their example. To Mary it would have been an unforgivable dereliction of duty – the duty so clearly laid upon her by the Almighty – if she had not tried by every means at her disposal to save her unhappy subjects from themselves.

It was against this background of uncertainty and fear, made even more depressing by a wet summer when the corn failed to ripen, that the tragic farce of the Queen's false pregnancy played itself out. By April all was ready for the arrival of the 'young master'. Midwives, nurses and rockers were in attendance, the cradle prepared and waiting, and the court crowded with noble ladies come to assist at the Queen's delivery. At daybreak on 30 April, a rumour circulated in the capital that Mary had given birth to a son the night before 'with little pain and no danger'. So circumstantial was the report that it was generally believed and, before anyone could stop them, the citizens had shut up shop and surged into the streets in search of the customary free food and drink. Bonfires were lit and 'there was great ringing through London, and in divers places Te Deum Laudamus sung'.[2] It was afternoon before messengers returning from Hampton Court brought the dispiriting news that not only had there been no safe delivery, but that it was not even imminent.

The days lengthened into weeks, weeks into months, gossip in the alehouses grew more and more ribald and eventually the fact had to be faced that there was no 'young master' or mistress either, and had never been one. The amenorrhea and digestive troubles to which Mary had always been subject, possibly, too, an incipient tumour, had combined with her desperate longing which – according to the omniscient Venetians – even produced 'swelling of the paps and their emission of milk' to create that pathetic self-deception.

For Elizabeth the tension of those early summer months must have been especially trying. If, against all the odds, Mary were now to bear a child, then, of course, her own prospects would be ruined and she would probably be reduced to accepting whatever marriage Philip and the Queen chose to arrange for her. Anxiety about the future apparently drove her surreptitiously to consult the famous astrologer, Dr Dee. Someone laid information, and Dee and three of Elizabeth's servants were arrested for having conspired to calculate 'the King's and Queen's and my Lady Elizabeth's nativity'. Elizabeth herself contrived to avoid direct involvement. Perhaps the report that both the informant's children had been stricken 'the one with present death, the other with blindness', discouraged too close an investigation.³

Elizabeth also took the opportunity to embark on a cautious flirtation with Philip, while Mary remained lurking miserably in the increasingly foetid atmosphere of the Palace. The Princess was as interested in her brother-in-law's friendship as he in hers, and there is evidence to suggest that he found her physically attractive. Two years later, when the Venetian ambassador, Giovanni Michiel, was compiling a detailed report on his tour of duty in England for the Senate, he observed that 'at the time of the Queen's pregnancy, Lady Elizabeth . . . contrived so to ingratiate herself with all the Spaniards, and especially with the King, that ever since no one has favoured her more than he does'. So much so that, in Michiel's opinion, it implied 'some particular design on the part of the King towards her'.⁴ Years later still, according to the account of William Cecil's son Thomas, Philip himself was heard to admit that 'whatever he suffered from Queen Elizabeth was the just judgement of God, because, being married to Queen Mary, whom he thought a most virtuous and good lady, yet in the fancy of love he could not affect her; but as for the Lady Elizabeth, he was enamoured of her, being a fair and beautiful woman'. As for Queen Elizabeth, she was to boast cheerfully that since their enmity had begun with love no one need think they could not get on together at any time she chose. The Queen was never afflicted with false modesty about her conquests, real or imaginary, though it is not likely on this occasion that she expected to be taken seriously. All the same, there is something curiously poignant in the picture of those two life-long antagonists – the elegant, fair-haired little Prince, heir to half the thrones of Europe but always careful of his dignity, as if to compensate for his unfortunate lack of inches, and the pale, red-headed girl of doubtful birth and dubious reputation, whose regality was yet instinctive and unconscious – walking together in the gardens of Wolsey's sumptuous red-brick mansion or under the dripping trees in the Park in the intense greenness of that far-off English summer, Elizabeth exerting herself to charm as only she knew how and acutely aware of Philip's enigmatic gaze upon her.

By the end of July, the situation at Hampton Court was becoming too embarrassing to continue any longer. Something had to be done to put a stop to the daily processions and prayers for the Queen's delivery, and on 3 August the court moved away to Oatlands in a tacit admission that Mary had given up hope. Elizabeth did not accompany them. According to Michiel, she was given permission to withdraw with all her attendants to a house distant three miles from her Majesty's. He added that she was not expected to return, 'as she is completely free'.[5] There had been more talk of sending her to Brussels but, when it was pointed out to the Emperor that any attempt to take the Princess Elizabeth out of the kingdom 'would certainly cause too great disturbance and most certain mischief', the plan was dropped without further comment.

Philip, however, was making definite preparations for his own departure. He had spent over a year in a country he disliked, among people who had not hesitated to slight him at every opportunity. He had been unfailingly kind and considerate to a wife more than ten years older than himself who did not attract him and could not produce an heir. He considered he had done as much as could reasonably be expected of him. Mary, having just come through the most appallingly humiliating experience any woman could suffer, now had to come to terms with the fact that the husband she adored with all the strength of her passionate, affection-starved nature, was determined to leave her. For a while she struggled against the inevitable, but Philip assured her patiently that he still loved her, explained that he had urgent business to attend to in his father's dominions and promised he would only be away for a few weeks. Mary had no alternative but to believe him and she gave in. He was to embark at Dover as soon as the escorting fleet was ready, and at the end of August the court went down to Greenwich to see him off. On the twenty-sixth, King and Queen rode in state through the City to Tower Wharf where 'they took their barge' to complete the journey by river. After all the conflicting rumours which had been flying about, many people believed Mary to be dead and, when she appeared now for the first time since her long retirement, the London crowds, whose unpredictability was the despair of all foreign observers, ran wild with joy at the sight of her.[6] Elizabeth was also bound for Greenwich but she had no part in the triumphal procession, making the trip entirely by water, according to de Noailles in a plain barge with only a few attendants. Philip left for Dover on 29 August but before he went, again according to de Noailles, he particularly commended Elizabeth to Mary's good will and was soon writing from the Low Countries to repeat what was virtually a command to handle her sister with kid gloves, as well as secretly leaving similar instructions with the Spaniards who remained in London.[7]

The Queen intended to stay at Greenwich until her husband's return, and Reginald Pole was given lodgings in the Palace, so that he might 'comfort and keep her company, her Majesty delighting greatly in the sight and presence of him'.[8] Elizabeth also stayed at Court, although it is doubtful whether her presence caused Mary any particular delight. Appearances, however, were being carefully kept up. The Queen, in deference to Philip's wishes, dutifully choked back her antipathy and treated her sister graciously in public, only conversing with her about 'agreeable subjects'. Elizabeth, too, was on her best behaviour. At Woodstock she had gone to confession and received 'the most comfortable Sacrament'. Now she attended Mass regularly with the Queen, and on 4 September joined in a three-day fast to qualify for indulgence from Rome. To the outward eye her Catholicism seemed beyond reproach – the time for doctrinal hair-splitting was long past – but many people, Simon Renard for one, remained unconvinced.

In spite of the Queen's laborious amiability, the atmosphere at Greenwich cannot have been very enlivening. Mary spent a good deal of her time weeping in corners, where she thought she was unobserved. Cardinal Pole treated Elizabeth with cold reserve, and the other members of the court were still a trifle wary of being seen too frequently in the Princess's company. In the circumstances, she probably took particular pleasure in renewing her acquaintance with one old friend. After a period of diplomatic service abroad, Master Roger Ascham was back in England. Being one of those Protestants who had found it prudent to conform to the new scheme of things, he now held the position of Latin Secretary to the Queen, and was able to resume his sessions with his old pupil. In September 1555 he wrote to his friend Sturm with all his old enthusiasm: 'The Lady Elizabeth and I read together in Greek the orations of Aeschines and Demosthenes on the Crown. She reads it first to me, and at first sight understands everything, not only the peculiarity of the language and the meaning of the orator, but all the struggles of that contest, the decrees of the people, the customs and manners of the city, in a way to strike you with astonishment.'[9]

Meanwhile, a dismal summer had turned into a dismal autumn. On 29 September 'was the greatest rain and floods that ever was seen in England'. Men and cattle were drowned. Worse still, 'cellars both of wine and beer and ale' in London and elsewhere were flooded out and a great deal of other valuable merchandise was lost.[10] October came in with no sign of Philip's return, and Mary had to leave Greenwich for St James's for the opening of Parliament. Elizabeth was given permission to go back to the country, and on 18 October she passed through the City on her way to Hatfield. The people turned out to give her a rousing send-off but, heartened though she always was by the evidence of her popularity, Elizabeth had no desire to give the Queen any unnecessary cause for offence and, according to de Noailles, she sent some of her gentlemen into the crowds 'to calm and restrain them'.[11]

Settled once more at Hatfield, she began to take up the threads of her old life. Katherine Ashley was back with her. So was Thomas Parry, and Roger Ascham came out to see her and read with her whenever he could get leave of absence. If it does not sound a particularly exhilarating programme for an energetic young woman of twenty-two, Elizabeth knew that time was on her side. She seems to have been perfectly content to wait, concentrating on keeping out of trouble and perhaps making a few tentative preparations for the future. Although no documentary proof has survived, it seems highly probable that she was now unobtrusively resuming her contacts with William Cecil. After all, he was still her Surveyor. Cecil, living quietly at his house in Wimbledon, was another of the prudent conformers and, although he held no office under Mary, the government had found itself obliged from time to time to make use of his services and experience on an *ad hoc* basis. Like the Princess, William Cecil had demonstrated a remarkable talent for survival. Like her, he was content to wait for better days.

All things considered, from Elizabeth's point of view, the situation looked a good deal brighter than it had done at the time of her previous retreat from court. She had made a powerful ally in Philip. Simon Renard was no longer dropping poison into Mary's ear – he had left England in September. But, in any case,

Renard was coming round to Philip's way of thinking in regard to Elizabeth. Another gap appeared in the ranks of her enemies that November with the death of Stephen Gardiner. Although 'wily Winchester' had, in fact, scarcely lived up to his title of 'bloody Bishop', luridly depicted by John Foxe as dedicated to hunting down the rightful heiress by fair means or foul, it is not likely that Elizabeth greatly regretted his departure from the scene. But, although 'some hope of comfort' was appearing 'as if out of a dark cloud', her troubles were not yet over. Indeed, as the winter wore on, the events of two years before began to repeat themselves with sinister exactitude.

Mary, left to struggle single-handed with a suspicious and refractory House of Commons, was making little headway. She was acutely short of money, but Parliament's normal reluctance to grant a subsidy was on this occasion not unnaturally exacerbated by the Queen's conscientious determination to relinquish that part of her income which derived from the first fruits and tenths of benefices appropriated by Henry VIII after the breach with Rome. A Bill directed against the English Protestant refugees abroad was defeated and Mary dared not even raise the project closest to her heart and Philip's – that his courtesy title of King should now be made a reality by coronation. But the Commons knew it was in her mind, and fears that this might prove a first step towards letting 'the absolute rule of the realm' pass into Philip's hands stiffened their generally unco-operative attitude. The members, too, remained preternaturally sensitive on the subject of Church property and Church revenues. The merest suggestion that any of this might be surrendered was enough to set alarm bells ringing, and Spanish and Popish influence was seen behind the most harmless measures. De Noailles was once more busily stirring the pot of suspicion and resentment; the only too evident weakness of the crown encouraged malcontents and hotheads; and by the early spring of 1556 the smell of conspiracy was once more in the air.

The Dudley plot as it became known, after one of its ringleaders, Henry Dudley, a distant connexion of the Duke of Northumberland, resembled Wyatt's in that its avowed intention was 'to send the Queen's Highness over to the King [but more likely to dispose of her in a more permanent fashion] and to make the Lady Elizabeth Queen and to marry the Earl of Devonshire to the said lady'.[12] Unlike the Wyatt rebellion, however, it relied heavily on French assistance and on the English *émigrés* being sheltered by the King of France. The Dudley conspirators, too, numbered a good many dubious characters – soldiers of fortune, restless exiles, unpaid royal officials and professional trouble-makers – who were moved less by genuine reasons of patriotism than by hopes of personal profit. Nevertheless, the movement was symptomatic of a deep-rooted and widespread discontent, and the fact that it came to nothing does not mean that the threat it represented was not real and immediate. Too many people were involved in the actual plot for it to remain a secret for long. One of its many ramifications was a scheme to raid the Exchequer where the Queen's hard-earned subsidy now reposed, and it was at this point that the first leak was sprung when, early in March, one Thomas White went to Cardinal Pole and told all he knew. The first arrests were made on 18 March, and as the Council began painfully to thread their way through a maze of confessions and depositions the names of Elizabeth's friends started to appear with ominous frequency. As for the Princess herself, the conspirators apparently regarded her hopefully as 'a jolly liberal dame, and nothing so unthankful as her sister'. Inevitably Elizabeth was the lodestone which drew 'the affections and wishes of the majority'. She was young and healthy. She would bear sons. Above all, she was an Englishwoman through and through. Inevitably, as Giovanni Michiel was later to remark, 'never is a conspiracy discovered in which either justly or unjustly she or some of her servants are not mentioned'.[13]

In April 1556 the Venetian picked up a report that there was a plan to send Elizabeth to Spain – a plan linked perhaps with the bizarre proposal originally put forward the previous autumn to marry her to Don Carlos, Philip's ten-year-old son by his first wife. Later in the month, Michiel heard that the idea of sending Elizabeth abroad was being 'earnestly canvassed' by the Queen in person, who, he wrote, 'conceives that by removing her bodily from hence, there will be a riddance of all the causes for scandal and disturbances'. He added that Elizabeth was saying plainly she would never marry, 'even were they to give her the King's son or find any other greater Prince'.[14]

So far there was no suggestion that the Princess was personally implicated in the Dudley conspiracy. It is true that in February, while the plot was still hatching, the Constable of France had sent a letter to de Noailles instructing him to be careful and 'above all, restrain Madame Elizabeth from stirring at all in the affair of which you have written to me; for that would be to ruin everything'.[15] Fortunately for Elizabeth this letter was not intercepted, but even if it had been it would not have been direct proof against her. The French, it seems, were still taking a good deal for granted where she was concerned.

All the same, the scent was beginning to lead the Council's bloodhounds uncomfortably close. Some time in May, Somerset House, still her London residence, was searched and a coffer full of seditious, anti-Catholic literature discovered. These were the tracts, ballads and broadsheets which continued to cause the government considerable annoyance, and their ownership was traced to no less a person than Katherine Ashley. Mistress Ashley, Elizabeth's Italian master Baptista Castiglione, Francis Verney (one of those gentlemen whose visits to The Bull at Woodstock had caused Bedingfield so much anxiety), and a fourth person were arrested for questioning. Katherine Ashley denied any knowledge of the conspiracy. Her mistress's feelings were such, she declared, that it would be as much as her place was worth to harbour any evil thoughts of the Queen. But all those 'writings and scandalous books' were apparently hers and the governess spent three months in the Fleet prison. She was once more dismissed from her post and ordered not to see Elizabeth again on her release. Castiglione seems to have cleared himself but Francis Verney was tried and convicted of treason, although subsequently pardoned.

It was the official attitude adopted towards Elizabeth herself which showed how much times had changed. Apart from the obvious danger of public disorder if any arbitrary action was taken against the Princess, Mary would not move without first consulting Philip. Michiel reported to the Doge on 2 June that a special courier had been hastily despatched to Brussels. 'It being credible', he wrote, 'that nothing is done, nor does anything take place, without having the King's opinion about it and hearing his will.'[16] It was presumably according to Philip's will that Sir Edward Hastings and Francis Englefield were sent to Hatfield bearing a kind message from the Queen, assuring her sister of her good will and using 'loving and gracious expressions, to show her that she is neither neglected nor hated, but loved and esteemed by her Majesty'. Michiel added significantly that this had been very well taken by the whole kingdom. The messengers were also instructed to condole with Elizabeth on the loss of her servants, but to point out that their arrest had been necessary in view of the licentious lives they were leading, 'especially in matters of religion'; and the fact that some of them were undoubtedly involved in the conspiracy was exposing her 'to the manifest risk of infamy and ruin'.[17]

The words were honeyed, but Mary did take the opportunity of reorganising the household at Hatfield. 'A widowed gentlewoman' was supplied in place of Mrs Ashley, and Sir Thomas Pope, 'a rich and grave gentleman of good name both for conduct and religion', installed as Governor. Although Sir Thomas himself 'did his utmost to decline such a charge', Elizabeth accepted him with good grace.[18] Thomas Pope was a very different proposition from Henry Bedingfield. For one thing, he was no stranger, having been a member of the household at Ashridge in 1554. He was also a witty, cultivated man, the founder of Trinity College, Oxford, and a pleasant companion whose presence would relieve her of responsibility.

Throughout the remainder of the summer, a hot dry one this year with a four-month drought, the aftermath of the Dudley plot continued to smoulder beneath the surface. In July a feeble attempt was made to stir up the dying embers when a Suffolk schoolmaster named Cleobury created some local disturbance by pretending to impersonate Edward Courtenay and proclaiming 'the Lady Elizabeth Queen and her beloved bedfellow, Lord Courtenay, King'. Thomas Pope was instructed to acquaint the Princess with 'the whole circumstance', so that 'it might appear how little these men stood at falsehood and untruth to compass their purpose and how for that intent they had abused her Grace's name'.[19] Elizabeth promptly improved on the occasion by writing to Mary in her most windy and high-flown style. 'When I revolve in mind (most noble Queen)', she began, 'the old love of paynims to their prince, and the reverent fear of Romans to their senate, I can but muse for my part, and blush for theirs, to see the rebellious hearts and devilish intents of Christians in name, but Jews in deed, toward their anointed king.' She ended by wishing 'that there were as good surgeons for making anatomies of hearts, that might show my thoughts to your Majesty, as there are expert physicians of the bodies. . . . For then, I doubt not, but know well, that whatsoever other should suggest by malice, yet your Majesty should be sure by knowledge; so that the more such misty clouds offuscate the clear light of my truth, the more my tried thoughts should glister to the dimming of their hidden malice.'[20] This choice specimen of her sister's epistolary art – a closely written page in Elizabeth's most elegant hand – can scarcely have failed to irritate Mary profoundly.

The Queen was enduring a miserable summer. She seldom appeared in public and trusted only a tiny handful of loyal Catholic councillors. As one of her frequent envoys to Brussels had told Philip the previous December, 'when she looks round and carefully considers the persons about her, she hardly knows one who has not injured her or who would fail to do so again, were the opportunity to present itself '.[21] Nicholas Heath, the new Lord Chancellor, was a poor substitute for Gardiner, and Mary was coming to lean more and more on Reginald Pole, the frail, middle-aged, idealistic scholar who had become Cardinal Archbishop of Canterbury in March. She yearned for Philip, but still there was no sign of his return. The old Emperor, preparing to bow off the stage and spend his last years in the monastery of Yuste, had now handed over all his burdens, save the Empire and Burgundy, to his son. Philip, as King of Spain, Naples and Sicily and Lord of the Netherlands, would have less time than ever to spare for England in the future. He was not pleased by his wife's failure to secure him the crown matrimonial and sent only promises – promises repeatedly and cynically broken – in reply to her self-abasing pleas that he should come back to her. Mary's last birthday had been her fortieth and, as the months passed, she could only rage and despair by turn while her stubborn hopes of bearing children were mocked by her husband's absence.

In September 1556 one of the anxieties shared by the Tudor sisters was removed by the death, in Padua, of Edward Courtenay. The disappearance of that sad, shadowy figure, chosen by popular acclaim to be Elizabeth's husband, was apparently a signal for Philip to renew his efforts to arrange her marriage to Philibert of Savoy. The Princess paid a visit to court that winter. On the twenty-eighth day of November, recorded Henry Machyn, 'my good lady Elizabeth's grace' came riding through Smithfield and

Old Bailey and on down Fleet Street to Somerset House, handsomely escorted by 'a great company of velvet coats and chains, her Grace's gentlemen' and upwards of two hundred horsemen wearing her own livery of red trimmed and slashed with black velvet.[22]

Her arrival caused a flurry of interest among the members of the diplomatic corps, all of whom were eager to find out whether Elizabeth was in town on business or pleasure. Giovanni Michiel heard that she had not been sent for, but had herself 'with great earnestness solicited to come'. She got, as usual, a rapturous welcome from the Londoners and although none of 'the Lords or gentlemen of the Court' had ventured to go out and meet her, many of them had since been to pay their respects at Somerset House.[23] Antoine de Noailles was no longer at the French embassy. After the Dudley fiasco England had become rather too hot for him and he had been replaced by his younger brother François, the Bishop of Acqs. The Bishop was longing to send a message to the Princess to enquire whether her patience was exhausted and if she had any plans for the following summer; but she was so closely surrounded that he hesitated to risk discovery which, he remarked, was only too probable with people who were incapable of concealing anything, and prudently decided to wait 'until God should give him a better opportunity'.[24]

Elizabeth duly went to see the Queen and was received, according to Michiel, 'very graciously and familiarly'. She even had an interview with Cardinal Pole – apparently the first time they had met, in spite of having been near neighbours at Greenwich for more than a month in 1555. Everything seemed to be going smoothly. Michiel planned to pay the Princess a courtesy visit, and it was generally thought that she would stay over the Christmas festivities. Then, on 3 December, less than a week after she had come to London, Elizabeth and her entourage were riding through the City again on their way back to Hatfield. The Venetian intelligence service was usually excellent but on this occasion Michiel had no comment to offer, except that the Lady Elizabeth departed so suddenly that he had had no time to call on her, and his visit would have to be reserved for another occasion.[25]

The solution of the mystery was to be provided by no less a person than the King of France, in a conversation some three weeks later with Giacomo Soranzo, Venetian ambassador to the

French Court. On being asked by Soranzo if he had any 'advices' from England, the King said he had been told that the Queen had sent for the Lady Elizabeth and proposed to marry her to the Duke of Savoy. The Princess had responded by bursting into floods of tears, saying that she had no wish for any husband and her afflictions were such that she only wanted to die. She wept so bitterly that tears came to Mary's own eyes, but all the same the interview had ended painfully. Faced with her sister's obduracy, the Queen had dismissed her from the court and 'purposed assembling Parliament to have her declared illegitimate and consequently incapable of succeeding to the crown'.[26]

Elizabeth's refusal to marry the Duke of Savoy is perfectly understandable. Naturally she would resist to the uttermost any attempt to tie her hands in this way before she ever came to the throne. Her aversion to the idea of marriage in general is also surely not very difficult to understand. All her life, ever since she had been a small child listening to her maids as they gossiped over their sewing, she had heard story after story and seen illustration after illustration of what women could be made to suffer at the hands of men: Mary's mother and her own; Jane Seymour, who had endured a labour lasting three days and two nights giving birth to the heir; even poor, dull Anne of Cleves, contemptuously rejected and condemned to a life of arid chastity, however full of creature comfort. There had been Katherine Howard's terrible end, and Katherine Parr betrayed by Tom Seymour and then killed bearing his child. If any further warning were needed, she had now before her eyes the dreadful example of how marriage was destroying Mary, a reigning queen. But Elizabeth had not forgotten the lessons she had learnt before she was sixteen; with that ice-cold brain and steely inner core of pride and self-knowledge to support her, she was to be able to say – and mean – that never would she trust her body or her soul to any man.

Nevertheless, the violence of her reaction on this particular occasion was uncharacteristic and a little surprising. If Michiel was right and Elizabeth had invited herself to court, it is possible that she had become a trifle overconfident and was taken off-balance by Mary's sudden, determined assault. But she must have known that the Queen, much as she wanted to please Philip, no longer had the power to force her into marriage or otherwise dispose of her against her will – the threat to disinherit her was

an empty one and both knew it. Elizabeth had so far successfully
evaded all matrimonial entanglements, and now that her position
was stronger than it had ever been she had only to stand firm and
keep her head to go on evading them. Were all those tears and
protestations just histrionics, or were they symptomatic of some
deeper emotional upheaval? If the French ambassador can be
regarded as a reliable witness, it appears that there was rather
more involved than yet another routine refusal to get married, for
according to the Bishop of Acqs a very curious incident indeed
took place during Elizabeth's visit to London. In a letter to a
friend, written in December 1570, the Bishop related how the
Countess of Sussex, who was attached to the Princess's household,
had come to see him twice, secretly and in disguise, to tell him
that Elizabeth's servants were urging her to extricate herself from
her problems by fleeing the country and had asked him if he could
arrange to get her across to France. The Bishop, however, so he
says, strongly advised against such a desperate course of action.
Elizabeth should remember and profit by her sister's example at
the time of Northumberland's attempt to deprive her of her
inheritance, and stay where she was whatever happened. When the
Countess came again, he said flatly that if the Princess ever hoped
to succeed to the throne she must on no account leave England.
He boasted, in fact, that by following his advice Elizabeth owed
her crown to him.[27]

If this astonishing story is true, and on the face of it there seems
little reason why François de Noailles should have gone to the
trouble fourteen years later of inventing such a circumstantial
account, it reveals Elizabeth in a state of very considerable emotional upheaval. Certainly in normal circumstances she would not
have needed anyone to tell her that flight, and to France of all
places, must inevitably have led to total disaster. Was it simply
that she had temporarily lost confidence in her own judgement
and her ability to deal with Mary? Or was she suffering from a
sudden, uncontrollable revulsion of feeling, now that the prize
which for so long had lain glittering before her as if at the end
of a dark, endless tunnel – the sort of prize one dreams of and
struggles for but yet somehow never quite believes in – was at
last becoming a reality? Perhaps some change in her ageing,
unhappy sister's appearance over the past year had brought it
home to Elizabeth, with a sudden blinding flash of realisation,

that quite soon now, possibly even within a matter of months, she would be Queen of England and just for a little while she was afraid. On the other hand, the whole hare-brained scheme may have been the invention of the Countess of Sussex who, un-deterred, went over to France, presumably to explore the situation on the spot, and was closely questioned by the Privy Council about her doings when she returned.[28] We are never likely to know for certain just what did lie behind this episode, but it is sobering to remember that Antoine de Noailles was not likely to have behaved in such a statesmanlike fashion as his brother apparently did, and Elizabeth might well have found the trap closed on her before she had had time to repent. In the event, she was able to go back to sanctuary at Hatfield and recover from whatever nervous crisis had overwhelmed her.

She was undoubtedly feeling the strain of her position as the *de facto* but so far officially unrecognised heiress-presumptive, and it is natural enough that she should have known moments of exhaustion and despair. Once, in later years, she was to refer briefly to that period of her life when she had been 'a second person'. She had tasted of the practices against her sister, she remarked enigmatically, and had herself been 'sought for divers ways'. In 1556 she was still assimilating the hard lessons of the world about her – the hardest and most important being that one who aspired to take, and keep, the highest place could not afford to give way to moments of human weakness, however natural. Fortunately for England and for herself, Elizabeth learnt that lesson and only on rare occasions was she tempted to forget it.

CHAPTER XIII

England's Elizabeth

IN March 1557 Mary's prayers were answered and Philip came back to England after an absence of nineteen months. The chief reason for his visit was to use his wife's devotion as a lever to force her reluctant countrymen into active embroilment in the perennial Franco-Spanish quarrel – just as the King of France and every other opponent of the Spanish marriage had always feared sooner or later that he would. Philip was also increasingly anxious to settle the question of Elizabeth's future. His sister, the Duchess of Parma, and his cousin, the Duchess of Lorraine, crossed the Channel with him, and the Venetian ambassador in France heard that 'the cause of their ladyships' going was that on their return they might bring with them "Madama" Elizabeth of England to give her for wife to the Duke of Savoy'.[1]

Philip succeeded in his first objective but, in spite of Mary's eager assistance and the fact that a considerable proportion of the Privy Council were accepting pensions from him, the task was not easy. He might even have failed if there had not been another particularly foolish attempt to disturb the Queen's peace that spring. Towards the end of April, Thomas Stafford – another of those disgruntled Englishmen who were being petted and paraded at the French court – together with a small force of the raff and scaff of the exiles collected with beat of drum off the back streets of Rouen, was landed from a French ship on the Yorkshire coast. Stafford, a scion of the noble House of Buckingham and descended of the old blood royal on both sides, seized the town of Scarborough and proceeded to issue an inflammatory proclamation. He and his companions had come, he said, 'with the aid and help of all true Englishmen, to deliver our country from all present peril, danger and bondage, whereunto it is like to be brought by the most devilish device of Mary, unrightful and unworthy Queen of England'. He accused the Queen of 'showing herself a whole Spaniard and no Englishwoman in loving Spaniards and hating

Englishmen' and raked up all the old bogeys about oppression by proud, vile and spiteful Spaniards.[2] But this time the cynical French policy of deliberately fomenting civil unrest and anti-Spanish feeling had overreached itself. Home-grown rebellions were one thing. Invasion – even by other Englishmen – was another. Local support for Stafford proved minimal and the whole silly affair was quickly put down by the Earl of Westmorland. It had caused a good deal of alarm in the North, however, as a sizeable French army was known to be quartered just over the border in Scotland and it undoubtedly smoothed Philip's path for him. On 7 June England declared war on France, and a month later Philip had gone. This time, as if she realised she would not see him again, Mary went with him to Dover down to the water's edge.

That other piece of business which the King had hoped to see concluded was making no progress and Elizabeth remained undisturbed. In April, the Bishop of Acqs had sent her a warning via the Marchioness of Northampton that there was a plan to take her to Flanders and marry her to Savoy. Elizabeth thanked him and sent a message in reply that she would rather die before either of these things should come to pass.[3] The visit of the two duchesses does not appear to have been a great success. The Queen did not take to them and, as far as we know, Elizabeth did not even meet them. At any rate, they had both returned home by the beginning of May. Philip, however, had not given up, and during the summer of 1557 he made another determined effort to get Elizabeth married to his friend and dependant Emmanuel Philibert, and recognised by the Queen as heir to the throne. Philip had long since resigned himself to the fact that Elizabeth would succeed her sister. She might be a doubtful quantity in many ways, but she was still infinitely preferable to Mary Queen of Scots; from Philip's point of view almost any successor would have been preferable to the King of France's daughter-in-law. He therefore sent his confessor, Francisco de Fresneda, to try again to persuade the Queen to push the marriage through without further delay, and if necessary without the consent of Parliament. De Fresneda had instructions to explain that it was for 'all the considerations both of religion and piety, and of the safety of the realms, and to prevent the evils which might occur were the Lady Elizabeth, seeing herself slighted, to choose . . . to take for her husband some individual who might convulse the whole kingdom into confusion'.[4]

But opposition to this sensible plan was by no means all on Elizabeth's, or Parliament's side, as de Fresneda soon discovered. According to a secret report relayed by one of the Venetian ambassadors, apparently on good authority: 'For many days during which the confessor treated this business, he found the Queen utterly averse to giving the Lady Elizabeth any hope of the succession, obstinately maintaining that she was neither her sister nor the daughter of the Queen's father, King Henry. Nor would she hear of favouring her, as she was born of an infamous woman, who had so greatly outraged the Queen her mother, and herself.'[5] Philip, naturally exasperated by his wife's behaviour, made his displeasure plain; but Mary, although miserable in the knowledge that she was alienating whatever affection he still felt for her, remained impervious to blackmail. In a long, anguished, self-exculpatory letter written about this time, she promised not to be stubborn or unreasonable; she would listen 'with a true and sincere heart' to any persons her husband thought fit to appoint to speak to her about the affair but, she added, 'that which my conscience holds, it has held for this four and twenty years'.[6] It was four and twenty years since Elizabeth's birth and, for all Mary's rationalisations and excuses, this apparently obscure phrase probably contains the nub of the matter. As little as Simon Renard did she believe in Elizabeth's conversion, but not even the argument that a Catholic husband would keep her sister in the fold could move her. Old wrongs cast long shadows and to Mary, now facing the ruin of all her hopes, the bitter past was as real as the bitter present. Once she had acknowledged Elizabeth as her legitimate successor, she would have publicly admitted that Anne Boleyn and her daughter had won. Not even for Philip, not even for the Church, could Catherine of Aragon's daughter bring herself to do that.

Philip was busy with the war and once again the question of Elizabeth's future had to be shelved. Giovanni Michiel left England early in 1557, but in his final report he included a detailed account of the Princess on whom the eyes of all Europe were now turning. 'My Lady Elizabeth', he wrote,

is a young woman whose mind is considered no less excellent than her person, although her face is comely rather than handsome, but she is tall and well formed, with a good skin, although sallow. She has fine eyes and above all a beautiful hand of which she makes a display; and her intellect and understanding are wonderful, as she showed very plainly by her conduct when in danger and under suspicion. As a linguist she excels the Queen, for besides Latin she has no slight knowledge of Greek, and speaks Italian more than the Queen does, taking so much pleasure in it that from vanity she will never speak any other language with Italians. She is proud and haughty, as although she knows that she was born of such a mother, she nevertheless does not consider herself of inferior degree to the Queen, whom she equals in self-esteem. . . . She prides herself on her father and glories in him; everybody saying that she also resembles him more than the Queen does.[7]

Elizabeth was still making do on the income of £3000 a year as provided by her father's Will, but this was no longer really adequate for her needs. Michiel remarked that she was always in debt, and would have been much more so had she not been careful to keep the numbers of her household within bounds. This was not easy, since there was scarcely a lord or gentleman in the kingdom who had not tried to enter her service or place a son or brother in it, 'such being the love and affection borne her'. However, went on the ambassador, 'when requested to take servants she always excuses herself on account of the straits and poverty in which she is kept, and by this astute and judicious apology she adroitly incites a tacit compassion for herself and consequently yet greater affection, as it seems strange and vexatious to everybody that being the daughter of a King she should be treated and acknowledged so sparingly.'[8]

Elizabeth might not hesitate to turn her straitened circumstances to good account but, in fact, even if their relationship had been different, there was not much that Mary could have done to help her. The crown itself was frighteningly short of money and, although this was not really the Queen's fault, the military adventure she had now embarked on had added an additional burden which the country was ill-equipped to carry. The war in France had begun well with an Anglo-Spanish victory at St Quentin, but then the tide turned, and 1558 opened with disaster. On 10 January came the news that Calais had fallen 'the which was the heaviest tidings to London and to England that ever was heard of '. The town of Calais and the Pale, some 120 square miles of French territory, although no longer of any very great strategic importance, represented the last outpost of England's cross-Channel empire and possessed considerable sentimental value – recalling as it did the glorious days of Crécy and Agincourt, of the Black Prince and King Harry V. Its loss was a national humiliation on a grand scale.

For Mary it was to be followed by yet another personal grief. During the Christmas holidays, with a dreadful pathos which still comes raw and shocking across the centuries, she had told Philip that she was pregnant again, having kept the news a secret for nearly seven months 'in order to be quite sure of the fact, lest the like should happen as last time'.[9] Did she really believe it, or was it just a final desperate attempt to bring her husband back to her? It did not bring him but Count de Feria was despatched to England, ostensibly bearing congratulations but more likely to find out if there was, in fact, any possibility of another pregnancy. There was not, as de Feria presently reported.

Elizabeth paid a short visit to London at the end of February 'with a great company of lords and noblemen and noblewomen'. In all probability this was the last occasion on which she appeared in public before her accession and the last time she saw her sister.[10] De Feria wondered whether he should go to see her while she was in town, but decided against it for fear of upsetting the Queen and having been given no definite instructions on the matter.[11]

There was a brief flare-up on the matrimonial front in April, when the Protestant King of Sweden sent an ambassador to propose a marriage between Elizabeth and his eldest son, Eric. Gustavus Vasa, however, so far forgot the proprieties as to address himself directly to the Princess without first observing the formality of asking the Queen's permission – a social gaffe which gave Elizabeth all the excuse she needed for sending the envoy about his business. When news of this affair reached Mary she worked herself into a state of violent agitation, apparently fearing that Philip would blame her for having allowed such an unsuitable proposal even to be suggested, and that he might make it the occasion for renewing his pressure on her to come to a decision about her sister. Sir Thomas Pope was ordered to speak to Elizabeth to try and discover from her own lips what her attitude to the Swedes really was, and also if she had any plans about marriage in general. Elizabeth reiterated her settled preference for a spinster's life, and with regard to the Swedish offer declared that she had liked both the message and the messenger so well that she hoped never to hear of either of them again. Thomas Pope, probing a little further, ventured to remark that he thought 'few or none would believe but her Grace would be right well contented to marry, so there were some honourable marriage offered her by the Queen's highness, or with her Majesty's consent'. He got nothing out of Elizabeth, however, beyond the calm reply: 'What I shall do hereafter I know not, but I assure you, upon my truth and fidelity, and as God be merciful unto me, I am not at this time otherwise minded than I have declared unto you. No, though I were offered the greatest prince in all Europe.' Sir Thomas, of course, did not take her seriously for a moment. As he commented in his report, 'the Queen's majesty may conceive this rather to proceed of a maidenly shamefacedness, than upon any such certain determination'.[12] It is unlikely that Mary believed in Elizabeth's expressed determination to stay single any more than Thomas Pope did, but after hearing from Hatfield de Feria was able to tell Philip that the Queen had calmed down, although she was still taking a passionate interest in the affair.[13]

De Feria remained in England for several months charged with the thankless task of trying to wring further supplies of men and money for the French war out of an obstructive and apathetic Privy Council. He did, however, make the journey into Hertfordshire to see Elizabeth in June, and the encounter was apparently satisfactory to both parties.[14]

It was a restless, uneasy summer. The sense of great changes impending rumbled in the air like distant thunder and every man's mind was 'travailed with a strange confusion of conceits, all things being immoderately either dreaded or desired'. The Queen was now a very sick woman. She could not sleep and suffered from long, stupent fits of melancholy and a 'superfluity of black bile'. Early in September she had a high fever, a new symptom for her, although the doctors maintained there was no cause for alarm.[15] But as the autumn approached excitement mounted. Rumour ran riot and 'every report was greedily both inquired and received, all truths suspected, diverse tales believed, many improbable conjectures hatched and nourished'.[16] The English people had suffered, more or less patiently, a decade of weak, factious government, internal dissension and bad housekeeping. Above all now they wanted peace, stability and the sort of leadership which would enable them to get on with their own concerns, undistracted by fear of strangers without or civil strife within. After their current experience of that unnatural phenomenon, a woman ruler, considerable uncertainty prevailed in some circles as to whether 'the succeeding Prince' would be able to give them that stability. In the words of the historian John Hayward, 'the rich were fearful, the wise careful, the honestly-disposed doubtful, the discontented and desperate, and all such whose desires were both immoderate and evil, joyful, as wishing trouble, the gate of spoil'. The inarticulate masses, though, just waited stoically and longed for 'their Elizabeth'.

Elizabeth was ready now, receiving visitors and quietly completing her preparations. There were no more nerve storms, no more fears or hesitations. During these last two years of comparative tranquillity she had been able to recover from the stress and strain of her teens and early twenties; to digest the experiences of that hectic period; to mature and develop. By the late summer of 1558 all her astonishing faculties were tuned to concert pitch and she stood in the wings, waiting composedly for her cue to step out into the dazzle of the spotlight and take her place upon the stage. Her twenty-fifth birthday came and went. The trees in Hatfield Park turned to red and yellow, and at St James's Palace Mary's life was drawing to its close.

By 22 October the news reaching Philip in Flanders had become sufficiently serious for him to send de Feria back to England 'to serve the Queen during her illness'. The Venetians heard that the Count's mission was to make a last-minute attempt to get Elizabeth suitably married and induce the Queen 'to give her the hope of succeeding to the Crown'. De Feria reached London on 9 November, but his instructions were already out of date and he was received, so he said, 'as a man who came accredited with the Bulls of a dead Pope'. Three days earlier the Privy Council, taking advantage of one of Mary's more lucid intervals, had spoken to her 'with a view to persuading her to make certain declarations in favour of the Lady Elizabeth concerning the succession'. Mary was too tired to struggle any longer, and on the day before de Feria's arrival the Comptroller and the Master of the Rolls had gone down to Hatfield to inform Elizabeth that the Queen was willing she should succeed in the event of her own death, but asked two things of her; that she would maintain the old religion as Mary had restored it and pay the Queen's debts.[17]

Realising that there was nothing more to be done at St James's, de Feria lost no time in joining the throng of courtiers already taking the Hatfield road. Elizabeth received him well, but not quite so cordially as she had done before. However, she invited him to supper and seemed pleased to see him. She went on to speak of her gratitude for Philip's good offices in the past and for his assurances of continued friendship. But when the ambassador, not very tactfully, began to indicate that she owed the recognition of her claim not to the Queen or the Council but to Philip, Elizabeth pulled him up sharply. She expressed considerable indignation at the treatment she had endured during her sister's reign and declared that she owed her crown not to Philip or even to the nobility 'but to the attachment of the people of England, to whom she seemed much devoted'. De Feria proceeded to offer much the same sort of advice about caution and moderation as Renard had once given Mary but, although Elizabeth remained perfectly amiable, discussed several of the Councillors with him, and even laughed with him about the idea of her marrying the Earl of Arundel, she gave little away and de Feria was left with an uneasy suspicion that she meant to be governed by no one. She was very vain, he reported, very acute and clearly an enthusiastic admirer of her father's methods and policies. He was afraid she would be unreliable on religious matters, for she appeared to favour those councillors who were suspected of heresy and he was told that all her ladies were similarly inclined. In fact, remarked de Feria bitterly, there was not a traitor or heretic in the country who had not risen, as if from the tomb, to welcome her accession.[18]

The Queen died at six o'clock in the morning of Thursday, 17 November, and later that same day, closing a chapter with unusual tidiness, the Cardinal of England, Reginald Pole, died too at Lambeth. There was little pretence of public mourning, and it is not likely that Elizabeth felt any personal grief for her sister. In spite of some sentimental stories that there had been a reconciliation between them during the last months of Mary's life, all the reports of the diplomatic observers indicate that they continued to dislike each other to the end, and really there was no reason why it should have been otherwise. A deputation led by that serviceable pair, the Earls of Pembroke and Arundel, brought the news to Hatfield, and Elizabeth is said to have fallen on her knees, exclaiming: 'A Domino factum est illud et est mirabile in oculis nostris!'[19] That afternoon the citizens of London rang the church bells 'and at night did make bonfires and set tables in the streets, and did eat and drink and make merry for the new Queen Elizabeth'.[20] Holinshed's Chronicle, admittedly with the benefit of hindsight, waxes lyrical on the subject of the accession.

> After all the stormy, tempestuous and blustering windy weather of Queen Mary was overblown, the darksome clouds of discomfort dispersed, the palpable fogs and mists of most intolerable misery consumed, and the dashing showers of persecution overpast; it pleased God to send England a calm and quiet season, a clear and lovely sunshine, a quietus from former broils . . . and a world of blessings by good Queen Elizabeth.

The transition to the new reign had been accomplished with remarkable smoothness. Mary notwithstanding, Elizabeth had long been generally accepted as the heir, but she had taken certain precautions and would have been ready to fight for her throne if necessary. Fortunately there was no need. In some ways she had been lucky. The death of Reginald Pole was, of course, an unexpected advantage, but after the disastrous humiliation of the French war there were few Englishmen ready to contemplate inviting Mary Stuart across the Channel and there was no other obvious alternative to whom the Catholics might have rallied. All the same the change-over was facilitated by the statesmanlike behaviour of the Lord Chancellor, Nicholas Heath. Parliament was then in session and, on the morning of 17 November, Heath sent for the Speaker and 'the knights and burgesses of the nether house' to come immediately to the Lords. He proceeded to announce the news of Mary's death and went on:

> Which hap as it is most heavy and grievous unto us, so have we no less cause another way to rejoice with praise to Almighty God for that He hath left unto us a true, lawful and right inheritrice to the crown of this realm, which is the Lady Elizabeth, of whose lawful right and title we need not to doubt. Wherefore the lords of this

house have determined with your assents and consents, to pass from
hence into the palace, and there to proclaim the said Lady Elizabeth
Queen of this realm without further tract of time.[21]

There were no dissenting voices and the Chancellor, by his
prompt action, had not only ensured Elizabeth's solemn recognition by Parliament before it was automatically dissolved by the
death of the reigning monarch; but, as himself a leading Catholic,
had secured the loyalty of any doubtful members of his party for
the new sovereign.

Elizabeth spent the next few days holding court at Hatfield and
consolidating her position. Nicholas Throckmorton, who had
achieved the distinction of being acquitted of treason shortly after
the Wyatt rebellion, had sent a long memorandum of advice to
the new Queen in which he counselled her to move warily at first,
so that neither 'the old or the new should wholly understand
what you mean'. It was the sort of advice which Elizabeth was
superbly equipped to follow. On 20 November she held her first
Council meeting, and William Cecil was sworn in as Principal
Secretary of State. Thus virtually the first act of the reign was to
inaugurate a partnership which was to last for forty years, and
must surely count as the most famous and successful in English
history. Elizabeth's words to her old friend and new Secretary on
that auspicious occasion are well known but still bear repeating.
'I give you this charge', she said,

> that you shall be of my Privy Council and content to take pains for
> me and my realm. This judgment I have of you that you will not be
> corrupted by any manner of gift and that you will be faithful to the
> state; and that without respect of my private will you will give me
> that counsel which you think best and if you shall know anything
> necessary to be declared to me of secrecy, you shall show it to myself
> only. And assure yourself I will not fail to keep taciturnity therein
> and therefore herewith I charge you.[22]

Other old friends were remembered during that exciting week.
Fat Thomas Parry was knighted, given the post of Controller of
the Household and made a member of the Privy Council. Kate
Ashley became chief Lady of the Bedchamber, and her husband
Keeper of the Jewel House. Robert Dudley was created Master

of the Horse, a position which entailed close attendance on the Queen.

On 23 November Elizabeth set out for London where she stayed at the Charterhouse; 'in which removing and coming thus to the City, it might well appear how comfortable her presence was to them that went to receive her on the way and likewise to the great multitudes of people that came abroad to see her Grace'.[2] Five days later, on Monday, 28 November, the Queen, wearing purple velvet with a scarf about her neck, the trumpets blowing before her and 'all the heralds in array', rode in procession to the Tower, while the City literally exploded with joy all around her.[24] The entry into the Tower can scarcely have failed to be a highly charged moment for the Queen, and for her Master of the Horse riding close behind her. Elizabeth summed up the situation with masterly simplicity, saying to those about her: 'Some have fallen from being Princes of this land to be prisoners in this place; I am raised from being prisoner in this place to be Prince of this land. That dejection was a work of God's justice; this advancement is a work of His mercy.'[25]

She remained in residence at the great fortress palace for nearly ten days, still feeling her way, holding Council meetings and taking the first cautious steps in the mystery of her craft. In spite of the general atmosphere of optimism and rejoicing, few English monarchs have ever had to contend with so many dangers and difficulties in the first few months of their reigns. Armagil Waad, Clerk of the Council under Edward, had drawn up a succinct list of some of the most pressing problems facing the new administration:

The Queen poor, the realm exhausted, the nobility poor and decayed. Want of good captains and soldiers. The people out of order. Justice not executed. All things dear. Excess in meat, drink and apparel. Divisions among ourselves. Wars with France and Scotland. The French king bestriding the realm, having one foot in Calais and the other in Scotland. Steadfast enmity but no steadfast friendship abroad.[26]

On the political front at home the religious question loomed large and threatening. Already 'the wolves were coming out of Geneva' as the Marian exiles prepared to return home eager to build the new Jerusalem. On this especially sensitive issue Elizabeth was moving with especial care, but it was obvious that a new settlement would have to be worked out as soon as possible. The Protestants, who regarded her as their saviour, the 'new star' which the Lord had caused to arise, and who had supported her in her darkest days, could not be disappointed now; but her Catholic subjects must not be driven to desperation and neither must the Catholic powers of Europe be too deeply offended. Abroad, the barometer pointed to storm. Young Mary of Scotland was openly quartering the royal arms of England on her shield and once those two colossi, Philip II of Spain and Henri II of France, had settled their differences, which they were now in the process of doing, it seemed only too likely that they would proceed to dismember England between them at their leisure. All over Europe bets were being laid that the new Queen of England would not keep her rickety throne for six months.

If the new Queen of England was at all daunted by the prospect before her, she certainly did not show it. The Court moved to Whitehall for Christmas and was apparently given over to merry-making. De Feria, who was becoming progressively more dis-enchanted with the new régime, had told Philip in November that Elizabeth was 'very much wedded to the people and thinks as they do, and therefore treats foreigners slightingly'. In December he was complaining querulously:

It gives me great trouble every time I write to your Majesty not to be able to send more pleasing intelligence, but what can be expected from a country governed by a Queen, and she a young lass who, although sharp, is without prudence and is every day standing up against religion more openly? The kingdom is entirely in the hands of young folks, heretics and traitors, and the Queen does not favour a single man whom her Majesty who is now in heaven would have received.[27]

But however much de Feria might regret the lowered moral and social tone of the court, he was obliged to admit that Elizabeth seemed 'incomparably more feared than her sister, and gives her orders and has her way as absolutely as her father did'.

Already the Queen was giving clear promise of her matchless abilities as a ruler, and already she was capturing the devotion of her subjects. The warmth and spontaneity of the welcome she had received, even from those 'whose fortunes were unlike either to be amended or impaired by change', had exceeded her expectations and during those early weeks she worked singlemindedly to foster and promote that love affair with the English people which was to be such a great source of her strength. 'If ever any person had either the gift or the style to win the hearts of people', wrote John Hayward,

> it was this Queen; and if ever she did express the same, it was at that present, in coupling mildness with majesty as she did, and in stately stooping to the meanest sort. All her faculties were in motion, and every motion seemed a well guided action; her eye was set upon one, her ear listened to another, her judgment ran upon a third, to a fourth she addressed her speech; her spirit seemed to be everywhere, and yet so entire in herself, as it seemed to be nowhere else. Some she pitied, some she commended, some she thanked, at others she pleasantly and wittily jested, contemning no person, neglecting no office; and distributing her smiles, looks and graces so artificially, that thereupon the people again redoubled the testimonies of their joys; and afterwards, raising everything to the highest strain, filled the ears of all men with immoderate extolling their Prince.[28]

In one sense, the consummation of the marriage between Queen and people can be said to have taken place at her coronation procession; in another, it only marked the beginning of the continuing drama to be played out on both sides for nearly half-a-century. On 12 January 1559 Elizabeth went by river from Whitehall to the Tower – not quite five years since the last time she had made that particular journey. Now, as she was rowed downstream, surrounded by her court and attended by the Lord Mayor and aldermen and all the crafts of the City in barges decorated with streamers and banners of their arms, the spectacle reminded an Italian observer of Ascension Day at Venice, when the Signory went out to espouse the sea.[29] To the crowds lining the river banks and clinging perilously to every vantage point on London Bridge, it was the living embodiment of a fairy tale, the perfect illustration of a moral – of virtue rewarded, the Cinderella princess coming to her own.

Two days later, on Saturday 14 January, at two o'clock in the afternoon, the Queen mounted an open litter trimmed to the ground with gold brocade and her great cavalcade, 'richly furnished and most honourably accompanied, as well with gentlemen, barons and other the nobility of this realm as also with a notable train of goodly and beautiful ladies', set off from the Tower to make the recognition procession through the City. No one looking at the jewels and gold collars, at the cloth of gold and crimson velvet, at the Queen herself, 'dressed in a royal robe of very rich cloth of gold with a double-raised stiff pile', would have guessed that the Treasury was empty, that there was a huge foreign debt and that Sir Thomas Gresham was already in Antwerp raising further loans on his country's virtually non-existent credit. These uncomfortable facts were not allowed to obtrude. Elizabeth, like her father and grandfather knew when it paid to put on a splendid show, and now if ever was the time to dazzle friend and enemy alike.

It was a cold day with flurries of snow in the air and muddy underfoot, but no such minor discomforts as wet feet could spoil the unalloyed success of the occasion. Everywhere the Queen was greeted with 'prayers, wishes, welcomings, cries, tender words and all other signs which argued a wonderful earnest love of most obedient subjects towards their sovereign'. And Elizabeth responded 'by holding up her hands and merry countenance to such as stood far off, and by most tender and gentle language to those that stood nigh unto her Grace, did declare herself no less thankfully to receive her people's good will than they lovingly offered it unto her'. All along the route, at Fenchurch Street and Gracious Street, Cornhill and Cheapside, St Paul's, Fleet Street and Temple Bar, there were pageants, presentations and loyal orations in Latin and English. Even Anne Boleyn had been rehabilitated, and in a tableau representing the Queen's lineage was placed next to Henry VIII 'apparelled with sceptre and diadem'. Everywhere Elizabeth had an appropriate word of thanks and appreciation. Her reply to the Recorder of London, who offered her a purse of crimson satin richly wrought with gold and containing a thousand gold marks, was considered especially pithy. 'Whereas your request is that I should continue your good lady and Queen', she said, 'be ye assured that I will be as good unto you as ever Queen was to her people. No will in me can lack, neither do I trust shall there lack any power. And persuade yourselves, that for the safety and quietness of you all, I will not spare if need be to spend my blood.'

No incident was too small for her comment and attention. 'About the nether end of Cornhill' an old man who turned his head away and wept was pointed out to her, but Elizabeth was not dismayed and exclaimed, 'I warrant you it is for gladness.' In Cheapside she was seen to smile 'for that she heard one say "Remember old King Henry the eight"'. 'How many nosegays did Her Grace receive at poor women's hands?' demanded Holinshed's Chronicle rhetorically. 'How oftentimes stayed she her chariot when she saw any simple body offer to speak to her Grace?' She kept a branch of rosemary, given to her with a supplication by a poor woman at the Fleet Bridge, in her litter all the way to Westminster, 'not without the marvellous wondering of such as knew the presenter and noted the Queen's most gracious receiving and keeping the same'.

As well as her gentle condescension to the 'base and low', it was noted with approval that the Queen showed no signs of forgetting her debt to the Almighty, who had 'so wonderfully placed her in the seat of government'. When she was presented with an English Bible at the little conduit in Cheapside, she took it in both hands, kissed it and laid it upon her breast 'to the great comfort of the lookers on', who felt that God would undoubtedly preserve a princess who took her beginning so reverently.[30] Temple Bar had been decorated with images of the giants Gog and Magog and there the City which, 'without any foreign person, of itself beautified itself' and had spared no expense in the process, reluctantly parted with the resplendent golden figure of the Queen. And so, as the short winter day closed in, borne along on the great warm wave-crest of her subjects' joyful approbation England's Elizabeth came home to Westminster by torchlight for her crowning.

If one were to try to draw up a balance sheet of all the qualities Elizabeth owed to her progenitors, one might say she inherited her fine eyes, rather sallow complexion, sharp features and sharp tongue from her mother; together with Anne Boleyn's considerable ability as an actress, her bourgeois determination to drive a hard bargain and her hysterical tendencies. From her father, with his strong Plantagenet streak, came the red gold hair, physical energy, family pride, self-confidence, vanity, personal magnetism and sure political instinct. From her grandfather, that wise and prudent prince who in some ways she resembled most of all, came the cold, calculating brain, shrewdness in statecraft, opportunism and exact knowledge of the value of money – not to mention an unswerving resolution to hold on to her sceptre against all comers. Perhaps, too, beneath it all, there was an element of the earthy, peasant cunning of those Welsh hill farmers from whom had sprung the seneschal to the rulers of Gwynedd.

How much did she owe to all the varied men and women who had filled the crowded canvas of her girlhood? A store of memories and twenty-five years of experience from which she had learnt discretion, self-discipline, patience and self-reliance; to know herself and her fellows and a strong distaste for the practice of making windows into men's souls. But whatever Elizabeth Tudor drew from her ancestry and her background, she had a magic that was all her own which made her the steely, subtle, enigmatic genius, the Faerie Queen who enthralled, baffled and infuriated her contemporaries for forty-five years and has en-thralled, baffled and infuriated every enquirer for four centuries since. Even those among her contemporaries who knew her best never really understood her. Perhaps Robert Cecil came nearest the mark when he said of the Queen that she 'was more than a man, and (in troth) sometimes less than a woman'. And yet Gloriana always knew exactly how to use her femininity to disarm criticism and whistle justly irritated councillors back into puzzled subjection. She kept her secret then. She keeps it now, and is likely to go on keeping it for all time. The one thing that can be said of her with absolute certainty is that she loved England and England's people with a deep, abiding, selfless love. When de Feria remarked that she seemed 'wedded to the people' he spoke no more than the literal truth, and it is one of the happy accidents of history that she and they came together at exactly the right moment for them both.

Notes

ABBREVIATIONS

A.P.C.	*Acts of the Privy Council*, ed. J. R. Dasent
Ascham, *Works*	*The Whole Works of Roger Ascham*, ed. Rev. Dr Giles
Bedingfield, *Papers*	Henry Bedingfield, *Papers*, ed. C. R. Manning
Chron. Greyfriars	*Chronicle of the Greyfriars*, ed. J. G. Nichols
Chron. Henry VIII	*Chronicle of King Henry VIII of England*, trans. and ed. Martin A. S. Hume
Chron. Queen Jane	*Chronicle of Queen Jane and Two Years of Queen Mary*, ed. J. G. Nichols
C.S.P. Dom.	*Calendar of State Papers*, Domestic, ed. Robert Lemon
C.S.P. Span.	*Calendar of State Papers*, Spanish, ed. Gayangos, Hume and Tyler
C.S.P. Span. Eliz.	*Calendar of State Papers*, Spanish, Elizabeth, ed. Hume
C.S.P. Ven.	*Calendar of State Papers*, Venetian, ed. Rawdon Brown
Foxe	John Foxe, *Acts and Monuments*, ed. Cattley and Townsend
Hall	Edward Hall, *Chronicle*, ed. Sir Henry Ellis
Haynes	Lord Burghley, *State Papers*, ed. Samuel Haynes
Hayward, *Annals*	John Hayward, *Annals of the First Four Years of the Reign of Queen Elizabeth*, ed. John Bruce
Hayward, *Life of Edward VI*	John Hayward, *The Life of Edward VI*
Hearne, *Sylloge*	Thomas Hearne, *Sylloge Epistolarum*
Holinshed	Rafael Holinshed, *Chronicles*
L. & P.	*Letters and Papers, Foreign and Domestic, of the Reign of Henry VIII*, ed. Brewer, Gairdner and Brodie
Machyn, *Diary*	Henry Machyn, *Diary*, ed. J. G. Nichols

MacNalty, *Elizabeth Tudor*	Sir A. S. MacNalty, *Elizabeth Tudor – The Lonely Queen*
MacNalty, *Henry VIII*	Sir A. S. MacNalty, *Henry VIII – A Difficult Patient*
S.P. Dom.	State Papers, Domestic
S.P. Henry VIII	*State Papers*, Henry VIII, vol. I
Strickland, *Lives*	Agnes Strickland, *Lives of the Queens of England*
Strype, *Aylmer*	John Strype, *Life of John Aylmer*
Strype, *Memorials*	John Strype, *Ecclesiastical Memorials*
Tytler	P. F. Tytler, *England under the Reigns of Edward VI and Mary*
Vergil	Polydore Vergil, *English History Comprising the Reigns of Henry VI, Edward IV and Richard III*, ed. Ellis
Wriothesley	Charles Wriothesley, *A Chronicle of England during the Reigns of the Tudors*, ed. William D. Hamilton

PROLOGUE

1. Hall
2. *Chron. Henry VIII*
3. Wriothesley

CHAPTER I. A GENTLEMAN OF WALES

[1] D. Williams, 'The Family of Henry VII', *History Today*, vol. IV (1954).

[2] Sir Thomas Artemus Jones, 'Owen Tudor's Marriage', *Bulletin of the Board of Celtic Studies*, vol. XI (1943).

[3] *Proceedings and Ordinances of the Privy Council*, ed. N. H. Nicolas, vol. V (1835).

[4] *Chronicle of London*, ed. N. H. Nicolas (1827).

[5] T. Rymer, *Foedera*, vol. X (1704).

[6] *William Gregory's Chronicle*, ed. J. Gairdner (1876).

[7] Vergil, ed. Ellis.

[8] John Stow, *Annals* ed. E. Howes (1631).

[9] Vergil.

[10] Vergil.

[11] Vergil.

[12] Hall.

CHAPTER II. THE KING'S GREAT MATTER

[1] *Epistles of Erasmus*, ed. F. M. Nichols (1901).

[2] Sebastian Giustinian, *Four Years at the Court of Henry VIII*, trans. and ed. R. Brown (1854) vol. 1.

[3] R. W. Chambers, *Thomas More* (1935).

[4] *Four Years at the Court of Henry VIII*, vol. 2.

[5] *L. & P.*, vol. 2, pt 1 (1113).

[6] Hall.

[7] W. Roper, *Life of Sir Thomas More*, ed. D. P. Harding (1935).

[8] G. Mattingly, *Catherine of Aragon* (1942).

[9] G. Cavendish, *Life and Death of Cardinal Wolsey*, ed. R. S. Sylvester (1959).

[10] *C.S.P. Ven.*, vol. IV (824).

[11] Cavendish, *Life and Death of Cardinal Wolsey*.

[12] Hall.

[13] *C.S.P. Span.*, vol. IV, pt 1.

CHAPTER III. 'AN INCREDIBLE FIERCE DESIRE TO EAT APPLES'

[1] H. F. M. Prescott, *Mary Tudor* (1952). See also P. Friedmann, *Anne Boleyn* (1884).

[2] *S.P. Henry VIII*, vol. 1 (1830).

[3] *C.S.P. Span.*, vol. IV, pt 2.

[4] State Papers.

[5] *Chron. Henry VIII*.

[6] *C.S.P. Span.*, vol. IV, pt 2.

[7] *C.S.P. Span.*

[8] State Papers.

[9] Ibid.

[10] *C.S.P. Span.*, vol. IV, pt 2.

[11] Wriothesley.

[12] *C.S.P. Span.*, vol. IV, pt 2.

[13] Hall.

[14] *C.S.P. Span.*, vol. IV, pt 2.

[15] *L. & P.*, vol. VI.

[16] Ibid., vol. VI.

[17] Ibid., vol. VI.

[18] *C.S.P. Span.*, vol. IV, pt 2.

[19] State Papers.

[20] *C.S.P. Span.*, vol. IV, pt 2.

[21] Wriothesley.

[22] *L. & P.*, vol. VII (509).

[23] *C.S.P. Span.*, vol. V, pt 1.

[24] State Papers. See also *L. & P.*, vol. IX (568).

[25] *C.S.P. Span.*, vol. V, pt 1.

CHAPTER IV. 'ANNE SANS TÊTE'

[1] Wriothesley.

[2] *L. & P.*, vol. X.

[3] Ibid., vol. X.

[4] Hall.

[5] Wriothesley.

[6] *L. & P.*, vol. X.

[7] Ibid., vol. X.

[8] Ibid., vol. X.

[9] Ibid., vol. X.

[10] Ibid., vol. X.

[11] Ibid., vol. x.
[12] C.S.P. Span., vol. v, pt 2.
[13] L. & P., vol. x.
[14] Chron. Henry VIII.
[15] C.S.P. Span., vol. v, pt 2.
[16] Wriothesley.
[17] Hearne, Sylloge.

[18] Ibid.
[19] Ibid.
[20] Wriothesley.
[21] C.S.P. Span., vol. v, pt 2.
[22] L. & P., vol. xi.
[23] Ibid., vol. xi.

CHAPTER V. 'THE KING'S DAUGHTER'

[1] C.S.P. Span., vol. v, pt 2.
[2] Hearne, Sylloge.
[3] L. & P., vol. xi.
[4] Wriothesley.
[5] L. & P., vol. xii, pt 2.
[6] Ibid., vol. xi.
[7] Hearne, Sylloge.
[8] L. & P., vol. xiv, pt 2.
[9] Ibid., vol. xv.
[10] Ibid., vol. xvi.
[11] T. Heywood, England's Eliza-

beth, Harleian Miscellany (1813).
[12] Ibid.
[13] Letters of Queen Elizabeth, ed. G. B. Harrison (1935).
[14] J. J. Scarisbrick, Henry VIII (1968) p. 485 and n. See also MacNalty, Henry VIII.
[15] F. A. Mumby, Girlhood of Queen Elizabeth (1909).

CHAPTER VI. ELIZABETH'S ADMIRAL

[1] Tytler.
[2] A.P.C., vol. 2.
[3] L. & P., vol. xvi.
[4] Hearne, Sylloge.
[5] Ibid.
[6] Strickland, Lives, vol. 5.
[7] Strickland, Lives.
[8] Mrs Everett Green, Letters of Royal and Illustrious Ladies (1846)
[9] Strype, Memorials.
[10] Haynes.
[11] Ibid.
[12] H. Clifford, Life of Jane Dormer, ed. J. Stevenson (1887).
[13] Haynes.

[14] Ibid.
[15] S.P. Dom., Edward VI, vol. 6.
[16] Haynes.
[17] Ibid.
[18] Ascham, Works, vol. 1.
[19] Ascham, Works.
[20] Hayward, Life of Edward VI.
[21] Haynes.
[22] F. L. G. von Raumer, History of the 16th and 17th Centuries (1835), vol. 2.
[23] Ascham, Works.
[24] Ascham, Works.
[25] Haynes.
[26] Tytler.

CHAPTER VII. 'THE PERIL THAT MIGHT ENSUE'

1 Haynes.
2 Ibid.
3 Tytler, vol. 1.
4 Hearne, *Sylloge*.
5 Ibid.
6 Tytler, vol. 1.
7 Haynes.
8 *S.P. Dom.*, Edward VI, vol. 6.
9 Tytler, vol. 1.
10 Haynes.
11 Tytler, vol. 1.
12 Haynes.
13 Ibid.
14 Tytler, vol. 1.
15 Haynes.
16 *S.P. Dom.*, Edward VI, vol. 6.

17 Haynes.
18 Ibid.
19 *S.P. Dom.*, Edward VI, vol. 6.
20 *A.P.C.*, vol. 2.
21 Haynes.
22 Tytler, vol. 1.
23 Haynes.
24 Ibid.
25 Ibid.
26 Ibid.
27 Ibid.
28 Ibid.
29 Ibid.
30 Ibid.
31 Agnes Strickland, *Life of Queen Elizabeth I* (1906).

CHAPTER VIII. SWEET SISTER TEMPERANCE

1 *A.P.C.*, vol. 2.
2 Ibid., vol. 2.
3 Ibid., vol. 2.
4 Ibid., vol. 2.
5 Ibid., vol. 2.
6 Ibid., vol. 2.
7 Ibid., vol. 2.
8 Ibid., vol. 2.
9 Strype, *Memorials*, vol. 2, pt 1.
10 Ibid., vol. 2, pt 1.
11 Clifford, *Life of Jane Dormer*, ed. Stevenson.
12 Strickland, *Life of Queen Elizabeth I*.
13 Haynes.
14 Tytler, vol. 1.
15 Strype, *Memorials*, vol. 2, pt 2.
16 Holinshed, vol. 3, p. 1014.

17 Ascham, *Works*, vol. 1, pt 1.
18 Ascham, *Works*.
19 Strype, *Aylmer*.
20 *C.S.P. Span.*, vol. IX, p. 489.
21 Hearne, *Sylloge*.
22 *A.P.C.*, vol. 3.
23 *C.S.P. Span.*, vol. x.
24 Ibid., vol. x.
25 R. Naunton, *Fragmenta Regalia*, ed. E. Arber (1895).
26 Strickland, *Life of Queen Elizabeth I*.
27 Strype, *Aylmer*.
28 Tytler, vol. 1.
29 *Household Expenses of the Princess Elizabeth*, ed. P. C. S. Smythe (1853).
30 Machyn, *Diary*.

CHAPTER IX. THE QUEEN'S SISTER

1 Hearne, *Sylloge.*
2 *C.S.P. Span.*, vol. XI.
3 H. Chapman, *The Last Tudor King* (1958).
4 *Chron. Greyfriars.*
5 G. Howard, *Lady Jane Grey and Her Times* (1822).
6 Machyn, *Diary.*
7 Wriothesley, vol. 2.
8 *Chron. Queen Jane.*
9 Ibid.
10 Wriothesley.
11 Prescott, *Mary Tudor.*
12 *A.P.C.*, vol. 4.
13 *C.S.P. Span.*, vol. XI.
14 Mumby, *Girlhood of Queen Elizabeth.*
15 *C.S.P. Span.*, vol. XI.
16 Ibid., vol. XI.
17 Ibid., vol. XI.
18 Ibid., vol. XI.
19 Ibid., vol. XI.
20 Wriothesley and Machyn.
21 *C.S.P. Span.*, vol. XI.
22 Ibid., vol. XI.
23 Clifford, *Life of Jane Dormer,* ed. Stevenson.
24 Mumby. *Girlhood of Queen Elizabeth.*
25 *C.S.P. Span.*, vol. XI.
26 Ibid., vol. XI.
27 Ibid., vol. XI.

CHAPTER X. 'WE ARE ALL ENGLISHMEN'

1 *C.S.P. Span.*, vol. XI.
2 Tytler, vol. 2.
3 Mumby, *Girlhood of Queen Elizabeth.*
4 *Chron. Queen Jane.*
5 Ibid.
6 Ibid.
7 Hearne, *Sylloge.*
8 Strype, *Memorials*, vol. 3, pt 1.
9 *Chron. Queen Jane.*
10 Ibid.
11 Tytler, vol. 2.
12 MacNalty, *Elizabeth Tudor.*
13 *C.S.P. Span.*, vol. XII.
14 Machyn, *Diary.*
15 *C.S.P. Span.*, vol. XII.
16 Holinshed, vol. 4.
17 Tytler, vol. 2.
18 Foxe, vol. VIII.
19 Foxe.
20 *S.P. Dom.*, Edward VI and Mary.
21 *C.S.P. Span.*, vol. XII.
22 Foxe.
23 Foxe; Holinshed; *Chron. Queen Jane.*

CHAPTER XI. ELIZABETH, PRISONER

1 *C.S.P. Span.*, vol. XII.
2 Ibid., vol. XII.
3 Foxe, vol. VIII.
4 Sir John Harington, *Nugae Antiquae*, ed. T. Park (1804).
5 *C.S.P. Span.*, vol. XII.
6 Foxe.
7 Ibid.

[8] Strype, *Memorials*, vol. 3, pt 2.
[9] *C.S.P. Span.*, vol. XII.
[10] Foxe.
[11] Mumby, *Girlhood of Queen Elizabeth*.
[12] Foxe.
[13] Bedingfield, *Papers*.
[14] Foxe.
[15] Bedingfield, *Papers*.
[16] Ibid.
[17] Ibid.
[18] Ibid.
[19] Foxe; Holinshed, vol. 4.
[20] Strickland, *Life of Queen Elizabeth I*.
[21] Bedingfield, *Papers*.
[22] Ibid.
[23] *C.S.P. Span.*, vol. XIII.
[24] Bedingfield, *Papers*.
[25] Prescott, *Mary Tudor*.
[26] Foxe.
[27] Ibid.

CHAPTER XII. 'A SECOND PERSON'

[1] *C.S.P. Ven.*, vol. VI, pt 1.
[2] Machyn, *Diary*; *C.S.P. Ven.*, vol. VI, pt 1.
[3] Tytler, vol. 2.
[4] *C.S.P. Ven.*, vol. VI, pt 2.
[5] Ibid., vol. VI, pt 1.
[6] Machyn, *Diary*; *C.S.P. Ven.*, vol. VI, pt 1.
[7] L. Wiesener, *Youth of Queen Elizabeth* (1879).
[8] *C.S.P. Ven.*, vol. VI, pt 1.
[9] Ascham, *Works*.
[10] Machyn, *Diary*.
[11] Wiesener, *Youth of Queen Elizabeth*.
[12] See D. M. Loades, *Two Tudor Conspiracies* (1965).
[13] *C.S.P. Ven.*, vol. VI, pt. 2.
[14] Ibid., vol. VI, pt 1.
[15] Wiesener, *Youth of Queen Elizabeth*.
[16] *C.S.P. Ven.*, vol. VI, pt 1.
[17] Ibid., vol. VI, pt 1.
[18] Ibid., vol. VI, pt 1.
[19] Strype, *Memorials*, vol. 3, pt 1.
[20] Ibid., vol. 3, pt 1.
[21] *C.S.P. Ven.*, vol. VI, pt 1.
[22] Machyn, *Diary*; *C.S.P. Ven.*, vol. VI, pt 2.
[23] *C.S.P. Ven.*, vol. VI, pt 2.
[24] Wiesener, *Youth of Queen Elizabeth*. Also E. H. Harbison, *Rival Ambassadors at the Court of Queen Mary* (1940).
[25] *C.S.P. Ven.*, vol. VI, pt 2.
[26] Ibid., vol. VI, pt 2.
[27] Wiesener, *Youth of Queen Elizabeth*. Also Harbison, *Rival Ambassadors*.
[28] *A.P.C.*, vol. VI.

CHAPTER XIII. ENGLAND'S ELIZABETH

[1] *C.S.P. Ven.*, vol. VI, pt 2.

[2] Strype, *Memorials*, vol. 3, pt 2.

[3] Wiesener, *Youth of Queen Elizabeth*, vol. 2.

[4] *C.S.P. Ven.*, vol. VI, pt 3.

[5] Ibid., vol. VI, pt 3.

[6] Strype, *Memorials*, vol. 3, pt 2. See also Prescott, *Mary Tudor*.

[7] *C.S.P. Ven.*, vol. VI, pt 2.

[8] Ibid., vol. VI, pt 2.

[9] Ibid., vol. VI, pt 3.

[10] Machyn, *Diary*. See also Wiesener, *Youth of Queen Elizabeth*, vol. 2, pp. 246–55.

[11] *C.S.P. Span.*, vol. XIII.

[12] Harleian MS., quoted in Strickland, *Life of Queen Elizabeth I*.

[13] *C.S.P. Span.*, vol. XIII.

[14] Ibid., vol. XIII.

[15] Prescott, *Mary Tudor*.

[16] Hayward, *Annals*.

[17] *C.S.P. Span.*, vol. XIII.

[18] Gonzales, *Documents from Simancas Relating to the Reign of Elizabeth*.

[19] Naunton, *Fragmenta Regalia*.

[20] Machyn, *Diary*.

[21] Holinshed, vol. 4.

[22] Quoted in C. Read, *Mr Secretary Cecil and Queen Elizabeth* (1955).

[23] Holinshed.

[24] Machyn, *Diary*.

[25] Hayward, *Annals*.

[26] Quoted in Read, *Mr Secretary Cecil*.

[27] *C.S.P. Span. Eliz.*, vol. I.

[28] Hayward, *Annals*.

[29] *C.S.P. Ven.*, vol. VII.

[30] Holinshed, vol. 4.

Select Bibliography

MANUSCRIPT SOURCES

State Papers, Domestic. In the Public Record Office.

PRINTED SOURCES (CONTEMPORARY)

Acts of the Privy Council, ed. J. R. Dasent, vols. 1–6, 1890.

Ascham, Roger, *The Whole Works of Roger Ascham*, ed. with a Life of the Author by Rev. Dr Giles, 1865.

Bedingfield, Henry, *Papers*, ed. C. R. Manning, Norfolk and Norwich Archaeological Society, 1855.

Burghley, William Cecil, Lord, *State Papers*, ed. Samuel Haynes, 1740.

Calendar of State Papers, Domestic, ed. Robert Lemon.

Calendar of State Papers, Spanish, ed. Gayangos, Hume and Tyler.

Calendar of State Papers, Spanish, Elizabeth, ed. Hume.

Calendar of State Papers, Venetian, ed. Rawdon Brown.

Cavendish, George, *The Life and Death of Cardinal Wolsey*, ed. Richard S. Sylvester in *Two Early Tudor Lives*, New Haven, Conn., 1962.

The Chronicle and Political Papers of King Edward VI, ed. W. K. Jordan, 1966.

Chronicle of King Henry VIII of England, trans. and ed. Martin A. S. Hume, 1889.

A Chronicle of London, ed. N. H. Nicolas, 1827.

Chronicle of Queen Jane and Two Years of Queen Mary, ed. J. G. Nichols, Camden Society, 1850.

Chronicle of the Greyfriars, ed. J. G. Nichols, Camden Society, 1852.

Clifford, Henry, *Life of Jane Dormer*, ed. Joseph Stevenson, 1887.

Elizabeth I, *The Letters of Queen Elizabeth*, ed. G. B. Harrison, 1935.

Erasmus, Desiderius, *The Epistles of Erasmus*, trans. and ed. Francis Morgan Nichols, 1901.

Foxe, John, *Acts and Monuments*, ed. S. R. Cattley and G. Townsend, 1839.

Giustinian, Sebastian, *Four Years at the Court of Henry VIII (1515–1519), A Selection of the Despatches of Sebastian Giustinian*, trans. and ed. Rawdon Brown, 1854.

Gonzales, Tomás, *Documents from Simancas Relating to the Reign of Queen Elizabeth (1558–1568)*, trans. and ed. Spencer Hall, 1865.

Green, Mrs Everett, *Letters of Royal and Illustrious Ladies*, 1846.

Gregory, William, *William Gregory's Chronicle. The Historical Collections of a London Citizen*, ed. J. Gairdner, Camden Society, 1876.

Hall, Edward, *Chronicle*, ed. Sir Henry Ellis, 1809.

Harington, Sir John, *Nugae Antique*, ed. Thomas Park, 1804.

Hayward, John, *Annals of the First Four Years of the Reign of Queen Elizabeth*, ed. John Bruce, Camden Society, 1840.

—, *The Life of Edward VI*, in White Kennett *et al.*, *Complete History of England* (1706), vol. II.

Hearne, Thomas, *Sylloge Epistolarum*, in Titus Livius, *Viva Henrici Quinti*, ed. Hearne, 1716.

Heywood, Thomas, *England's Elizabeth*, Harleian Miscellany, 1813.

Holinshed, Rafael, *Chronicles*, 1807–8.

Household Expenses of the Princess Elizabeth, at Hatfield, 1551–2, ed. P. C. S. Smythe, Camden Miscellany 2, 1853.

Leti, Gregorio, *Historia o vero vita di Elizabetta, regina d'Inghilterra*, French, translation, 2 pts, Amsterdam, 1692.

Letters and Papers, Foreign and Domestic, of the Reign of Henry VIII, ed. Brewer, Gairdner and Brodie, 1862.

Machyn, Henry, *Diary*, ed. J. G. Nichols, Camden Society, 1848.

Madden, F., *The Privy Purse Expenses of the Princess Mary*, 1831.

Mumby, F. A., *The Girlhood of Queen Elizabeth*, 1909.

Naunton, Robert, *Fragmenta Regalia*, ed. Edward Arber, 1895.

Nichols, J., *Progresses and Public Processions of Queen Elizabeth*, 1823.

Proceedings and Ordinances of the Privy Council, ed. N. H. Nicolas, 1835.

Raumer, F. L. G. von, *History of the 16th and 17th Centuries*, 1835.

Roper, William, *The Life of Sir Thomas More*, ed. Davis P. Harding in *Two Early Tudor Lives*, New Haven, Conn., 1962.

Rymer, Thomas, *Foedera*, vol. x, 1704.

State Papers, Henry VIII, vol. I, 1830.

Stow, John, *Annals*, ed. E. Howes, 1631.

Strype, John, *Ecclesiastical Memorials*, 1822.

—, *Life of John Aylmer*, 1821.

Tytler, P. F., *England under the Reigns of Edward VI and Mary*, 1839.

Vergil, Polydore, *The Anglica Historia of Polydore Vergil (1485–1537)*, ed. Denys Hay, Camden Society, 1950.

—, *English History Comprising the Reigns of Henry VI, Edward IV and Richard III*, ed. Ellis, Camden Society, 1844.

Wriothesley, Charles, *A Chronicle of England during the Reigns of the Tudors*, ed. William D. Hamilton, Camden Society, 2 vols, 1875.

LATER WORKS

Bindoff, S. T., *Tudor England*, Harmondsworth, 1950.

Chamberlin, Frederick, *The Private Character of Queen Elizabeth*, 1921.

Chambers, R. W., *Sir Thomas More*, 1935.

Chapman, Hester, *The Last Tudor King*, 1958.

Chrimes, S. B., *Lancastrians, Yorkists and Henry VII*, 1964.

Evans, H. T., *Wales and the Wars of the Roses*, 1915.

Friedmann, Paul, *Anne Boleyn, a Chapter of English History, 1527–1536*, 1884.

Gairdner, James, 'Mary and Anne Boleyn', *English Historical Review*, vol. 8 (1893).

Harbison, E. H., *Rival Ambassadors at the Court of Queen Mary*, Princeton, N.J., 1940.

Howard, G., *Lady Jane Grey and Her Times*, 1822.

Howe, Bea, *A Galaxy of Governesses*, 1954.

Jenkins, Elizabeth, *Elizabeth the Great*, 1958.

Jones, Sir Thomas Artemus, 'Owen Tudor's Marriage', *Bulletin of the Board of Celtic Studies*, vol. xi (1943).

Jordan, W. K., *Edward VI: the Young King*, 1968.

Loades, D. M., *Two Tudor Conspiracies*, 1965.

Mackie, J. D., *The Earlier Tudors*, 1952.

MacNalty, Sir A. S., *Elizabeth Tudor – The Lonely Queen*, 1954.

—, *Henry VIII – A Difficult Patient*, 1952.

Mattingly, Garrett, *Catherine of Aragon*, 1942.

Muir, Kenneth, *Life and Letters of Sir Thomas Wyatt*, Liverpool, 1963.

Neale, J. E., 'The Accession of Elizabeth I', in *Essays in Elizabethan History*, 1958.

—, *Queen Elizabeth I*, 1934.

Parsons, W. L. E., *Some Notes on the Boleyn Family*, Norfolk and Norwich Archaeological Society, 1935.

Prescott, H. F. M., *Mary Tudor*, revised ed., 1952.

Read, Conyers, *Mr Secretary Cecil and Queen Elizabeth*, 1955.

Routh, E. M. G., *A Memoir of Lady Margaret Beaufort*, 1924.

Rowse, A. L., *Bosworth Field and the Wars of the Roses*, 1966.

Ryan, Laurence V., *Roger Ascham*, Stanford, Calif., 1963.

Scarisbrick, J. J., *Henry VIII*, 1968.

Storey, R. F., *The Reign of Henry VII*, 1968.

Strickland, Agnes, *Life of Queen Elizabeth I*, Everyman ed., 1906.
—, *Lives of the Queens of England*, 8 vols, 1875.
Temperley, Gladys, *Henry VII*, 1914.
Wiesener, Louis, *The Youth of Queen Elizabeth I*, trans. C. M. Yonge, 2 vols, 1879.
Williams, David, 'The Family of Henry VII', *History Today*, vol. IV (1954).
Williams, Neville, *Elizabeth: Queen of England*, 1967.

Index